THE ENTREPRENEURIAL SPIRIT OF AFRICAN AMERICAN INVENTORS

PATRICIA CARTER SLUBY

 PRAEGER

AN IMPRINT OF ABC-CLIO, LLC
Santa Barbara, California • Denver, Colorado • Oxford, England

Library of Congress Cataloging-in-Publication Data

Sluby, Patricia Carter.
   The entrepreneurial spirit of African American inventors / Patricia Carter Sluby.
     p. cm.
   Includes bibliographical references and index.
   ISBN 978-0-313-36335-1 (hardback) — ISBN 978-0-313-36336-8 (ebook)
1. Inventions—United States—History.   2. African American inventors—
History.   3. African American business enterprises—History.   4. United States—
Race relations—History.   I. Title.
   T21.S58 2011
   338.6'42208996073—dc22   2010047613

ISBN: 978-0-313-36335-1
EISBN: 978-0-313-36336-8

15   14   13   12   11   1   2   3   4   5

This book is also available on the World Wide Web as an eBook.
Visit www.abc-clio.com for details.

Praeger
An Imprint of ABC-CLIO, LLC

ABC-CLIO, LLC
130 Cremona Drive, P.O. Box 1911
Santa Barbara, California 93116-1911

This book is printed on acid-free paper ∞

Manufactured in the United States of America

To my maternal great-grandfather Giles Beecher Jackson Esq.,
a passionate businessman and ardent believer in black
enterprise, and to my father, William A. Carter Jr., and
his father, William Sr., both pioneer entrepreneurs.

Contents

Preface

In past centuries, American people of color were acknowledged by whites for their talent for music and dance, but any mention of the "Negro's" innate ability in the realm of inventive genius was considered fantasy. Thought of as having little if any originality, they were presumed to possess mental deficiency in the mechanical and industrial arts and to be incapable of original thought. Even people of color themselves, coming from the previous condition of bondage and having very little opportunity for gaining knowledge in science, fine art, or literature, were unaware of members of their race who had the faculty for discovery. Whites reasoned that the black man could not perform like any person of the majority race. But the general assumption by whites that blacks were not capable of becoming inventors or had no business acumen was far from truthful. The paternalistic and denigrating attitudes of white supremacists permeated Western society, but in spite of their power and opinion, notable black ability and ingenuity prevailed.

Numerous accounts reflect innovative efforts of Americans of African descent, of those who believed in self-reliance and self-motivation. In earlier centuries blacks developed a strong business tradition. These stalwart, creative men and women helped make a better America, and they displayed entrepreneurial spirit identical to that of other immigrants in America. Free inhabitants in Northern and Southern cities and towns received considerable income from barbering, tailoring, catering, and the clothing business.[1] Livery stable enterprises afforded freedmen another profitable effort.

Let's go back in history to set the stage. Expounding in 1833 on the skillful-ness of the Negro, U.S. Representative Edward H. Everett (later president of Harvard University) gave an address before the Massachusetts Colonization Society wherein he asserted that in the history of the black race, "In the period of their glory, when they occupied the forefront in the march of civilization," one should "see what they were and what they did three thousand years ago."[2]

The oldest remains of humans have been found in Kenya, the heart of the African continent. Only two types of artifacts from this early period remain today—partial skeletons and the tools with which people worked. The human who first took up the stone ax, the arrowhead, and the flint knife lived in in-nermost Africa, home of the darker races. Obviously, then, prehistoric man's presence gave rise to certain items of necessity and convenience. Ali A. Maz-rui in *The Africans* reveals that "Africa is not merely the probable cradle of Man and his initial culture: the continent is also the genesis of civilisation. Eastern Africa provided the birth of humanity and culture: several regions of Africa made a major contribution to the development of agriculture; and northern Africa initiated grand civilisation."[3]

The denizens of Africa worked in metal by fashioning spears, knives, and death masks of copper and iron. They were creating arts while the tribes of Europe and Asia were not yet born. They were so advanced in the sub-Saharan region that they skipped a phase of cultural development, advancing directly from the Stone Age to the Iron Age, bypassing the Bronze Age entirely be-cause natural iron supplies were more abundant in the southern Sahara than copper.

During the first half of the 16th century, Affonso I, the king of the Congo, was the first monarch to modernize Africa on a large basis. He encouraged Christian beliefs and brought about the practice of using modern skills in masonry, carpentry, and agriculture. He improved Congo politics and resisted the lures of the slave trade.

For nearly 400 years after reaching the shores of America, the darker-hued race conceived remarkable, clever inventions. Then exploited as slaves, legally cast as chattel, blacks displayed abundant ingenuity during the developing years of America. To know the history of America is to be aware of the cultural and social changes brought about by the result of African Americans' inspira-tions. Their mental prowess is legendary.

Like their forebears, early Africans in America were expert artisans, mak-ing pottery, weaving textiles, carving wood, and sculpting ivory and metal, the mainline crafts practiced by free and enslaved souls. Moreover, as masters in a myriad of trades, Africans excelled in mining, metal tooling, and construction. The skill of the newly enslaved African swiftly was used for the construction of plantation buildings, stately manor homes and their outbuildings. Slaves alongside freemen made, designed, and fashioned as well much of the fine silverware and furniture commonly viewed in these households. However, the majority labored on plantations as skilled agrarian workers, mostly in the tobacco and cotton fields. The Carolinas in America's South were ideal for cultivating rice, a staple of the regional economy. Here, enslaved Africans who came from the region along the Gambia River and in Sierra Leone where rice was grown had their knowledge of rice growing exploited by their masters, earning for them an enormous profit on this cash crop.

Superior skill and natural inherent talent are found in the stories of extraordinary people of color, whether bondsmen or free. In an example, Stephen L. Bishop (?–1857), a Kentucky slave who spoke Latin and Greek, was renowned for his adroitness and extraordinary skill in the exploration of the gigantic Mammoth Cave in Kentucky. Moreover, two famous musicians, the ragtime impresario Scott Joplin (1868–1917) and eminent author, composer, and arranger Justin Holland (1819–1887), who was a classical pioneer and the most pivotal American guitarist of the late 1800s, both accentuate the creative genius of Americans of color.[4]

During military conflicts of 18th- and 19th-century wars, African Americans served honorably as soldiers and sailors. Free blacks eagerly responded to the call to fight for the nation. Throughout their service, they invented and developed intricate weaponry and crafted mariners' tools, devices, and ornaments. Scrimshaw art was a common skill among mariners during idle times.

In reflection on mankind's ingenuity, the stone or wooden wheel of the ancient past evolved into the automobile's modern steel-belted tire. The printing press revolutionized our way of receiving knowledge, and the pine torch, the tallow drop, the candle, and oil lamp fell obsolete to the illumination of the electric light. Ancient hooks or other unprotected metal shafts used to fasten clothing, boots, and shoes gave rise to the safety pin and then Velcro fastenings. Today, even the sounds of typewriter keys and the familiar busy line signal heard over the telephone have given way to the genius of technology-minded engineers. Ideas for such items emanate from individuals known as inventors, whether female or male, black or white. Discoveries and improvements have taken place for millions of years, *beginning with the darker races.* Therefore, an account of human inventiveness gives insight into society's ever-changing needs. And black Americans helped create those needs in spite of racial prejudices and rabid discrimination.

By turning their inventions into wealth, a measurable number of African American patentees pushed hard to exploit their patented concepts through business ventures to gain what they generally believed would improve the human condition and would bring them, the inventors, greater economic security and higher social status, though such rewards were restricted given the systems of slavery and segregation that permeated society. Facing an ever-present climate of bigotry and stereotypical beliefs, black innovators continually empowered and reenergized their efforts to succeed. The earliest patentee of ebony hue, Thomas Jennings, a free man in the 1800s, did achieve great success along these lines, and a few, such as Norbert Rillieux and James Forten, came into prominence in business in those early years. However, the majority of black inventors were not so lucky financially. In the latter decades of the 20th century, when segregation policies were struck down by federal legislation, bringing in the age of integration, black inventors saw adjustments in hiring practices and in the social, political, and economic mindset, but discrimination and racism marched on nonetheless.

Benevolent and self-help societies sprouted in the 19th century to aid the black citizenry. As technology advanced and time marched on, alliances for specialty groups such as scientists, inventors, nurses, lawyers, architects, engineers, physicians and dentists, chemists and physicists, and other tradesmen have platforms expressing the importance of minority participation in the mainstream of society that historically rejected them. Their emphasis on programs and strategies is essential to the survival of these trades. This work is not intended to explore the efforts of all African Americans engaged in entrepreneurial ventures, for many are very worthy of mention, but is directed toward African American patent and trademark holders who pressed on in business enterprises as an outgrowth of their intellectual property, regardless of ever-present oppression and roadblocks.

The advancement of *Homo sapiens,* the modern man, on planet Earth was gradual but steady over eons. Dynasties arose and then faded way, kingdoms endured but fell to ruin from the heaviness of time. A few thousand years ago, man founded towns and cities, and a few hundred years ago the Industrial Revolution dawned. The last quarter of the 20th century to the present is known as the information age, and it has embodied rapid technological advances. Astounding progress from the scientific genius of people of color along with those of a paler hue spawned new problems to solve. So where do we go from here? The drums that beat the pace will forever accelerate the urges to improve what has gone on before. Black Americans will demand their share in this now global enterprise system through an entrepreneurial ethos.

Pat Sluby
November 2010

Acknowledgments

The idea of writing this book was compelling for several reasons. After my initial interest in inventions and in inventors was aroused, I wanted to do something about the story of African American inventiveness. My study of this creative genius began when I was a patent examiner at the U.S. Patent and Trademark Office. While there, I heard many stories from African American inventors and listened to their desires to turn a profit from businesses initiated as outgrowth from their patents. The world should know the story of how they brought their dreams to reality. It is a pleasure to reach the point of acknowledging the notable and celebratory entrepreneurial achievements of these brave, unintimidated inventors. All has been a journey into the unexpected realm of writing.

In the course of my patent career and afterward at various stages of my research, I received support from many colleagues working in the field of intellectual property. I deeply appreciate the use of many research facilities and the quiet, steadfast perseverance of archivists and librarians, but particularly I am indebted to Library Program Specialist Margaret J. Collins at the Illinois State Library for her diligence and strong support throughout this effort. She was a treasure.

It is with deep gratitude that I thank Maceo C. Dailey for his encouragement and patient guidance. I give grateful thanks to Adam Mandell for his immeasurable assistance and aid. I am grateful to Charlotte Douglas, Art Molella, Julie Winch, and Andrew D. Hirsch for their willing support. Freely sharing information were Sherry Davis, Mary C. Williams, Terry Phillips, and

Gail E. Wright. To many friends and others whom I have not mentioned by name, I voice my heartiest thanks.

With endless gratefulness I richly thank all the inventors who assisted me. The number is so great that I dare not list them for fear of an omission. Readily, these extraordinary and giving talents were forthcoming with information about their enterprises.

I acknowledge the generous support of my early editors, Elizabeth Demers, Brian Foster, and Tisha Hooks, and of editorial operations coordinator Erin Ryan. I especially thank editor Emily Birch, who was positive and very attentive to the writing details of this project as it came to completion. I richly thank Barbara Walsh for her fine copyediting of the manuscript, and I thank the production staff at Praeger.

My family was always at my side, pushing and encouraging me at every turn. My mom, Thelma, and my dad, William A. Carter Jr., a businessman and entrepreneur, provided the love and support I needed from birth, pleased and proud at each success. My husband, Paul E. Sluby Sr., stepped into my life at a time needed for giving me unending assistance and sage advice. I owe him deep gratitude. My daughters, Felicia and Julia, are precious to me, and I thank them for belief in their mother.

Introduction

The Congress shall have power . . . to promote the progress of science and useful arts, by securing for limited times to authors and inventors the exclusive right to their respective writings and discoveries.

—*The U.S. Constitution, Article I, Section 8*

Before I became a patent examiner at the U.S. Patent and Trademark Office, I knew very little about patents or inventors. I, like many consumers, had knowledge of patent leather shoes (made by a once-patented process), but after I entered the patent examining corps I received firsthand information about the term *patent*.

A federally protected grant, resulting from the product of an inventor's brainchild, is called intellectual property. Patents (along with trademarks, trade secrets, and copyrights) are representative of this property and are of great value to anyone who wants protection for an invention or innovation. Possession of this property is extremely valuable because the rights can be sold, transferred, inherited, mortgaged, and taxed. Rights and protection for those who own such property are founded on laws specific to the particular property.

Patents of today push forward new ideas for a better world tomorrow. Through the years, science and industry have spawned and developed countless invaluable concepts. Most of today's patents are improvements on known products and represent the fruit from the seeds of earlier conceived ideas. More abundant commodities at lower cost result in better living for all of humankind. The primary beneficiary of the patent system is the consumer, a reality that makes patents valuable to the public. In a time when technological improvement is exceedingly important, patents will be a great incentive to effect the necessary investment and invention.

Countless applicants have succeeded in receiving the desired federal patent protection, but the names of only a few patentees have become household words. Such inventors as Alexander Graham Bell, Thomas Alva Edison, Henry Ford, or George Goodyear are quickly recognized; however, patentees like George Washington Carver, Granville T. Woods, Jan Matzeliger, Percy Lavon Julian, Lewis Howard Latimer, and Elijah McCoy are not well known to the general public. Historically, the names of African Americans have generally been excluded from publication lists that highlight inventors. Nonetheless, at a time when African Americans were classified as chattel and deprived of their human rights, the patent system provided the opportunity for free blacks to be known for their genius. Yet, for the most part, their ingenuity and creativity went unobserved since persons of color were ignored or ridiculed. In fact, though, the earliest black patent holder received the patent in 1821, a year when slavery was still alive and well in this country, *and* later made a fortune from the marketed invention.

The ever-increasing number of African American inventors is a vital and productive force in our economy. Although they did not gain patents in great abundance in the 1800s, a few of them reaped enormous benefit from their protected concepts. By the 1900s they secured a host of patents, with many still going to market successfully. Evidence of their presence in the new millennium guarantees more revelations. From their emergence as inventors, African Americans have received many thousand U.S. patents out of the more than seven million grants of records. The number will grow as sable inventors continue to apply for proprietary rights. Weekly issuance of these grants holds promise.

As an examiner, I had the opportunity to witness the total picture of U.S. and foreign ingenuity. Firsthand knowledge of developments in all phases of endeavor is at the fingertips of an examiner so that the breadth and depth of creative genius can be viewed. I became aware of numerous black inventors, many of whom were successful in obtaining patent grants. However, others became frustrated with the system's failure to issue the coveted documents. Indeed, it is a difficult process to traverse.

The inventor's patent application must pass the rigid examination system and other technical requirements before the grant is issued, officially known as a U.S. Letters Patent. The patent professional applies the three tests of patentability—novelty, usefulness, and unobviousness. If these tests are satisfactory and other technicalities are met, the examiner allows the inventor to receive the patent.

Nearly all inventors want monetary gain besides personal satisfaction from their inventiveness. This is quite understandable inasmuch as the path from creation to production can present substantial financial demands. Those inventors who choose to protect their product with a patent before going to market find that it is very expensive to have their application travel through the complexities of patent examination. Subsequently, additional time, energy, and money are spent to manufacture the product for its general or specialized purpose, whether patented or not protected. At this point, all must dig deep into their pockets, since obtaining a patent does not ensure pecuniary rewards. This must come from individual effort.

While a copyright is a form of protection given by law to authors of literary, dramatic, musical, artistic, and other intellectual works, and a trademark is an arbitrary word, name, symbol, device, or slogan used by a manufacturer, seller, or other outlet for goods or services, a patent is granted by the government to an inventor to stop others from making, using, or selling the invention throughout the United States. There are three basic types of patents for which an inventor can specifically apply: utility patents (the best-known and largest type applied for), design patents, and plant patents. The utility patent is issued to anyone who invents or discovers a new and useful (having utility) process, machine, manufacture, or composition of matter, or a new and useful improvement, subject to certain conditions. The design patent is granted to any person who has invented a new, original, and ornamental design for an article of manufacture. The plant patent may be issued to a person who invents or discovers and asexually reproduces a distinct and new variety of plant. The inventor is not rewarded unless the invention benefits the consumer since the buyer will not purchase it otherwise, and surely the patentee wants the creative effort to be salable so that he or she can recoup the expenses necessary to produce the product plus make a profit from the ingenuity.

This writing attempts a study of the African American patent holder's entrepreneurial spirit from the earliest time to the present. In completing this task, though, errors inescapably may appear, or some names may be overlooked. Indeed, it is a very difficult task to harness each and every inventor of color for a myriad of reasons; one, in part, is that applications for patents and trademarks do not require ethnic or gender identification. Various publications address the subject of patent ownership by African Americans; nevertheless, these works mainly concern inventions of popular or famous personalities. Here, many hidden names come to the public's attention for the first time, appearing with the more recognized talents. Although a sizeable number of minorities have secured patents in the United States and abroad as well, only domestic patents are of concern herein.

To put this writing into perspective, I must mention that it is not a full scholarship on entrepreneurship among African Americans or any other group. I leave that subject to educators and researchers careered in that discipline. The central purpose of this work is to bring to the fore enterprising achievements of gifted thinkers and tinkerers of African descent who bring a more satisfactory level of living to the marketplace. To put it another way, this effort focuses on black enterprise of a special class of people—those who hold patent rights.

My previous work, *The Inventive Spirit of African Americans: Patented Ingenuity*, presented a full study of past and present innovators often overlooked in the annals of human endeavor, bringing a stirring account of the toughness of the human creative spirit in the face of enormous obstacles. After its publication I realized that a sizable number of modern inventors are successful entrepreneurs, adding to the list of those enterprising developers of yesteryear.

The instant effort should be useful to students in secondary education and those in higher economic and intellectual pursuits who are concentrating on business enterprises and entrepreneurship; on African American history, achievement, and emerging industries; or on the social, health, and physical sciences. The abundant intellectual property of black patent holders should interest scholars working in the field of patents and trademarks and in the inventive process itself.

The appendix, "Roster of African American Patentees," lists the inventor's name, the patent title, its number, and the date of issue. While a significant number of black inventors own scores of grants, all their documents may not be listed. Inclusive of Henry E. Baker's research, the roster embraces inventors who have utility patents for inventions that have use in the general chemical (inclusive of biotechnical concepts), mechanical, and electrical areas (inclusive of computer science and business practices). Also included are the inventors who have secured design patents for inventions that have an ornamental look. For some entities or persons having trademarks I refer you to my earlier work mentioned previously.

1

Setting the Stage: Early Inventive Spirit

The wheel of fortune revolves slowly, but surely . . . and the wrecks along the shore and memories of others handed down to us are convincing proof of the statement made.

—*James E. Shepard, National Negro Business League, Boston, 1900*

During the early building of the United States of America, bondsmen created implements pertaining to farm equipment and household utilities that made their work somewhat easier. After the period of slavery ending in 1865, those previously held in bondage were freed and thus became citizens through the ratification of the Thirteenth Amendment of the U.S. Constitution. Freed souls bought land or were given property by their former owners and thereby had their own farms or plots of land to tend. Success came to some who used various inventions of their own. In fact, they were considered wealthy in terms of the standards of the day.

The early successful patentees of color exhibited extraordinary fortitude, tenacity, and perseverance given the prevailing attitude and conditions under which they existed. Albeit, their "wheel of fortune" moved slowly but steadfastly against the tide of racism and hostility. Despite the barriers that excluded them from formal schooling and access to centers of research and business development, early black inventors were active in the field of invention and made meaningful contributions to science and industry.

Most people of color did not have an education in the formal sense (which was also a reality among a large population of white Southerners). Being denied basic freedoms because of insidious laws designed to keep them ig-norant, freed men and women studied independently, mostly in secret. Some freeborn or manumitted persons were educated by others of their race; by brave and considerate masters; or by abolitionists, primarily Quakers who es-tablished schools for blacks in certain regions. Then, too, religious groups in benevolence also educated the illiterate. Unquestionably, this underprivileged segment of the population had a talent for learning and for creative work.

For the most part it was a hardship for *free* Americans of color to engage in an enterprise because they were not treated as fully free citizens with all inalienable rights in a free society. Practically, papers of freedom meant half bondage in view of severely restrictive laws in area jurisdictions. State leg-islators enacted statutes in the 1700s and 1800s to harness all activities of Africans out of bondage, designed to protect the white community against free black uprisings. The District of Columbia enforced offensive policies re-flected in black codes that had an effect on all slaves, and freed persons as well. For example, all secret, private, and religious meetings of "colored" persons were prohibited freedoms beyond the hour of 10 at night. Bondsmen were punished "with any number of stripes on the bare back" for breaking lamps, and for "bathing in certain waters between sun-rise and sun-set." Terms were even set forth "upon which free colored persons are permitted to reside in the City of Washington."[1] The neighboring states of Virginia and Maryland like-wise passed repugnant slave codes. In fact, in *all* the Southern states, nowhere could both free and enslaved people of color travel or settle without some law dictating their daily routine.

Out West, the Oregon Territory in the early 1840s did not want minorities of color living in that Pacific Coast region at any cost and passed an exclusion-ary act. In 1844, after slavery was declared illegal there, a law was enacted to whip the freed twice a year until they abandoned their habitat and left. In 1862, this hateful "Lash Law" was replaced with other legislation, somewhat less harsh but just as prejudicial and racist, that charged African Americans, Chinese, Hawaiians, and mixed races a tax of five dollars, payable annually, for the privilege to live in that territory.[2]

In the North, slave catchers roamed freely, kidnapping many freed blacks and runaways seeking freedom and returning them to bondage. A fugitive-slave case reached great notoriety in 1842, involving George Latimer, the father of illustrious inventor Lewis Howard Latimer. The police arrested the father in Boston four days after his arrival when Latimer's owner appeared before authorities demanding his imprisonment until Latimer returned to slavery. News of the arrest spread. Abolitionists and friends such as William Lloyd Garrison, a close ally of innovator and sailmaker James Forten, and Frederick Douglass supported the call for Latimer's release, raising $400 to purchase his freedom. This case was Boston's first famous fugitive-slave action and, along with several other cases of fame, resulted in the passage of a Massachusetts law prohibiting state employees from searching for fugitive slaves.[3]

In the late 1700s, Philadelphia was thriving as a bustling port city on the Delaware River, teeming with sailmakers, shipbuilders, craftsmen, and mariners. By the early 1820s Philadelphia, a sizable city in the state of Pennsylvania, lost its economic stronghold as a shipbuilding center to New York, a city closer to the open seas and where a few thousand free Americans of African descent lived. The country had survived the Revolutionary War (1775–1783) and second war with Great Britain begun in 1812, but economic upheavals plagued Philadelphia and other cities across the nation as well. However, the port city of New York was favored by British traders, and New York was off to a running start. In these Northern enclaves in spite of the specter of forced return to slavery, free black Americans in the late 18th and 19th centuries successfully engaged in businesses and trade.

John Sibley Butler notes in his work *Entrepreneurship and Self-Help among Black Americans:*

> Although the literature has overlooked the Afro-American experience, the group has been involved in enterprise since the inception of the nation. Free Afro-Americans in the 1700s and 1800s laid the foundation for the Afro-American business tradition. Even under the system of slavery, there are historical accounts of enterprise by Afro-Americans.[4]

Most free blacks, though, were fearful of being captured and enslaved. Yet a prominent ebony-hued American apparently felt confident enough to live in New York City on the Atlantic Coast and operate a thriving business resulting from his creative genius. Indeed, Thomas Jennings is the earliest identified African American patent holder and an early successful African American entrepreneur in that rarified sphere. In the words of Butler, "Despite harsh reality, free Afro-Americans were able to generate a measure of economic stability."[5] Jennings, the inventor, entrepreneur, and activist of great talent born in 1791, went on to set the standard for black inventors in taking an invention from creation to production and finally to financial success.

Residing in New York City, he fought for the abolition of slavery in the early 1800s, operated a boardinghouse, and backed his community activism with earnings from his business. His beliefs in parity for his people inspired him to organize protests and to challenge Jim Crow practices on public conveyances such as railroads, steamboats, omnibuses, and ferryboats. A fervent fighter against peonage, he would be forcibly ejected by the police from white railcars during demonstrations. His feisty daughter Elizabeth, a schoolteacher, helped break up segregated streetcars in New York City when one Sunday morning she was thrown from a horse-drawn streetcar designated for whites. She retained none other than future president of the United States Chester A. Arthur to take her lawsuit to the Supreme Court, and they won the case against the railway company. Jennings also was a leading member of the National Colored Convention Movement and helped found organizations such as the Wilberforce Benevolent Society, the Legal Rights Association of New York, and the Abyssinian Baptist Church (a powerful entity in the mid-1900s under the pastoral leadership of Congressman and Reverend Adam Clayton Powell Jr.).[6]

After an apprenticeship with a renowned New York tailor, Jennings founded his own successful clothing establishment that became one of the largest clothing stores in the city. He reaped direct benefit from the exclusive right to exclude others from making, using, or selling, for a specified length of time, his invention based on his federally protected improved process for "dry-scouring" clothes (a method for renovating or cleaning clothes), securing for him an impressive and stunning accomplishment at that time in history. It was a dream realized for an American of African descent 44 years before the demise of slavery.

The primary objective of inventing is to advance science and the useful arts, a process that spurs the economy by encouraging the consumer—the primary beneficiary—to purchase the product. Minus the consumer, the invention concept is without merit, doomed to failure. Patents, of course, have value when there are customers. Thomas Jennings gave the public a better product and was rewarded by his customers' patronage, a perfect demonstration of a patent's value, as his patent not only benefited him but also provided a better level of living. The clothing and tailoring business was a trade that free people of color could endeavor in generally without repercussion due to its servile status; it was an enterprise mostly avoided by whites, giving free blacks an advantage where they derived considerable income. Jennings, hence, was industrious in this arena. Given Jennings's success, it can be reasoned that competitors appeared with improvements, sparking more inventions.

Jennings's "Letters Patent" (the official name), preserved in a gilded antique picture frame that hung above his bed at the time of his death in 1859, was signed by U.S. Secretary of State John Quincy Adams and by Attorney General William Wirt. Jennings's success led to opportunities and success for his family members. All of his children were educated, and each prospered in his or her enterprise. His son William was a progressive New York businessman, and another son, Thomas, built a large dental practice in New Orleans. His daughter Matilda became a dressmaker and his other daughter, Elizabeth, having a propensity for activism, taught school in New York City before and after marrying.[7]

In the course of events since Article I, Section 8 of the federal Constitution gave "Congress the power . . . to promote the progress of . . . useful arts by securing for limited times to . . . inventors the exclusive right to their discoveries," the basis for the patent system, the governing laws went through periodic changes, but at no time did the periodic changes in the laws reflect the difference between kinds and types of inventors in reference to race, color, creed, religion, gender, or any other limitation other than nationality; thereby the government distinguishes inventors by nation and not by race. The story of the early black American patent holder before slavery's end who attempted to receive federal protection is found in the *legal status* of the person rather than in patent law itself. Jennings, a case in point, born a slave in 1791 and subsequently emancipated, held a new status as a free human who could make a "contract" like any other citizen in 1821, the year his patent was issued. Patent applicants were, and still are, compelled to sign an oath or declaration containing a clause reciting their citizenship. Moreover, a patent is a contract—an enforceable agreement between the federal government and the patentee(s). Inasmuch as enslaved individuals (chattel property) could not perform this function in reference to citizenship, in turn they were prohibited from enjoying any rights pertaining to the document.[8]

The innovative craftsman, remarkable merchant, and abolitionist James Forten, born of free American parents of color in 1766 in Philadelphia, allegedly received a patent on an improved contraption to manage sails. Extensive efforts have been made to locate the document in the U.S. Patent and Trademark Office's published records and patented files, but none has been found.[9] Forten, a former sailor, superbly trained by his employer Robert Bridges in the techniques of how to make or repair all types of sails, easily could have devised a novel process, or he could have developed a new type of hardware to manufacture sails with ease, but if he engineered any such device, he never gained a patent grant. What we do know is that James Forten, who became a man of great import, earned substantial income, reportedly more than $100,000, from his keen business insight, astute real estate endeavors, and productive management of his sail loft where he employed black and white employees. It was from these monies that Forten bankrolled his antislavery activities and became a prominent abolitionist pamphleteer and antislavery representative.

Although Forten held no patent, his achievements in business and in trade are worth mentioning in this work because of his extraordinary success during the turbulent formative years of America. Philadelphia was the nation's capital and a growing seaport city that suffered through the disastrous yellow fever epidemic of 1793, an epidemic that returned again and again. Vessels coming up and down the Delaware River, outfitted with sails, needed new ones or were in need of repair. Sailmakers were plentiful and in heavy competition. African

Americans there controlled this profitable business in the early 1800s. In the work *A Gentleman of Color,* author Julie Winch reflects on Forten:

> In the decade and a half after his return from England in 1785 James Forten not only made the transition from apprentice to master crafts-man but established himself as a man of influence within Philadelphia's free community of color. During the next decade and a half, from 1800 to the end of the War of 1812, he would build on those foundations. In terms of his business career, these were the years when he began to branch out, buying real estate, extending loans, forging ties with white businessmen.[10]

A prominent agent against slavery, Forten denied sale of his sail-rigging and sail-handling tool for slave ships. He is credited with influencing his close friend, the abolitionist William Lloyd Garrison, editor of the *Liberator,* to stand against the evils of colonization. Forten even helped Garrison out of finan-cial difficulties due to the indebtedness of the *Liberator.* In 1841, at age 75, and now a wealthy entrepreneur and ardent abolitionist, the former sailor and sailmaker became very ill and died on March 4 the following year, leaving a sizable monetary estate.[11]

As good fortune would have it, a gifted grandson inherited James Forten's mechanical skills and his business acumen as well. William B. Purvis, born in Philadelphia in 1841 and living in Bucks County, Pennsylvania, in 1850, was classed as mulatto. He held about 12 patents on a paper-bag machine, a mechanism that squared off the bottom of the bag, called "satchel-bottoms," and formed "bellows side folds," between 1894 and 1897. Additionally, he held a patent on a metallic pronged paper-bag fastener (avoiding cord). These dis-coveries established him as a successful creative genius who made a career out of inventing. Purvis, the son of the prosperous Joseph and Sarah (Forten) Purvis, classified as white in one federal census, set up the Union Electric Construction Company of New York at the beginning of the 20th century to handle his manufacturing enterprise. He well knew how to handle a business, being born into an elite free black Philadelphia family whose wealth stemmed from ownership of large properties and farms in the early 1800s.

During his productive entrepreneurial years, Purvis, self-taught, labored on a variety of concepts and modifications other than paper-bag machinery. These ideas, too, matured into patents: on three improved electric railway sys-tems, a distinct fountain pen with a holder "adapted to general use and which may be carried in the pocket," a self-inking hand stamp, and a magnetic car-balancing device. His patented cutter for paper wound on rolls is reported to be one of the first designs of its kind. He had an extraordinary knack for work-ing out ordinary problems. He was a problem solver who turned obstacles into opportunity. The holder of diverse patents found the opportunity to sell the patent rights to his unique paper-bag machine to the New York Union Paper Bag Company. It was needed and therefore extremely vital to the economy. Unmarried, Purvis resided with his sister, Annie, in the town of Darby, Pennsylvania, until his death in 1914, and he was buried in the cemetery of the Church of St. James the Less in Philadelphia beside his mother, the daughter of James Forten.[12]

Industrial enterprises undertaken by blacks centered mostly around manufacturing and building. The story of Henry Boyd, a successful cabinetmaker and inventor but not a patent holder, is recounted here because it demonstrates some of the issues in the struggles of blacks to make it in a business. A number of inventors thought that a business partnership and indirect patent protection through the name of white business associates were best for them. Such was the thinking of Henry Boyd, who formed a commercial venture with a white cabinet manufacturer. Given this racial cooperation, Boyd avoided the obstructions he faced as his own representative in a prejudicial environment. Born a Kentucky slave, Boyd purchased his freedom following an apprenticeship as a cabinetmaker under the tutelage of his master. Migrating to Cincinnati in 1826, he was unable to find work and hired himself out as a stevedore. Eventually, after a stint as an independent carpenter, Boyd partnered with a white craftsman. By 1835, he had accumulated $3,000 and also secured the freedom of his brother and sister. As a talented bed-frame designer and an accomplished shop owner, Boyd wanted protection for his unusual sturdy frames, so he allowed his partner to get a patent in 1835 on the "Boyd Bedstead" design. Later, he invented a device for turning the rails of a bed but did not pursue patent protection. By this time he employed dozens of black workers, and white men as well. Afterward, competitors saw immense benefit in the invention, and Boyd did what he thought was the next best thing to protect his designs. In 1845, as Cincinnati's premier manufacturer of bedsteads selling on a national level, Boyd started identifying the profitable object by stamping his name on each product. However, his detractors did not appreciate the practice. As a result, several fires were started deliberately at his manufacturing facility, but each time he reconstructed the site where he built all kinds of furniture. Finally, in 1863, he was compelled to retire since he was too much of a risk for insurance companies.[13]

Some free Americans of the darker hue in the 1800s had resources. In Louisiana a goodly number of them owned plantations and slaves who labored on the land. Remarkably, one such landowner was a woman, Marie Metoyer of Natchitoches Parish, who had ownership of a 2,000-acre estate and more than 50 slaves in the early decades of the 1800s. Coming from a privileged New Orleans background, the brilliant inventor Norbert Rillieux was born into circumstances quite different from those of most free Southern blacks. Rillieux, who was freed at birth, was born on March 17, 1806, to Constance Vivant, a slave, and Vincent Rillieux, a wealthy white engineer, inventor, and French planter. Designated a quadroon, Norbert Rillieux was baptized in St. Louis Cathedral and because of his father's position received the privileged education of the colored Creole. His father then packed him off for further schooling in Paris, where he studied engineering at L'École Centrale, the finest institution in France. After graduating at age 24, he became an instructor in applied mechanics, the youngest person ever to achieve this position. Having an interest in sugar-refining techniques, he was captivated by thermal dynamics and steam power and published a series of papers on steam engines and steam economy.[14]

Rillieux attempted to interest Parisian investors in his theory of multiple-effect evaporation, but without success. As a youngster he was exposed to the age-old processing of sugar on his father's Louisiana plantation and observed the crude refining of the sugarcane and beets. Until 1846 slaves performed the dangerous, backbreaking work of hand-ladling the boiling cane juice from one open vat to another to produce a dark, sticky sugar, a method popularly known as the "Jamaica Train." The process was tedious, slow, and expensive, yielding a thick syrup. In 1840 Rillieux returned to his native city with the hope of finding someone there to put money into his revolutionary system, which produced a refined, granulated sugar at a reasonable cost.

Several scientists had previously designed vacuum pans and condensing coils, but without much success. Accomplishing the goal of inventing a new and useful improvement, the well-trained inventor designed an ingenious procedure that used an evaporating pan or boiler having an enclosed series of condensing coils in vacuum chambers. This clever design reduced labor and saved fuel since the saccharine juices and syrup boiled at a lower temperature, producing a better product. Rillieux filed for a patent and was issued his first grant, number 3,237, in 1843 for this improvement in sugar works. On December 10, 1846, Rillieux received another patent, number 4,879, for an improvement on his previous sugar-refining method. It was this second patent that captured the world's attention and virtually changed the entire sugar industry from initial processing to end product. It was the radical, special arrangement of the evaporators that led to the success of this truly efficient innovation. This success quickly spread in Louisiana and to the West Indies, setting the precedent for all evaporation systems. The extra revenues gained from the first sugarcane crop processed under the novel concept could be used by planters to purchase machinery.[15]

The world's premier vacuum evaporator system that made sugar abundant and cheap launched Rillieux as the most celebrated engineer in Louisiana. His innovations set precedents and standards in all segments of chemical engineering. On March 17, 1857, he became the owner of another patent (granted as a reissued document) on his sugar-refining process. As with most successful operations, Rillieux's ideas were copied and pirated. Even some of his designs were stolen and taken offshore to Europe; however, he was able to enjoy great wealth from the sale of his innovations. As a free person of color in Louisiana, however, he suffered professional discrimination and race restrictions. Becoming disenchanted with the deteriorating legal state of affairs for blacks in the mid-1800s in Louisiana, Rillieux returned to France, where he engaged in Egyptology and later in engineering research. In 1881, he received yet another patent on a method of heating sugar beet juices with vapors in a multiple-effect system. According to an associate, Rillieux, now in his 80s, lost the rights to a French patent for a combined process of heating juices with vapors in multiple-effect because experts failed to recognize its novelty. However, the process was later acknowledged by the industry and came into worldwide use in factories, cutting production costs while providing an improved sugar product. In spite of many obstacles, Norbert Rillieux took pleasure in the benefits from his inventions, and after his death on October 8, 1894, his widow was able to live a comfortable life until her death in 1912.[16]

The rail companies, kings of transportation, exploited unskilled and skilled workers alike. African Americans in the thousands worked as linemen and locomotive firemen. Many of them participated in the development of railways, offering solutions to help make the rail lines safer. The lines were extensive, and the engineer running the train on the tracks needed to know of hazards and the whereabouts of approaching trains to avoid accidents. The extraordinary, prolific inventor Granville T. Woods, a telegraphic and electrical wizard, solved numerous problems and eased a multitude of the engineer's concerns. Sometimes called "The Black Edison," a name created to equate him with the genius of Thomas Edison, Woods had a phenomenally gifted mind, triumphant in investigation into the field of electricity.

Woods, surely the most exceptional black inventor by the latter decade of the 1800s, was crafty when it came to certain business dealings. Though at one period he was outsmarted by a slippery swindler, Woods persevered and at the beginning of 1900 turned a marginal patenting existence into a distinct improvement in fortune. In the work Black Inventors in the Age of Segregation, author Rayvon Fouché asserts, "For Woods, invention was first and foremost an economic undertaking, a means to gain more capital to invest in future projects. But the grand ideas exemplified in his patents indicate that he also had a vision for modernizing America."[17]

The issues of where Woods was born and his formative technical training have been discussed in many writings. Granville Woods was born on April 23,

1856, a son of Tailer and Martha Woods. His death certificate identifies his place of birth as Australia, even though other sources commonly give his origin at Columbus, Ohio.[18] Author Rayvon Fouché proffers three other citations to support his Australian birthplace. However, the 1860 Federal Population Enumeration for the County of Knox in Ohio lists a Granville Woods, age 10, born in Ohio, and having an older sister named Henrietta and a younger sister named Rachel, plus several other siblings. Their mother is named Martha, born in Virginia, and the father, named "Cyrus" Woods, was born in "Ta" (possibly Tasmania, an island owned by Australia; there is no U.S. state or territory abbreviated with those letters). Granville indeed had two sisters with those given names.[19] Certainly, the Woods family was free in 1860; otherwise, as bondsmen they would not have been enumerated in the 1860 census by name as free head of a household.

Granville Woods attended school until he was 10 years of age, when he started to work in a railroad equipment repair shop in Columbus, Ohio. In his teens during Reconstruction after the Civil War he apprenticed under skilled tradesmen as a machinist and blacksmith. He had private instruction in mechanical engineering, but mostly he was self-educated, gleaning electrical knowledge from library books or those privately borrowed, books that fed his grasping intellectual desire for the subject matter. Woods was brilliant. His electrical cleverness may have budded at a very early age. In 1878, Woods, an employed engineer, embarked on a short stint onboard the British steamer *Ironsides*. Afterwards, he found work on several railway lines in Ohio that enabled him to learn railway technology. In his free time, a friendly telegraph operator in the city of Washington Court House taught him how to operate a telegraph. It was during these runs between cities that Woods became inquisitive about an elevator system, setting the stage for his inventive streak.[20]

Many inventors believe that they can be creative thinkers and at the same time seek venture capital and run a business that exploits their patents. These are not easy tasks. Crossing disciplines, from exerting energy to thinking out solutions to problems to endeavoring in the specialized field of marketing and entrepreneurship, are the most difficult of demands on an inventor. Tackling the intricacies of seeking venture capital, a vital tool to the success of any business, requires intuitiveness and skill, as does employing publicity strategies to advertise the business enterprise. Then there is the tricky marketing arena to consider. To do everything oneself and expect a favorable outcome is risky. Most inventors do not succeed in performing these multiple tasks. Granville Woods experienced a wild ride.

After arriving in Cincinnati in 1880, he encountered a hostile environment. During this period Woods was basically unemployed. Though the city

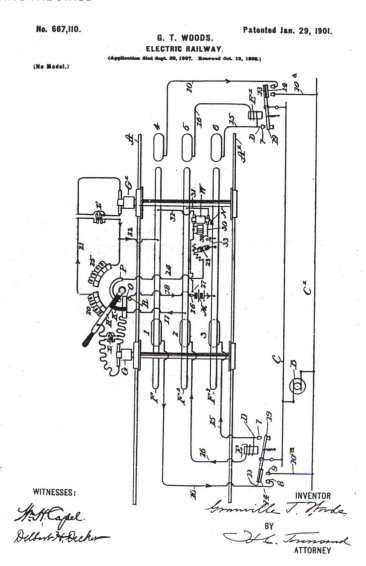

No. 667,110.   Patented Jan. 29, 1901.

G. T. WOODS.

ELECTRIC RAILWAY.

(Application filed Sept. 20, 1897. Renewed Oct. 19, 1900.)

(No Model.)

WITNESSES:

INVENTOR

BY

ATTORNEY

Electric Railway, patented invention of Granville T. Woods. (U.S. Patent and Trademark Office)

in the early decades of the 1800s had a liberal belief toward sable Americans, during the last half of the century, Southern whites streamed in, bringing with them racist attitudes that turned the tide for black residents. Jim Crow practices prevailed, so Woods did odd jobs to make ends meet and borrowed money from friends to finance his inventions. Between 1880 and 1885, Woods concentrated on his inventions, beginning with steam-driven engines and then induction signaling devices. In 1881, while trying to continue his railway endeavors, the area of his expertise, Woods lost momentum when he contracted smallpox, debilitating him for months. A year later he recovered and restarted his creative juices by conceiving a steam boiler furnace that matured into a patent in 1884, his first patent grant of many more to come. Immediately, he sold the rights to Ezra W. Vandusen for an amount coincidentally equal to the cost of the final application fee due for issuance of the patent. Since he owed a lender money, Woods used the amount to pay off his debt.[21] Woods traveled back and forth between Cincinnati and New York City during this time, probably to solicit venture capital for his concepts. He contacted Westinghouse Air Brake Company in 1883, hoping for outright purchase of his innovations.

In 1884, he acquired a patent on a telephone transmitter that sent sound over a distance by means of electric current. The following year, nine years after the invention of the telephone by Alexander Graham Bell, Woods received a patent on an apparatus for transmission of messages by electricity where transmitters used either Morse code or voice messages. He coined the word *telegraphony* for this technology, which combined the telegraph with the telephone. This patent grant strongly competed with the earlier Bell patent, and Woods sold the rights to the invention to the Boston-based American Bell Telephone Company for a modest sum, not the sizable amount he was thought to have received.[22]

Woods wanted his initial patents, which he dubbed "pot boilers," to generate immediate rewards so that he could continue to patent and develop his induction telegraphy system, a concept that would revolutionize rail communication. As with any innovation of this magnitude, Woods needed capital for research and development, but his plans did not materialize. Nonetheless, this setback did not deter him. He was too determined to move forward. In 1885 Woods discovered a novel system of inductive communication. Woods's inventive drive was awakened when he read an article in *Scientific American* that year on a competitor's invention almost identical to his. Woods thought that the induction telegraphy technology had not advanced to the level of review in the august journal. From this instant forward Woods, now highly motivated, devoted all his energy into beating the competitor to the patent office. Fouché writes of Woods that "this technology was his personal domain, and [he] was flabbergasted to see anyone working in his private area. He spent many years perfecting his system of inductive communication and was not ready to let it slip away to another inventor."[23] Now he needed a facility in which to practice his inventions.

Around 1886, Woods formed a business relationship with two Cincinnati financial backers who observed his potential to make money for them. These backers founded the Woods Electric Company in Kentucky and in Ohio as well. Woods desired to establish a company that would start producing his innovations, but, as it turned out, one of the backers wanted Woods to produce the patents for sale on the open market. Woods then became very disenchanted with the business practice of the financiers. He wanted to get out of the contract that he had signed with the company using his name. This was a difficult, costly, and long procedure. Wood finally extricated himself but then was penniless, so he opened a machine repair shop in Cincinnati with his brother Lyates to raise funds for his subsequent inventions.

In 1887, Granville Woods received a patent on one of his most important and controversial inventions—the induction telegraph system, a means for deterring accidents by keeping each train informed of the whereabouts of the one immediately ahead of or following it, and enabling communication between stations and moving trains as well, a phenomenal idea that companies in the industry quickly adopted.

His inventions on electrical railway telegraph systems competed with inventions of Lucius Phelps and Thomas Edison. They invented similar telegraph procedures and litigated to decide who was first to invent. Wood was victorious in the legal battle that put his inventions in the limelight, and he relished the celebrity, eclipsing that of Edison and other inventive luminaries. This good fortune rained on Woods in the form of extraordinary publicity. In 1886, the *Catholic Tribune* lauded Woods as "the greatest colored inventor in the history of the race, and equal, if not superior, to any inventor in the country [and he] is destined to revolutionize the mode of street car transit." The *Cincinnati Colored Citizen* in 1887 proudly acknowledged, "We take great pleasure in congratulating Mr. G. T. Woods on his success in becoming so prominent that his skill and knowledge of his chosen art compare with that of any one of our best-known electricians of the day." And the *American Catholic Tribune* the same year followed by declaring that "Mr. Woods, who is the greatest electrician in the world, still continues to add to his long list of electrical inventions. The latest device he invented is the Synchronous Multiplex Railway Telegraph . . . two hundred operators may use a single wire at the same time. Although . . . messages may be passing in opposite directions, they will not conflict with each other."[24]

In 1890 Woods moved to New York City to find more lucrative work for electrical engineers. Needing money badly, he associated himself with the American Patent Agency, but then found out that the agency was cheating and manipulating him. Feeling deprived from the firm's deceitful practices, Woods moved on. The company bearing his name never earned a reputation, but many corporations to which the Granville Woods patents were licensed or sold grew into gigantic conglomerates, famous for buying out competitors. Finally, Woods received financial success after a productive patenting stint from 1893 to 1896, when he bought a farm in New York.[25]

Woods put many ideas for the electric streetcar into practice and obtained patents on them. He conceived "dynamotors" that significantly diminished the threat of fires on streetcars. Additionally, Woods discovered a better system for transferring electric current to the electric cars and devised a grooved wheel, the troller, so the car could accept electric current while at the same time reducing friction. The common term *trolley car* is derived from the word *troller*. Woods patented more than 60 inventions, 35 of which were on electrical innovations and 15 of which dealt exclusively with electric railways. Nearly all of his patents were assigned, mostly to General Electric, Westinghouse, or to inventor H. Ward Leonard.

At one point in his life Woods may have married, a conclusion that possibly could be drawn from a certain news report. A scandal erupted in May 1896 when a news account reported that Granville Woods "sues a wealthy Poughkeepsie man because he will not discharge the former's alleged wife" from servitude. Through an agency in New York City, the man had hired a "comely colored girl" named Susie Elizabeth Woods, called Lizzie, who claimed to be the wife of Granville Woods.[26] On Woods's 1896 patent concerning a system of electrical distribution, Lizzie Woods is listed as one of three witnesses who signed the patent application papers on August 31, 1892. This document is assigned to S. E. Riley of New York. Just after 1900, Woods conceived an automatic air-brake system patented in 1902, assigned to Westinghouse Air Brake Company. Lyates Woods and S. E. Woods (likely Susie Elizabeth Woods) were listed as witnesses on the patent drawings. One year later, Lyates joined with his brother as coinventor on the electric railway apparatus, assigned to the General Electric Company. The brothers continued joint inventorship until 1907. With this new enterprise Woods furthered his inventive skills. His business ability to sell the coveted grants showed determination sprinkled with a level of success within his entrepreneurial spirit. While he gained no enormous wealth, Woods nonetheless secured enough economic reward to keep him in the inventive process in spite of the many costly patent interference cases he endured.

Granville Woods suffered a stroke and died on January 30, 1910, at Harlem Hospital in New York City. He is buried at St. Michael's Cemetery in Queens, New York. Louis Haber in his work *Black Pioneers of Science and Invention* eulogizes Woods with the following:

> Few inventors of any race have produced a larger number of appliances in the field of electricity, and few have done more for the electrical industry than Granville Woods. His work continued without interruption for over a quarter of a century.
>
> Today we owe much to the brilliance and industry of Granville Woods, who . . . gave us much of what we now take for granted in the field of electricity.[27]

Woods's inventive career went through a period of upturns and downturns, the downturns resulting mostly from poor business transactions and the lack of adequate funds for research and development. His accumulation of knowledge demonstrated the difficulty that small independent inventors experienced in participating in emerging new disciplines. Most inventors want monetary gain besides personal satisfaction from their inventiveness. This is quite understandable since the path from creation to production can present substantial financial demands. Those inventors who choose to protect their product with a patent before going to market discover that it is very expensive to have their application travel through the complexities of patent examination. Having a patent grant, though, does not guarantee success. This must come from individual effort—a lesson Granville Woods learned the hard way.

Inventing can be a practical occupation. Success as an inventor depends on how one proceeds to reap any benefit from one's effort, but it is luck mostly. Marketing the invention is the goal of any inventor who wants to recoup expenses from the inventive process. One must know the clientele to whom the effort is directed. If your product is popular or makes a significant change in the way one does business, there is a good chance of succeeding at selling your commodity; otherwise getting the buyer or investor to believe in your invention may prove difficult. Of course, using the services of a marketing professional who must be paid is an option, and the expense for the services can come from the profit made from sales.

For most of the early inventors of color, self-manufacturing and self-promotion seemed the best choice within the atmosphere of hostility toward blacks that was common during that era. Then, too, if the product was well received by customers, it sold itself, creating a solid economic base for the producer. One inventor and entrepreneur in particular enjoyed the benefits of his lucrative manufacturing business until changing trends in lifestyles forced him to adjust plans and diversify. Samuel Raymond Scottron, a New York–based manufacturer born in Philadelphia in 1843, understood the essence of diversification. Between the late 1870s and 1893, through trial and tribulation, he worked on his many inventions ranging from mirrors to window treatments to other domestic products. Scottron, grandfather of actress and singer Lena Horne, was a merchant of household goods who preferred to manufacture and market his own patented inventions. In 1849 his family moved to New York, where Scottron attended public schools. He married at the age of 19 and later began his inventing career.[28]

Recounting in the magazine *Colored American* in 1906, Scottron reasoned that a "patent which can be simplified by another is worth nothing. . . . knowledge of mechanics will show you how to use the simplest methods in obtaining certain desired results . . . [but contact] with the market will show you whether what you wish to accomplish will be worth anything . . . even if you succeed in making the thing." Scottron found that years "are spent by some in trying to do something by way of a patented article, that even if made, wouldn't be wanted by a sufficient number of persons to make it desirable."[29] The invention business was risky, to put it mildly.

Scottron began his business career as a merchant and trader, who was associated with others as a sutler of a regiment near the close of the Civil War. After mustering out in 1865, he first went to Florida and opened grocery stores, abandoned the unprofitable businesses, and then went North to Springfield, Massachusetts, where he established a barbershop. This business inspired his first profitable idea: an adjustable mirror wherein one's view of every side could be seen all at once. Scottron's Adjustable Mirrors were so arranged opposite each other to allow the full view of every side. After studying at night during a seven-year apprenticeship to a pattern maker and to a master mechanic to acquire the skill to make mirrors, such as learning the difference between cast and rolled metals, he became successful at the specialty, receiving a patent on the technology. However, diversification for Scottron was not so much a desired plan, but rather one forced upon him because of the downfall of three business partnerships and the consumer's rise and decline in taste in the window treatment industry.[30]

Ever the watchful eye for fashion trends, and now his own counsel, Scottron shifted his attention to inventing household products, including extension cornices for curtains. He abandoned the mirror business to manufacture cornices—a trendy product—under contract with H. L. Judd & Company of New York in the early 1880s. Promoting the extension cornice inventions secured him thousands of dollars. To his dismay, though, society swiftly abandoned cornices in favor of newfangled curtain poles, so he put his cornice patents out on royalties. Accordingly, the capricious trade again forced him to modify his choice of products to bring to market. Living on royalties until he got a footing in the ranks of the curtain-pole makers, Scottron began as a manager and salesman at a firm, staying the course for 15 years.[31] From that technology he made discoveries and patented two curtain-rod combinations, receiving one patent in 1892 and the second in 1893.

All was going well until Scottron, now sensitive to new enterprises, by chance found out how to make glass look like onyx and other stones. Setting off in still another direction, Scottron began to manufacture "porcelain onyx" in the form of cylinders or tubes that were useful to lamp and candlestick producers. Ultimately making an enormous income from sale of pedestals, tabourets, lamp columns, and lamp and vase bodies at his Monroe Street office in Brooklyn, Scottron held steadfast, employing his entire family of wife, son, and three daughters to assist him. He produced and marketed his creation of imitation onyx and various foreign and American pottery finishes as well, preferring to hold the process as a trade secret rather than patent it. At long last he had found a highly profitable and, more important, stable business enterprise.[32]

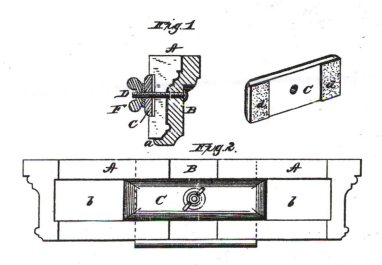

WITNESSES

F. L. Ourand

H. Aubrey Toulmin

INVENTOR

S. R. Scottron

Alexander Thaxton

ATTORNEYS

Adjustable Window-Cornice, patented invention of Samuel R. Scottron. (U.S. Patent and Trademark Office)

Scottron by now had adjusted to the mercurial nature of the marketplace. He was an active member of the National Negro Business League, where he was a delegate to its founding convention in 1900 and advised would-be inventors to go for simplicity in plans and construction and to always be familiar with the market.[33] He saw the advice as a beacon to show other inventors whether what they wish to accomplish will have any value in the system. Scottron's business philosophy can be expressed best by the old ditty "Paddle Your Own Canoe," which in part recites, "When the world is cold and dark, keep an aim in view. Toward the beacon mark, paddle your own canoe. Leave to heaven in humble trust all you will to do, but if you succeed, you must paddle your own canoe." The ditty represented the overall self-help attitude most black business talents adopted following Reconstruction.[34]

Given this position, the minority group had little alternative but to embrace it. After all, it seemed the most reasonable solution to their plight. The position enlightened not only their own race but the majority race as well of African Americans' achievements as businessmen, artisans, authors, military men, skilled practitioners of various professions, and inventors.

2

Self-Help—a Beginning: Business in the Making

When we recall the fact that the colored people have come so recently from savagery, through the barbarism of slavery, into the light of civilization, we should expect them to be slow in getting a footing in the shifting and uncertain sands of the business and commercial world. . . . The colored people are passing through a hard and severe economic struggle. . . . And yet, in spite of all these adverse conditions, a very creditable beginning has been made in the business world—a beginning that promises well for the future.

—Andrew F. Hilyer, "The Colored American in Business," Boston, 1900

Gradually, in the 19th century, various black business, mercantile, and professional groups established independent associations. Membership rolls of farmers' alliances and cooperative unions, agricultural and mechanic associations, and institutes for promotion of mechanic arts and sciences included black inventors. These important interests were vital to everyone's welfare regardless of vocation. In the early 1800s, the publishing business offered a few industrious freeborn and manumitted individuals an opportunity to express deep concern about their existence in a country struggling with the thorny slave problem as it transitioned from an agrarian society to an industrial commonwealth. With a wide minority readership, black news columnists praised the achievement of skilled tradesmen and craft experts, including the occasional inventor, whom they willingly promoted and proudly exalted. Although whites burned out some brave publishers and destroyed their presses, the power of the pen prevailed. Upon relocating west or north, these journalists simply reorganized and began other publications.

The rise of ebony Americans in business and in inventive thought during the antebellum period was promising in spite of the overwhelming odds due, in part, to oppression, prejudice, and deprivation. Walker in *The History of Black Business in America* states that within the context of U.S. law, "Race mattered a great deal." Nonetheless, she indicates the importance of the economic successes that free and slave enterprises exhibited, which can be "attributed to the remarkable business ability of antebellum black entrepreneurs to capitalize on the free-market system" and reasons that "the most successful antebellum black businesspeople must be considered entrepreneurs" within a limited context.[1] In discussing black business from the end of the Civil War to 1900, she says, "There was a continuation and expansion of entrepreneurship within the tradition of self-help activities that had distinguished black economic endeavors" starting at the beginning of the country.[2]

The South was in economic shambles after 1865. Farmland was devastated, and harvested crops were destroyed or confiscated. Houses and shelter were in ruin. At the end of the war goods and services were in need along with the critical need for food, clothing, and a place to live. Previously, slave labor sustained Southern agriculture with many of the craft and trade services being provided by former skilled bondsmen.

Some blacks continued their businesses from the antebellum period, mostly begun with marginal financial resources. Booker T. Washington affirms in *The Negro in Business* that

> [the Southern Negro] was . . . very often skilled in trades which proved to be for him the thresholds to business enterprise in a condition of freedom. The slave skilled as a butcher, for instance, after emancipation often opened a butcher shop of his own; the skilled carpenter taught himself to read and cipher and became a contractor; and the skilled plantation poultry-man in some cases gradually built up a trade reckoned by the car-loads.[3]

Among this group were innovative minds whose creative abilities sparked the desire to make improvements on what had come before.

At that time the conventional wisdom of the white power base, which had a pessimistic outlook, was that blacks were not mentally capable of or proficient at running a business. It was thought that they lacked basic education, but the need to learn the three introductory subjects—reading, writing, and arithmetic—was not as acute then as today. Hardly any business, white or black, recorded transactions of any nature as part of its day-to-day activities. If a person knew how to recite numerals in ascending order and could give exact change, then he could do business.[4]

Accompanying the development of business enterprise at this time was the active role of creative thinkers. Exceptional black talent repeatedly came to the forefront for being ingenious in manufacturing and in the sciences and the arts. If blacks were inherently inferior, how is it that so many achieved great distinction? Black inventors have contributed to the progress of the people through their inventive genius more than most ordinary men in modern civilization, spurring the nation's economy by revolutionizing industries. These include the genius of Granville Woods, Elijah McCoy, Jan Matzeliger, William Purvis, Norbert Rillieux, and George W. Carver, whose innovations helped make America prosper. Other inventive members of the race were not so extraordinary but did their part to encourage the growth of the nation, such as D. F. Black of Mechanicsburg, Pennsylvania, who invented several products and engaged in processing a coconut food, which he manufactured "with fair success."[5] Reverend John B. Randolph of Burlington, New Jersey, secured a patent in 1895 on a combined apparatus for heating and for cooking with the objective of saving one-half the fuel cost to heat a house.[6] Henry Creamer, an inventor from Brooklyn, New York, was granted patents between 1885 and 1888 on an automatic steam pump that was held in high regard.[7]

NATIONAL NEGRO BUSINESS LEAGUE

Founded by Booker T. Washington, the National Negro Business League aimed to stimulate and increase African American enterprise and capital. Washington desired first to concentrate on economic growth before beginning a fight for civil rights. Many inventors who had established businesses became staunch members of the influential organization. Being a member of the group meant having connections, especially with its founder, who was president of Tuskegee Institute and the leading black figure with ties to the White House.

See *The Negro in Business* by Booker T. Washington and *Proceedings of the National Negro Business League*, 1900.

Andrew Franklin Hilyer, a successful real estate investor in Washington, D.C., acquired two patents in 1890 for improved home heating devices. Hilyer, born a slave in 1858 in Walton County, Georgia, moved to St. Louis, Missouri, and then to Nebraska before moving to Minneapolis, where he attended the University of Minnesota and became its first black graduate. After relocating to the District of Columbia, he entered Howard University, graduating as valedictorian of his law class in 1885. The following year he received a master's degree in the field.

In 1890 he obtained two patents on wall registers. One invention concerned an improved water evaporator attachment for hot-air registers and the other was an improved evaporator for hot-air registers. It is not readily known if Hilyer sold his patent rights after issuance of the documents or established a business exclusively to promote the inventions; however, he did receive an income from his sanitary-valued water evaporator attachment.[8]

In the 1890s, Hilyer edited a catalogue of black businesses, organizations, and churches. In Boston in 1900, he delivered a lengthy address on the "colored" American in business before the national meeting of the National Negro Business League. In recalling that black people came from "the barbarism of slavery" into "the light of civilization" not far back, Hilyer presented, in part, a glowing detailed report. It was gleaned from the W.E.B. Du Bois 1899 conference investigation of the "Negro in Business" that cited "1,906 colored business men and women" and specified type of business, number of years in business, and amount of capital invested.[9]

Hilyer was particularly active in stimulating black business development and in promoting liberal and industrial education. He was appointed the secretary-treasurer of the Jamestown Negro Exhibit's promoting organization and sponsor, the Negro Development and Exposition Company, headed by its director-general and chief promoter, Colonel Giles B. Jackson. Living comfortably and described as one of the foremost advocates of black economic cooperation, Hilyer became ill with acute bronchial pneumonia and died at his home on January 13, 1925. Funeral services were held at Howard University's Rankin Chapel. Hilyer's eldest son, Franklin Nicholas Hilyer, a graduate of the Armstrong Manual Training School, exhibited an original design of an electric automobile at the 1907 Jamestown Negro Exhibit, where Hilyer himself showcased his inventions.[10]

In the 1800s and 1900s, technical, professional, and trade entities coexisted alongside the commonplace mutual benefit organizations, all established to articulate the concerns of the bondsman and of the free black. Instituted as forums, the worthy groups set forth strategies and programs for the poor and hapless. These organizations began training underprivileged citizens, giving them a support structure vitally needed during this hostile, racist period of the nation.

African American normal, mechanical, and agricultural schools also provided training, which brought forth a new breed of builders and craftsmen who were able to assist with rebuilding the South. Further, a new generation of professionally taught architects surfaced, some of whom formulated mechanical and building trade programs at several black college campuses. By the 20th century, these builders and architects founded businesses and designed black enclaves, hotels, commercial buildings, insurance companies, and banks for fraternal organizations.

Despite the sweeping restrictions placed on people of color, some found an economic niche carved from delivering a quality service such as barbering, catering, nursing, or laundering in the open market. They were law-abiding, churchgoing citizens, setting an example for their children, whom they sent to school for an education that they themselves had been denied. However, all was not well. Appearances were misleading.

Faced with an antagonistic society, which generally viewed them with contempt and disdain, these citizens saw the need to group together to protect themselves. As result, mutual aid efforts, secret fraternal orders, and burial societies were founded. Many became forerunners of black insurance companies that were by-products of these burying-ground groups and fraternal societies. Nearly all people of color at that time joined one society or another regardless of their profession, trade, or employment. Societies sprang up everywhere to assist the preacher, dressmaker, carpenter, inventor, lawyer, doctor, clerk, and dentist as well as the printer, blacksmith, and railway laborer.

Independent enterprises were flourishing due to the leadership of their black administrators. The community supported the efforts of groups like the True Reformers, which prospered in the early decade of the 20th century. This remarkable organization, led by a black Baptist minister, achieved extraordinary success. William Washington Browne, born in 1849, founded the benevolent Grand United Order of True Reformers in Alabama as the true way to "reform" adverse conditions of black people. When Browne relocated to Richmond, he reorganized the Virginia branch and renamed it the Grand Fountain of the United Order of True Reformers, which established a mutual benefit fund in 1883 that subsequently became a large insurance company. The Grand Fountain at Richmond provided significant employment for tradesmen and various craftsmen and built a hall, a hotel, and a home for "old folks" over several decades, putting the talents of black architects and building contractors into service.[11] Branches of the True Reformers were located in several jurisdictions, including Washington, D.C.

In 1888, the True Reformers chartered a savings bank, making it the first black-owned and black-operated bank in the United States, conceived in philanthropy. Additionally, the Reformers established a real estate agency, a building and loan association, and cooperative grocery stores, all in the political jurisdiction called Jackson Ward. Inhabited by blacks, Jackson Ward was configured by one of its members, prominent resident and avid black business promoter Giles B. Jackson, an attorney born enslaved in 1853. Jackson prepared the articles of incorporation for the True Reformers. During its growth the organization began a weekly newspaper as well. Benefiting from the thriving enterprises that generated millions of dollars, the Reformers profited immensely from the skills and business acumen of its members.[12] Unfortunately, in 1910 the True Reformer Bank, as it came to be known, failed from

MAGGIE LENA WALKER AND THE INDEPENDENT ORDER OF SAINT LUKE

One remarkable African American order, the Independent Order of Saint Luke, was founded by Mary Prout just 2 years after the end of the Civil War in 1867 in Baltimore. Organized exclusively for women, it provided health and death benefits to its members and was brought to prominence in Richmond by Maggie Lena Walker, who became the first woman to head a bank anywhere in the world. After taking over leadership of the benevolent order around 1899, Walker, a product of Richmond's Jackson Ward district born in 1867, accomplished amazing results in 10 years. Again, with the use of black skills, a beneficial organization prospered. Walker, a woman of great ability, rare tact, and business foresight, established a general department store and also began a weekly newspaper. These enterprises produced hundreds of thousands of dollars in assets. In 1903, she set up the Saint Luke Penny Savings Bank and by 1910 was its president. The institution, later known as the Consolidated Bank and Trust Company, was the model for other mutual benefit societies that flourished. Due to its conservative practices the Trust Company did not close during the infamous 1929 U.S. stock market crash. Although the Independent Order went out of existence some decades after Walker's death in 1934, its bank and branches thrived, thus attesting to the astute business practices of people of color.

Sources: Harris, *The Negro as Capitalist*, pp. 47–48; Jackson and Davis, *The Industrial History of the Negro Race of the United States*, p. 135; Ives, "Richmond's Black Heritage," p. 23; and Walker, *The History of Black Business*, p. 188.

mismanagement, but it succeeded in implanting "certain social and economic ideals in Negro life."[13]

The most innovative period in the nation's development occurred probably in the 1880s, when the country was shifting from agriculture to industry. This was when the trolley car, the automatic shoe-lasting machine, the steam turbine, the electric furnace, the electric light, and railroad concepts were patented. African American inventors were significant participants in this great display of creativity. Very naturally they began inventing agricultural implements and culinary utensils, as these were the classes of art with which they had the most experience, and which obviously called out their genius. After the end of the Civil War, they began securing patents in every possible range of subjects.

Black inventors surfaced in quick succession after Southern reconstruction. They were thrifty and industrious, advancing labor-saving tools, contraptions, mechanical processes, and chemical compositions.[14] Often, success for these inventors came from individual performance and lots of luck.

Efforts to capitalize on an invention are exhausting, and hence some black inventors who held patent rights often sold or assigned them to white businessmen, or they established limited companies that did not benefit them on a long-term basis. At times the assigned company would issue stock or hold a partnership with the patentee. These enterprises often were short-term schemes to provide the inventor with needed funds to develop ideas and to manufacture and market the invention; however, many black inventors were not able to fully capitalize on their patents as they envisioned. It was in that period of great intellectual development that the ubiquitous automatic shoe-lasting machine was invented in 1883 by Jan Matzeliger, an immigrant of mixed parentage from the country of Surinam in South America. Hoping to manufacture his revolutionary shoe device and its improvements, Matzeliger sorely needed funds and unfortunately traded his patent rights for stock in a company. The enterprise ultimately grew into a multimillion-dollar business after his death in 1889 at the age of only 36.[15]

Even though some early patentees were prolific, their interest in establishing manufacturing companies rested in research. The decision to follow this path put them in a less favorable position when it came to capital. Canadian-born inventor Elijah McCoy devised an automatic lubricator for steam engines and received 57 patents on improvements in the field. The automatic oiling process became so well known that railroad personnel and industrial engineers and mechanics would not use any new equipment or piece of machinery unless it contained the "real McCoy" device, an indication of the genuine apparatus.[16] As negotiable property, patents were sold for some form of profit. In McCoy's instance, he exchanged the patent rights for minor shares in the company bearing his name but enjoyed only meager profit. The assignment of these rights, recorded at the U.S. Patent and Trademark Office, might vary in specifying an individual assignor or a company or corporation as assignor.

Washingtonian Leonard C. Bailey was a very lucky inventor. Born in the nation's capital in March 1843, Bailey rose to prominence as an astute and shrewd businessman. He profited enormously from his patented combined truss and bandage concept. On June 30, 1883, Bailey filed an application on his improvement in trusses, or bandages relating to supporting an inguinal or scrotal hernia. The objective was to provide a simple and effective device for supporting "the reduced parts" of the body that would give superb relief to the patient and would affect an ultimate cure without the use of pads commonly used to retain the intestine. Just three months after filing Bailey became a patent holder. He appealed to the Army Medical Board to use his invention for soldiers having that need. His persuasiveness won over the authorities, who handsomely compensated Bailey. In time he netted millions of dollars from his invention. His achievement was most unusual given the unsettling racial attitudes of the time.

Having an entrepreneurial spirit, Bailey cofounded the Capitol Savings Bank and served as its treasurer and was director of its Industrial Building and Savings Company. The Savings Bank was one of the first black banks in the United States, organized in 1888, the same year that the True Reformers Bank of Richmond was chartered. The Savings Company, essentially a building and loan association, was organized in response to the demand of black men to do business.

Later, with more creative thought, Bailey conceived and then patented an improved folding bed in 1899. The portable device collapsed into a form that made it easily transportable. It primarily was useful for hospitals on account of its hygienic properties and the ease with which it could be kept clean and rendered antiseptic. It is not clear from records if he received any monetary reward for this concept. During his lifetime, Bailey became the director of the Manassas Industrial School in Virginia and was a member of the first integrated jury impaneled in the District of Columbia. He passed away suddenly on September 1, 1918, at his residence, survived by an adopted daughter.[17]

Bishop B. W. Arnett from Wilberforce, Ohio, in an 1896 account of the schools founded, manned, and supported by African Americans, declared

Leonard C. Bailey. (From the Patricia Carter Ives Sluby Collection)

that from that published work the world will be informed as to what the race is doing for its own education. Expounding on gender initiative, he let it be known that males and females alike have shown skill in the professions, and both have arrived at success in business.[18] William Lloyd Garrison in 1900 presented an assessment of race relations in the North and in the South. He proclaimed that "the colored people in the South are doing the necessary work, steadily gaining in wealth, self-reliance and intellectual power."[19] Garrison further urged African Americans to aim for self-employment and be self-reliant and self-supportive. He strongly suggested that blacks take a path for possession of property honestly earned.[20] Giving evidence of progress, G. F. Richings in his book of 1902 expressed similar sentiment, reasoning that the black race had not been fairly assessed in its ability to learn.[21]

At the turn of the 20th century when William McKinley was president of the United States, black Americans were subjected to one of the most devastating vehicles employed by powerful white forces to keep the races segregated and minorities under control. Disfranchisement and "Jim Crow" laws suppressed them at their every attempt to enjoy racial equality. Reconstruction had ended and the last African American elected to the U.S. Congress had left office.

In the former capital of the Confederacy, Richmond, Virginia, nearly half the population of 50,000 were African American, of which more than 5,500 were registered voters in the heavily black-populated Jackson Ward enclave. But by 1896, there were only about 3,000 registered voters.[22] Even worse, in September 1903, only 760 out of 8,000 voting age people of color in all of Richmond were qualified to vote. After 1902, the black vote was virtually eliminated from Virginia politics, largely through the efforts of ultraconservatives who felt that blacks did not merit the same position and status in society that they did. In 1901, a ridiculous education test and a poll tax were adopted, required as a prior condition for voting. Due to poverty and illiteracy, many blacks did not pay the required taxes. In 1903, a case was filed in the state courts testing the infamous voting restrictions. However, the effort was to no avail. On appeal the U.S. Supreme Court decided to favor the white majority, virtually eliminating the black vote from politics.[23] The Fourteenth and Fifteenth Amendments to the Constitution gave people of an ebony hue the right to vote and hold office; however, these privileges quickly disappeared in the South at the beginning of the 20th century. How did they persevere and sustain themselves during these onslaughts and escalating Southern lynching?

Even during these frightening, debilitating times in the nation, the wheels of invention by African Americans steadily turned over and over, changing obstacles and difficulties into advantage. The Negro Exhibit of the 1907 Jamestown tercentennial celebration was the site of choice for mechanical and inventive talent. There, Adolphus C. Howard, born a slave in 1863 in Mississippi, displayed his popular shoe polish product, manufactured at his well-equipped factory in Chicago and in New York as well. After about five years of formal schooling and self-reading in New Orleans, where his mother had taken him to find his grandmother in 1865, he started working at age 10 and later ended up in Boston. Before becoming a Pullman porter and an early ruling member of the National Negro Business League, Howard worked as a ship steward. He quit the porter position after saving about $180 and used the money to start his enterprise. He began by peddling his shoe-blacking composition to railroad porters and others on the street. His initial stock included $2 worth of cans and material. Then he spent $500 every two months on the tins alone. The business prospered rapidly, expanding to all the large department stores of both metropolises plus Philadelphia, then to neighboring Mexico. Much of his accomplishment can be attributed to his wife's assistance as a bookkeeper.

Howard's large and attractive display of a practical invention won him a bronze medal at the 1907 Jamestown Exhibit, setting an example of sable ingenuity and business acumen.[24] He was told that his photograph of a "colored" man on his boxes would ruin his business, but he found it no obstacle to his success and even acquired a registered trademark for the goods. Among orders he received was one from Bornn & Company of New York for 40,000 boxes and another from a Mexican company for 70,000 boxes. By 1907, Howard's receipts from the sale of the liquid and paste compositions were up to $20,000 per year.[25] Here, Howard gave the general population a better product for which he was richly rewarded.

Stalwart individuals such as A. C. Howard and other inventors demonstrated their ability to succeed in a chosen line of industry. From modest beginnings they built up great and profitable business ventures, and their efforts earned them respect from both blacks and whites in their local areas. Inventors who became successful businessmen in the early decades of the 1900s such as Howard and Samuel R. Scottron not only were members of the National Negro Business League but were anointed by its president, Booker T. Washington, to address the league at its national business sessions for the express purpose of telling those assembled how they succeeded in business. This was a distinct honor.

Jamestown exhibitor Aiken C. Taylor won prestigious awards in 1907 for two of his many inventions. Born in Charleston, South Carolina, in 1878, Taylor received a silver medal for a combined cotton planter and fertilizer distributor and a bronze medal for an extension stepladder. Also showcased among some of the best innovations was Taylor's convenient bedsprings that could be converted into a chair with the turn of a lever. The concept was not patented until 1918.[26] Of Taylor's 11 patented inventions, the property rights of 4 were transferred to Emanuel P. Summerfield of Norfolk, Virginia. The rights of his extension stepladder patent were transferred to the Extension Step Ladder and Speciality Company Inc. of Richmond, Virginia, around 1913, where Taylor

Ser. No. 60,836 CLASS 4. ABRASIVE, DETERGENT, AND POLISHING MATERIALS. THE A. C. HOWARD POLISH COMPANY, INCORPORATED, New York, N. Y. Filed Jan. 15, 1912.

was then living. Clearly Taylor was enterprising enough to reap some benefit from his innovations. By 1918 he had relocated to Washington, D.C., where he was granted a patent for a pivoted window sash, the rights of which were transferred to Summerfield also.

Hunter C. Haynes, who was born to former slave parents in Selma, Alabama, became a self-made entrepreneur through his extraordinary skill. In the late 1890s, he developed a razor strop that enabled a novice to sharpen a razor without cutting the strip of leather that formed the strop. The new and widely popular invention, called "The Twentieth Century Razor Stropper," has been mentioned to have had a patent pending; however, to date no record at the patent office has been uncovered to indicate this. In any event, Haynes filled orders for the device through his Haynes Razor Strop company, organized in Chicago in 1904, gaining thousands of dollars in profit.[27]

At the age of 10, to support his mother and sister, Haynes began to work, as did numerous children in the South, blacking boots and selling papers. Struggling to keep the family together, as a teenager he apprenticed with one of the oldest and best African American barbers in Alabama, becoming first-class in just 15 months. It was at this early age that he conceived of a ready-to-use razor strop. He held the idea dormant until he was able to save enough money to act on it, and he continued working as a barber in Chicago and then in San Francisco. On the West Coast he returned to the razor strop concept and built a small laboratory in a corner, where he produced a few strops. From the sale of this product he was able to secure enough funds to return to Selma but found the circumstances there inhospitable. Suffering from cruelty in a toxic area, he and his wife fled North, ending up penniless in Chicago in 1896.[28]

As fate would have it, the honorable trade of barbering for blacks had slipped from their hands. Times had changed in Chicago and elsewhere in the North, due in part to the proliferation of barber schools that shut their doors to blacks and concentrated on training whites. Consequently, newly trained, very skilled white barbers replaced African Americans in the finest shops in the country. Nonetheless, Haynes was not deterred by the change in attitude and turned a gloomy situation into a profit-making endeavor. Ever the intuitive talent, Haynes produced an article of manufacture he knew the white barbers would buy. He made a profit selling his best steel razors and used it to purchase more from a German manufacturer. This beginning later earned him the title of "king of razor-sellers."[29]

Finally, the business grew into a large enterprise. From its earnings he produced his remarkable, novel razor strop. After a brief period, Haynes realized enormous gains, well beyond his hopes. The Haynes Razor Strop was a roaring success nationally and abroad as well. His strops were sold exclusively in the barbershops of the Waldorf Astoria hotel and other prestigious establishments, even by the private barber to the emperor of Germany. In late 1899 his business made more than 1,000 strops, and in 1900 Haynes introduced his innovative article to about 200,000 barbers. He exhibited his popular strops and razors at the Indianapolis conference of the National Negro Business League in 1904.[30] Perseverance, strength, fortitude, and an extreme desire to succeed propelled Hunter C. Haynes into a sphere of endeavor he never imagined.

In 1918, Haynes passed away at his home in Saranac Lake, New York, where he and his wife had moved. Haynes had pursued another career in which he was quite prominent. He was a major figure in the motion picture business as a producer of comedies. His stellar production was *Uncle Remus' Visit to New York.*[31]

Like the Negro Exhibit that Colonel Giles B. Jackson (the title the lawyer preferred) sponsored for the Jamestown Exposition of 1907, the 1915 National Negro Exposition, held at Virginia's state fairgrounds in Richmond and also organized by Jackson, celebrated the 50th anniversary of the emancipation and achievements of blacks. The Negro Historical and Industrial Association promoted the exposition, which demonstrated the thrift, industry, and achievement of American blacks, whom 50 years earlier were thought incapable of existing as an industrious, enterprising group. The federal government endorsed and supported the effort by appropriating $55,000 to aid in its promotion. More than 25,000 black and white citizens visited the site. Exhibits were sent from every state and by every African American university and college. Adolphus C. Howard's manufactured Howard Shoe Polish was one of the more prominent exhibits.[32] More than likely a number of inventive talents, such as Aiken C. Taylor, who now lived in Richmond, also showcased their discoveries.

In the early 1900s, people of color in the South began migrating North to improve their economic conditions. There, the cities received a great influx of desperate Americans looking for a more equitable and tolerable job market. A few of them did realize a measure of success, but not without tribulation. Joining the ranks of minority inventors at the new century's turn was Shelby Davidson, born three years after the end of the Civil War. He moved to Washington, D.C., from Kentucky in 1887 to work in the auditing department of the U.S. Post Office Department. He was a lawyer but was curious about the functions of adding machines, and he hoped to improve the auditing method instantly used by the government. After diligent study in the first few years of the 1900s, he took up the matter with his superior and in turn made visits to the factory of the Burroughs Adding Machine Co., hoping for cooperation with them concerning the needs and possibilities of the parts' automatic grouping.[33] Davidson had encountered daily problems with tabulation and sought ways to overcome them. He was captivated by these mechanisms. His first solution, a paper rewind mechanism for adding machines, was patented in 1908.[34] The government utilized his concept with many of its

Cover of patent grant to Shelby J. Davidson, 1908. Reprinted in *Shelby Davidson, Inventor: In His Own Words* by Joellen ElBashir, HU ArchivesNet, The Electronic Journal MSRC-Howard University, February 2001, http://www.huarchivesnet.howard.edu/teachshelby3.htm. (U.S. Patent and Trademark Office)

No. 884,721.

PATENTED APR. 14, 1908.

S. J. DAVIDSON.
PAPER REWIND MECHANISM FOR ADDING MACHINES.
APPLICATION FILED MAR. 13, 1906.

3 SHEETS—SHEET 3.

Paper Rewind Mechanism for Adding Machines, patented invention of Shelby J. Davidson. (U.S. Patent and Trademark Office)

adding contraptions. Davidson worked alone to perfect his ideas; however, he faced the usual dilemmas inventors confront. After personal meetings with adding machine company executives, the sought-after support for production and marketing never materialized.

Although grievously disadvantaged, blacks went into business nonetheless. When making money, they invariably were able to save a portion. Patience and persistence paid off. Some of the most enterprising and successful of these businesspersons were those born in slavery, especially the enslaved who had prior training and experience. Additionally, their personal initiative and self-reliance counted for better progress. When black businesspeople dealt with the socially and economically disadvantaged of their race after the conflict between the North and the South, black businessmen took to the task of encouraging and educating them in thrift and in the management of their affairs, as well as in precision in meeting their obligations. All of this combined to make their businesses possible and profitable.

3

Following Their Passion—in the Marketplace

The true measure of a nation's worth is its contribution to the well being of the world. This can be applied equally well to races, and judging by this standard, the Negro has nothing of which to be ashamed.

—*Giles B. Jackson and D. Webster Davis, The Industrial History of the Negro Race, 1908*

In the first two decades of the 1900s, Americans experienced great benefit from mass production of goods, which became cheaper and more affordable to the average citizen. African American inventors played a vital role in this economic boom. They, along with black leaders, scholars, and businessmen, became a part of a greater movement to define who they were in a society that considered blacks second-class citizens.

In those years, the leaders Booker T. Washington and William E. B. Du Bois were rivals with opposing positions as to the best national posture for people of color. Washington urged the pursuit of industry and thrift, whereas Du Bois promoted higher scholarship and merit. In either case, a New Negro emerged from the growing middle class of men and women who challenged negative stereotypes. Courageous, bold, and fearless, the new mindset worked tirelessly to redefine the nation's concept of its black citizens.

After a time of expansion of African American business, the Great Depression hit the country during the 1930s, and blacks consequently suffered enormous hardships. The high unemployment rate among blacks took its toll on minority businesses, which depended nearly 100 percent on their patronage.

However, on the national level, whether during the Depression or otherwise, African Americans always spent largely at white businesses. One nationwide campaign, though, did help blacks find employment in white enterprises.

MARCELLUS CARRINGTON WALLER, A SELF-TAUGHT INNOVATOR

African Americans invented scores of devices of every kind, shape, or form, and, based on the innovation, a few of them founded small companies that endured generation after generation, providing a lasting livelihood for the progeny. Marcellus Carrington Waller was a self-taught jeweler who invented useful tools and parts to practice his craft because he could not afford to buy them. His uncle, a blacksmith, trained him to work with tools. In 1900, Waller, with only a third-grade education and during harsh racial discrimination and racism, founded M. C. Waller, Jewelers, in Richmond, Virginia, later becoming Waller & Company, Jewelers after a consolidation. Waller was gifted with a special ability to handcraft everything he needed. Although he did not patent any of his inventions, Waller is significant because he built a successful company around his remarkable ability. Practicing with him in this highly skilled discipline were three sons, Junius, Richard, and Thomas. Grandson Richard Jr. and his two sons, Richard III and David, carry on the business, operating under the name Waller & Company, Jewelers, more than 100 years later, assisted by Richard Jr.'s five sisters. Marcellus Carrington Waller, a pioneer entrepreneur, left an enduring legacy. The enterprise is one of the premier black businesses in the city, surviving two world wars, a depression, and numerous recessions.

Courtesy Waller & Company, Jewelers, Richmond, Virginia.

The Don't Buy Where You Can't Work campaign opened a few doors for minorities, but this concept was limited in scope. Among the desperate citizens seeking equity were the black creative geniuses. The Depression notwithstanding, a great number of patentees surfaced during this economic crisis. They were inventing a variety of useful but simple mechanic devices, toys, heating and refrigeration systems, musical instruments, engineering systems, and chemical compositions. Somehow, they found the resources for development and were victorious in traversing the costly patent system.

Between the 1920s and the 1940s, more black Americans became interested in the sciences and engineering; however, they lacked the opportunity to work at large manufacturing concerns due to severe hiring restrictions. More frequently, inventors became salaried workers and held advanced degrees in

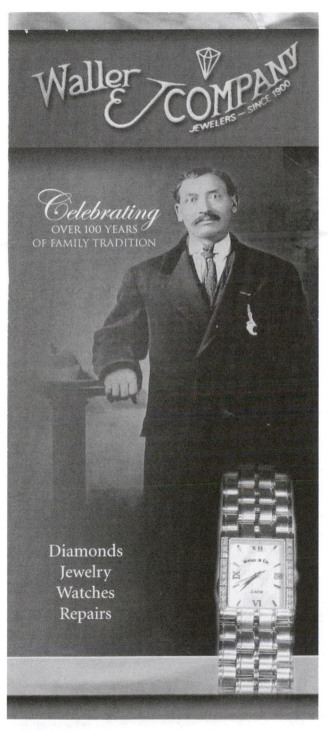

Business brochure of Waller & Company, depicting founder Marcellus Carrington Waller. (U.S. Patent and Trademark Office)

technical fields. When a few Americans of African descent obtained degrees in technology and engineering from predominately white colleges and universities, they sought employment at large companies. Hoping to participate on research teams, they applied but were rejected. As a consequence, most of them taught at colleges and universities designed for African Americans, such as inventors George Washington Carver and Percy Lavon Julian.

Then came World War II, which opened up new opportunities. The country needed scientists, and color did not matter. Minorities left academia and became employed at various corporations and manufacturing enterprises. Novel ideas emerged and inventions proliferated. Some were conceived individually, but others were produced in cooperation with fellow scientists at the facility. Still, others opened businesses to promote and market their patented inventions for profit.

PROGRESSIVE ACHIEVERS

The progressive achiever Percy Lavon Julian, born April 11, 1899, to a railway mail clerk and a schoolteacher in Montgomery, Alabama, seemed destined for greatness in chemistry and in the business world. From his early years, he embodied characteristics that molded a pioneer and role model for future researchers in chemistry. After graduating from the State Normal School for Negroes, Julian entered DePauw University and became its star chemistry pupil, graduating valedictorian of his class in 1920.[1]

Desiring to do immediate graduate study, Julian found his academic advancement temporarily stunted because of race prejudice. The graduate world did not accept him because professors feared they could not get him employed afterward. They reasoned that if he went into industry, white researchers, who would be his co-workers, would sabotage his work. Moreover, he was told that white universities would not hire him to teach. Thus, Julian was urged to instruct at black schools.[2]

In between teaching at Fisk University and then at Howard University, he received a Ph.D. from the University of Vienna in 1931. For a time he was a research fellow and professor of chemistry at his undergraduate alma mater. Then the Glidden Company, located in Chicago, hired him as a director of research, a move seen as a change in attitude toward the acceptance of black scientists in America. Julian began in 1936 in the Soya Products Division, where his research resulted in the development of a process to derive cortisone from a base of soybean oil. His pioneering research with the protein-rich soybean was of great use in seeking a solution to the worldwide problem of protein deficiency. The multitalented inventor discovered the base for a firefighting foam, called "Aero-Foam," used during World War II to extinguish gasoline and oil fires, and he isolated a soya protein that could be used to coat and size paper and textiles as well as to create cold-water paints.[3]

After receiving more than 40 patents while still at Glidden, Julian decided to go into business for himself. In 1954, he ended his employment at the Glidden Company and established his own Julian Laboratories in Chicago and the Laboratorios Julian de Mexico in Mexico City. He secured dozens more grants, including patents from Switzerland, Great Britain, Mexico, France, Australia, Canada, Germany, and the Netherlands. Louis Haber in *Black Pioneers of Science and Invention* writes that Julian "specialized in the production of his Substance S, synthetic cortisone, and found that the wild yams of Mexico were even better than soya beans as a source for his projects." Further, Haber records that the "first year resulted in a profit of $71.70, but the net profit for the second year was $97,000."

Success came to Julian Laboratories within a few years when it became a premier global producer of drugs processed from wild yams in Julian's Mexican plant. They were cultivated in Mexico but refined at another facility located in Oak Park, Michigan, near his home there. After seven years of good fortune, Julian made another decision that prompted even more prosperity. He sold his Oak Park Laboratory to the renowned pharmaceutical company Smith, Kline and French "for the sum of $2,338,000" and assumed the position of president with the firm "at a five-figure annual salary."[4]

Dr. Julian received numerous honors and awards during his lifetime. Julian's life in Chicago and in his professional career were often plagued by

Percy Lavon Julian. (Photographs and Prints Division, Schomburg Center for Research in Black Culture, The New York Public Library, Astor, Lenox and Tilden Foundation)

racism and discrimination; however, he rose above the hatred. Dr. Percy Lavon Julian passed away on April 19, 1975, in a Waukegan, Illinois, hospital. In 1990, he became the second African American to be inducted into the National Inventors Hall of Fame at Akron, Ohio, at the time of George Washington Carver's induction, both posthumously.[5]

PATENT CHARACTERISTICS

A patent is a document, issued by the U.S. Patent and Trademark Office, that grants to its owner a legally enforceable limited property right to bar others from practicing the invention, that is, from making, selling, or using the invention described and claimed in the written account. The inventor at this point is not necessarily required to produce the invention. The patent owner may sell all or partial rights to the patent or grant an exclusive or nonexclusive license for parties to practice the invention. Also, a patent or an application for a patent can be transferred as the result of a financial transaction.

Julian, like the black inventors who followed him as manufacturing and business practitioners, certainly discovered that income from possession of patents was very profitable. Alex Severinsky and Andrew Hirsch assert that the business of inventing alone has become an important economic phenomenon in the American economy. They report that "economic value generated by intellectual property is overtaking that created by manufacturing."[6]

Like Dr. Percy Julian, Dr. Lloyd Arthur Hall was a renowned, brilliant chemist and prolific inventor possessing more than 105 domestic and foreign patent grants; however, unlike Julian, Hall achieved his success in the form of a relationship with his employer, Carroll L. Griffith, a chemist who founded Griffith Laboratories in Chicago and hired Hall as a chief chemist and technical director. Hall remained with the company his entire career, spanning 34 years.[7] As an employee there, he acquired patents on sterilization methods of commercial products like drugs, food, medicines, cosmetics, and hospital supplies with ethylene oxide to kill germs, processes that revolutionized these businesses. These patents were necessarily assigned to Hall's employer because of a technical operation of law. As property of Griffith Laboratories the firm controlled how the patents would make money for the corporation. When the entire rights of a patent are transferred as the result of a financial transaction, the inventor loses all claim to any profit. Percy Julian, on the other hand, formed his own company and had complete control of its assets.

TRIBULATIONS AND ROADBLOCKS

Nearly all inventors crave financial reward from the sale of their inventions. This is natural. Inventors are curious people, good at coming up with ideas and solutions. A large number of them feel that they are the best people, too, to bring those ideas to the marketplace. However, these two functions require separate and distinct skills. Having the skill to perceive the problem and solve it, that is, conceive successful outcomes, such as inventions, does not equate to the inventor being the best person to commercialize inventions once they are patented. Only a very small percentage of inventors or patentees have been skillful at both ends of the spectrum, and their paths were filled with many tribulations and roadblocks. A few early black inventors like Woods, Scottron, and McCoy bridged both worlds, but only with great difficulty, and for some, little profit. It took Scottron many changes in course to finally turn the financial corner, but luck was a great part of the picture.

The inventor who cares little about financial reward is the inventor who devotes his talents solely to the development of his special interests. Nothing else seems to matter. Even food and sleep at times are not important. Obsessed and passionate, this extraordinary genius survives on the promise of the next dawn. George Washington Carver was in that number.

As a matter of course, during the industrial revolution in America, new inventions quickly superseded and rendered obsolete even newer concepts. Obsolescence for African American innovators was troublesome, but something more important handicapped them—lack of capital to practice the invention.

A working model was essential to iron out mechanical glitches. This was a requirement then (now long abolished) when applying for a U.S. patent. A model could be costly to make, particularly if the patentable innovation required the inventor to design intricate details. The need for currency was paramount if the inventor wished to attempt the next step. Money was needed for manufacturing, labor, materials, equipment, and marketing. The biggest roadblock was the combined racist and prejudicial attitude of white financial institutions that turned their back on the black community. Without adequate funds, the intellectual property owner cannot capitalize on the invention or concept, and thus there is no reward for labor, and no benefit to the consumer. With limited capital, minority innovators experienced overwhelming frustration. Somehow, though, a number persevered, adjusting to the America of that time in history.

AFTER THE BATTLEFIELD

During World War II, black businesses from the East Coast to the West Coast vied for defense contracts within a blatantly racial environment. After submitting numerous bids, several of them won contracts. Though they put forth a diligent effort, the businesses nonetheless failed within a year. At that time, a surge of inventions by blacks appeared on the landscape, showcasing a number of patent holders, a few of whom organized business enterprises around their federally protected commodities. One enterprise, the Washington Shirt Manufacturing Company, operating under the trademark "Dunbar Shirts" (named in honor of poet Paul Lawrence Dunbar), had annual sales in excess of two million garments. Founded by George J. Washington of Chicago in the late 1930s, the business became a hallmark in the clothing industry. During the war years Washington had a military contract to produce shirts for the armed forces and by the mid-1950s was the only black-owned shirt manufacturer in the nation. For many decades the items were sold in a large number of top national department stores.[8]

Returning home from World War II in 1945, after they had been fighting for their country in faraway places, African American servicemen dreamed and hoped for equitable jobs and improved housing. Looking for racial equality, the veterans in conjunction with the general black population pushed the federal government into providing civil, social, and economic relief during the 1950s and 1960s. In those decades across the country, many cities such as Chicago in the Midwest, Baltimore in the North, and especially the jurisdictions in the South were highly segregated and racist. Black Americans were pitted against complex and perplexing political systems and lashed out against inequities, especially in the South. In spite of the turmoil, the creative thinker of color pressed on with new and improved inventions.

As time progressed, a veteran of an earlier war made a tremendous impact on modern life. The brilliant Frederick McKinley Jones patented 40 concepts in the refrigeration field, where he designed and advanced the technology of refrigeration equipment. Overall, he held more than 60 patents covering other disciplines as well, all obtained over a 21-year span ending in 1960.

Jones, the first black member of the American Society of Refrigeration Engineers, had very little formal education, yet he amazed university-trained engineers with his skill and intellect. Born on May 17, 1893, in Covington, Kentucky, to John Jones, an Irish railroad worker, and a black mother, Frederick had a turbulent upbringing. His mother disappeared when he was an infant, so his father took him to nearby Cincinnati, where they moved from one rooming house to another. The father placed the child in the hands of landladies during the day.[9] With no real supervision, Frederick became very disorderly as the years passed. Urged by the women to get the boy an education, Jones took 7-year-old Frederick to Father Edward A. Ryan at the St. Mary's Catholic Church rectory and left, never to be seen again. To pay for his room and board, Frederick worked at the rectory. He soon tired of the routine and struck out on his own in Cincinnati at age 11 with only four years of schooling and an extraordinary inquisitive mind.[10]

After near starvation, much hardship, and years spent at odd jobs, Frederick Jones finally found mechanical work at a farm near Hallock, Minnesota. He acquired enough ability in engineering at age 20 to earn the highest grade for the Minnesota engineer's license. He toyed with racecars for several years, then enlisted in the 809th Pioneer Infantry in 1918 after the United States entered World War I. There he was given the task of repairing and working on mechanical engines and electrical devices.

Upon his return to Hallock after the war, Jones worked as a mechanic but obsessively tinkered with machinery. He began to invent things such as an improved microphone, called a "condenser type," and fiddled with wireless transmitters. Jones and a friend built a powerful 500-watt radio station that aired short programs three days a week. He aided a local physician by developing a novel portable X-ray, successfully used for years in the Hallock hospital. During the 1920s, Jones studied, researched, and experimented with ideas in rented facilities.[11]

When talking films (sound-on-film) arrived in Hallock, Jones, intrigued by the apparatus, became a projectionist. The projector was full of annoying vibrations, so he perfected it with inventive parts that he never patented. He never accepted compensation for his ingenuity. This was his way. All he wanted to do was tinker and think out solutions to the varied problems.

Ready to move on to find bigger challenges, Jones packed his belongings and headed for Minneapolis, where he found his niche and acceptance. As an experienced radioman and amazing inventor, he found that his reputation preceded him. A broadcasting company there had heard how successful his innovations were and invited Jones to work there. In 1930 fate intervened when before even entering the doors of the radio station, Jones came upon the Ultraphone Sound Systems Company. There, impressed by Jones's knowledge of sound systems, company owner Joseph A. Numero hired Jones, eventually becoming Jones's lifetime mentor, colleague, and friend. Although Jones was an American of color, it was his intellect that had an impact on Numero.

During the 1930s the giant companies Western Electric and American Telephone & Telegraph engaged in a lawsuit against Ultraphone, who they claimed was infringing on their patents. This litigation was the backdrop for Jones's expertise in the fields of electricity and engineering. He was called upon as an expert witness who had perfected amplifier circuits that were outstandingly superior to those of both companies. During the protracted litigation, Jones improved electronic sound systems and conceived his first patented invention. In 1939, he obtained a grant for a ticket-dispensing machine, assigned to Nation-Wide Manufacturing Corporation of New York City but built by Ultraphone for their theater.[12]

Around this time Jones labored on his most outstanding innovation, a refrigeration compressor. A company president who was a golf partner of

Numero was livid when one of his refrigerated transport trucks had engine failure on the road. It was filled with ice and salt to keep a load of poultry fresh, but the ice melted in the summer sun, and the goods subsequently spoiled. The executive complained to Numero, who owned an air-conditioned movie theater, that he wished Numero and Frederick Jones could find a way to keep a truck's contents from perishing in transport. This incident was the impetus that led Jones on a path to a long, meritorious patenting career in refrigeration.[13]

Jones proffered to have an air-conditioner unit ready for a transport trailer in a matter of weeks. Although other inventors had conceived plans to place a refrigerator apparatus on wheels, many and varied problems had not been solved. Jones took the challenge and produced a vastly superior mechanical device. The refrigeration concept was novel—the first of its kind. The invention, described as an air-conditioner for compartments of vehicle carriers, was projected as useful not only for trucks, but for railroad cars or other modes of transport as well. The apparatus provided "in conjunction with the compartment of a truck or van, means for circulating air within and through all parts of the compartment." Further, it comprised a gas engine and a starter unit controlled by a thermostat within a partitioned section of the vehicle. Frederick M. Jones and co-inventor Joseph A. Numero filed a patent application in 1939. Three years later, on December 1, 1942, they received the coveted grant.[14] The patent, assigned to the U.S. Thermo Control Company, an association comprising Numero and someone named M. Green, became the lynchpin of the new firm. This was Jones's second patent but the first of many on improved refrigeration systems. Nearly all bear his name as the sole inventor, and all were assigned to Thermo.

Numero's Ultraphone company was the agency that first produced the refrigeration unit, but he sold that enterprise to the Radio Corporation of America (RCA), which included Jones's exceptional electronic sound track and his ticket-dispensing machine, in favor of owning a new enterprise, the United States Thermo Control Company. Their appliances were known first under the name Thermotrol but afterward under Thermo King. In the mid-1950s, the company's name was changed to Thermo King Corporation to match the product name.[15]

Jones kept making improvements on the unit and coming up with new designs using interdisciplinary approaches. Now empowered with novel technology, Thermo Control became the leader in the transportation of perishables in such a way as to influence the beginning of fresh ideas about the use of refrigerated commodities. It was Jones's creative talent alone that carried Thermo Control into a realm beyond Numero's expectations; after all, his refrigeration concept put Numero in business. During World War II,

Jones's lightweight, compact refrigeration component with its radical space-saving design was chosen as the model equipment for all military transport vehicles. Additionally, he conceived an improved way to defrost refrigeration apparatus. At this time, Jones, accepted into the circle of armed forces engineers and officers, was given a position as consultant at the U.S. Defense Department.

Although he did not own any part of Numero's multimillion-dollar corporation, Frederick McKinley Jones was made vice president and top engineer in the experimental division. He instructed the company engineers in his creative method and singly held a multitude of patents for revolutionary two-cycle gas engines, a removable cooling unit, a rotary compressor, an engine-actuated ventilating system, and many more innovations for improving ways to preserve perishable foodstuffs in transit.[16]

Jones's patents, most valuable to the producers, had enormous benefit to people all over the globe. The corporation as owner or licensee of his technology had the advantage of enormous sales volumes. Because of its rapid growth, the company, then known as U.S. Thermo Control Company, was forced to expand its facilities and hire more employees. The success of the Jones's pioneering inventions in the field unquestionably launched a new growth industry—the frozen-food business and consequently the supermarket.[17] Revolutionizing the field, millions of jobs became available and new businesses sprang up. To this day, Thermo King equipment is found worldwide.

Joseph Numero took care of Jones, and Jones willingly labored and produced over and again for the corporation. He wanted it no other way. Money and possessions were of no consequence to him. He was offered high-salaried jobs at other firms but turned them down out of his love of Thermo King. Jones even declined an honorary doctorate degree from prestigious Howard University. By the 1950s, Jones was reputed nationally as a premier inventor, engineer, man of ideas, and expert mechanic, cited by one journalist "as the greatest colored scientist in America," equating him to Thomas Edison.[18]

Frederick Jones married a Swedish woman during his years in Hallock, but their relationship dissolved after a few months. Years later in 1946 in Minneapolis, he married another woman, Lucille, who survived him. Chronically ill for years, Jones died of lung cancer on February 21, 1961, at age 68. He is buried at Fort Snelling National Cemetery.[19] In 1977, Frederick McKinley Jones was inducted into the Inventors Hall of Fame of Minnesota.

Not all inventors have the financial security to manufacture, sell, and distribute the invention, so going into a joint venture with a partner or manufacturer is a clear option for many. Jones was determined, steadfast, and brilliant. He knew how to answer the question almost before it was asked. He knew his audience.

CAPITALIZING ON ANOTHER VALUABLE TYPE OF FEDERAL PROTECTION IN THE HAIR CARE AND BEAUTY TRADE—THE TRADEMARK

Many innovators employ several valuable types of intellectual property other than just patents to protect their creative concepts and, of course, to bring in capital. Trademarks and copyrights as well as trade secrets can be used as forms of protection. As we have seen, patents protect inventions of things that can be touched or handled. Trademarks protect things such as a word, name, or slogan that identifies the source of goods or services; and copyrights protect literary, dramatic, musical, artistic, and other intellectual works. Trade secrets are of value only while they remain secret; confidential information is an important asset to companies and businesses.

TRADEMARKS

A trademark is an arbitrary word, name, symbol, device, or slogan which is used by a manufacturer, seller, or other outlet for goods or services in an association with the goods or services to indicate the *source* of the thing or service, and to distinguish his or her goods from those of others. Service marks, collective marks, and certification marks are special trademarks. Trademarks are registered and can be renewed.

See *The ABC's of Intellectual Property* by Intellectual Property Owners Inc.; http://www.uspto.gov.

In the previous chapter mention was made of the use of a trademark to help protect an immensely popular shoe polish product with a name used by the manufacturer. The beauty manufacturing businesses created and run by African Americans established trademarked words and phrases to help protect their goods from those of others. Trademark rights are acquired or established by selling and shipping a product bearing the mark to a commercial client in interstate commerce. The highly sought after hair and cosmetic products were in great demand in the early decades of the 1900s when mail-order houses, door-to-door sales, and subscriptions were a popular and highly profitable method of selling merchandise in cities and locales across the country. A mass consumer culture arose in the early 20th century when women became the primary purchasers of goods.

For the leaders of the early African American beauty-care industry, the pioneers, all women, saw the clear advantage of uniting the consumer with the product. The practice became the hallmark of merchandising systems that envisioned economic freedom for black women who could improve on their appearance as well as gain the quality of being worthy of esteem and respect. Minority women found the hair care and beauty industry a sustainable source of income where they were their own boss, a welcome change from being a worker hired to perform a job. They put their hands and brains together to make work by way of entrepreneurship. The way African American women raised, made, and kept money is a testimony to their ingenuity, business skills, and ability to manage affairs—elements of value in the development and improvement of the minority enclave.

Annie Minerva Turnbo Pope Malone, a visionary, was the earliest beauty entrepreneur and millionaire. She predated the eminent Madam C. J. Walker in establishing a business. In fact, Walker worked for Turnbo as a sales agent in St. Louis for a short time around 1903.[20] Soon joining the lucrative trade with Malone and Walker were Sarah Spencer Washington and a few black males shortly thereafter—all becoming fierce rivals, each wanting to corner the market.

Female sales personnel and agents were trained in the business and handled the distribution and marketing of the commodities as well. Hundreds of thousands of dollars passed into the hands of these savvy business owners over many decades. A workforce of thousands was dutifully rewarded by employers for their diligence and team spirit. These business icons built magnificent complexes to house their learning institutions and a variety of businesses and enterprises as well, initiatives that inspired others to follow suit. They built empires based on beauty products that were diligently trademarked over many years. As millionaires, they did not forget their people and donated monies to charities, national entities, and the community for a variety of projects and efforts, committing themselves to social welfare and politics.

Annie M. Turnbo was born in 1869 in Metropolis, Illinois, a few years after the end of the Civil War and grew up with older siblings after the death of their parents. She endured prejudice and racism and struggled as a laundress. In her teen years she lived with a married sister in Peoria, Illinois, where she began high school but failed to complete her studies due to an energy-draining disease. Subsequently, her health improved and she became fascinated with ways to improve the appearance of African American hair textures. Looking to make her condition in life better after receiving an education, she developed ingredients for a hair formula from some basic schooling in chemistry and from her herbalist doctor aunt. Malone began manufacturing her "Wonderful Hair Grower" product, promoted to help heal scalp problems and to reduce hair loss, in a rented building at a cost of $5 per month in the black township of Lovejoy, Illinois, where she was now living.[21] Many African American women had problems managing their hair and suffered from a number of

Ser. No. 171,464. (CLASS 6. CHEMICALS, MEDI-
CINES, AND PHARMACEUTICAL PREPARATIONS.)
Annie M. Malone, doing business as Poro College, St.
Louis, Mo. Filed Nov. 1, 1922.

No claim is made in the exclusive use of the words "Trade
Mark."

Particular description of goods. — Liquid and Ointment
Preparations for Promoting the Growth of the Hair,
Preparations for the Treatment and Relief of Tetter;
Preparations for Promoting the Growth of Hair on the
Temples, Pressing Oils for Use in the Treatment of the Hair,
and Preparations for Use as Shampoo.

The trade-mark displayed as shown has been continuously
used since about Jan. 23, 1922, and the word "Poro" alone
since prior to Sept. 21, 1906.

Registered trademark of PORO. (U.S. Patent and Trademark Office)

adverse skin and scalp conditions for which ready-made products had been
prescribed. A regular shampoo routine, scalp massages, and a healthy diet
substantially improved these conditions, in addition to homogeneous mix-
tures and compositions containing the active ingredient sulfur, which for-
mulations were obvious to duplicate. Malone and other hair entrepreneurs,
though, hailed their "secret" portions as the ultimate solution.

In 1902, Malone relocated to a more lucrative locale in St. Louis, partly because the 1904 World's Fair was coming there. She married a Mr. Pope in 1903 and produced hair products under the name Pope-Turnbo, though the marriage was short-lived.[22] Not having access to standard distribution methods, she and a sister began a door-to-door campaign with several trained assistants who, in turn, recruited others. Malone also sold her products to some local drugstores. The move proved strategic. She profited well from her retail outlets and advertisements at the World's Fair, gaining new customers and agents. About this time she began using the word "Poro," which was registered as a trademark in 1906, to protect her product from ever-present imitators and deceivers. The trademarked products included liquid and ointment preparations for promoting hair growth and for the treatment and relief of tetter. Also, the "Poro" name described goods used as a shampoo and as a pressing oil in the treatment of the hair.[23]

Traveling to the South to expand her market, Malone gave demonstrations wherever she could. Her enterprise grew rapidly. She was a pioneer in utilizing women to exploit her products, giving them a source of employment when career opportunities then were quite limited. In 1913, 1914, and 1915, Malone purchased one-half interest in the four patents of Walter L. Majors, an inventor living in St. Louis.[24] Majors was a family man who worked as a mechanic.[25] His patent for a hair drier could be seen as useful for her hair-care method, but one would have to speculate on the reason a heater for motor vehicles, motor-controlling device, and coin-controlled taxicab controller would interest Malone. Perhaps she was aiding the inventor by helping him recover the cost of producing the invention or had some business venture in mind.

Malone herself held a design patent for "Sealing Tape." She filed on October 3, 1921, and received the patent on May 16, 1922, for a term of 14 years, the tenure of such grants.[26] Described as an "ornamental design" that had a lacy look, Malone used it as background for her "Poro" trademark.

DESIGN PATENTS

A design patent protects the way an article looks—its appearance—and not its structural or utilitarian features. A design consists of the visual ornamental characteristics embodied in or applied to an article of manufacture. The patent laws provide for the granting of design patents to any person who has invented any new, original, and ornamental design for an article of manufacture.

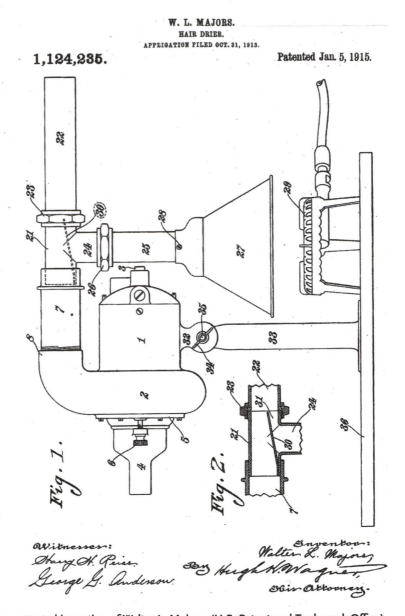

Hair Drier, patented invention of Walter L. Majors. (U.S. Patent and Trademark Office)

In 1918, Malone built a glorious multistoried building in St. Louis, recognized as Poro College, to house her fast-growing enterprise, consisting of a factory and beauty-training school accented with multiple needs and services to the general public. By the 1920s, Malone was probably worth around $14 million. In 1921, she challenged the registration of the trademark "Hay-Po," filed by Clarence C. Hay. She opposed the right to use the words, which she held infringed upon her registered mark. Malone won her case at the Court of Appeals of the District of Columbia that year.[27] At this juncture her industrial enterprise, known as Poro College Products Company Inc. was known internationally. Her business acumen had cornered the sales market, beating out fierce competition with an effectively functioning franchising method.

In 1914 she married Aaron E. Malone, who assisted her with the business, but divorced him 18 years later. Unfortunately, their difficulties spilled over into the huge beauty-care corporation, and the divorce settlement in 1927 eventually, in part, caused Malone to lose a chunk of her empire. Her troubles compounded as her holdings went into decline. She was repeatedly sued and owed the government a sizeable amount of back taxes because of her distaste for paying luxury and real estate taxes.

Although strapped with financial difficulties, Malone continued to register trademarks. In 1938, she moved all of her business to Chicago, where she already had a school and huge residence. In 1948, she registered "Poro," under Poro College Products Company Inc., a successor to the business of Annie M. Malone, nee Annie M. Pope, doing business as Poro College in Chicago, Illinois. The goods and services on the market included liquid and ointment preparations for the hair, scalp, and temples; pressing oils; shampoo preparations; brilliantine; croquignole oil; cold cream; vanishing cream; deodorant; talcum powder; face powder; lipstick; and rouge.[28] By 1951, though, she was insolvent, and the government took control of her business empire. She had accumulated the greatest fortune of any African American in the first decades of the 20th century. Childless, Annie Minerva Turnbo Pope Malone died of a stroke on May 10, 1957, in Chicago. What remained of her estate, estimated at a sum of $100,000, was left to her nieces and nephews.[29]

At this time in Chicago, Mayor Richard J. Daley was the undisputed boss who controlled the city politic with an iron hand. The African American population was swelling from Southern newcomers seeking a better life, but finding decent housing was mostly out of their reach because of segregationist practices designed to keep blacks in poor neighborhoods, mostly on the South Side. While overcrowded neighborhoods and schools were the norms for decades in this black enclave, this is where black entrepreneurs thrived and this is where brilliant entrepreneurs such as Malone, Walker, and Overton demonstrated their business acumen.

Trademarks facilitate selling and form connecting links between products, sales, and advertising. The wellspring of hair and beauty care products began with women who registered hundreds of trademarks for cosmetic treatments, principally in the first three decades of the 20th century. The

DESIGN.

A. M. MALONE.
SEALING TAPE.
APPLICATION FILED OCT. 3, 1921.

60,962.

Patented May 16, 1922.

Inventor:
Annie M. Malone,
by Rippey Kingsland
Her Attorneys.

Sealing Tape, patented design of Annie M. Malone. (U.S. Patent and Trademark Office)

federal government intervened when it saw that the industry needed to be watched. In part, health and sanitation issues raised concerns about the quality of products and procedures employed by practitioners. Thus, stringent laws were passed to regulate the business.

Madam C. J. Walker saw the immediate benefit of trademark protection. She also knew about patent protection; however, she was unsuccessful at receiving an exclusive grant after filing her application for an invention and concentrated exclusively on the trademark system.[30] Her million-dollar business initially developed from the trade slogan "Anti-Kink Walker System."

Walker was born in 1869 on a Delta, Louisiana, cotton plantation under a devastating sharecropping system just after the end of the Civil War. To escape poverty in the dire Southern circumstances she married Moses McWilliams, a Vicksburg, Mississippi, laborer, at age 14, and she became a widow with a daughter at age 20. Walker moved to St. Louis in 1888. There she found work as a washerwoman, during which time she had a short marriage to John Davis. Just a few years after the century's turn in 1900, during the World's Fair at St. Louis, Walker was hawking Poro's "Wonderful Hair Grower" door-to-door to augment her laundress income and help support her daughter. With self-determination and self-confidence, Walker got the idea to prepare a product to improve the condition of her thinning hair. From a dream in which the ingredients for a hair mixture were given, she developed a formula to help prevent her hair from falling out.

In 1906, now in Denver, Colorado, she married Charles Joseph Walker, popularly known as C. J, a sales agent for an African American newspaper, and embarked wholeheartedly in the hair preparation business. With the help of her husband's newspaper promotion experience, Walker manufactured and sold such products as "C. J. Walker's Blood and Rheumatic Remedy and the newly named Madame C. J. Walker's Wonderful Hair Grower."[31] She adopted the prefix Madame to bring appeal to her products and to give dignity to her image, for the polite term was a popular feminine undertaking. Soon disagreements erupted between the couple, which resulted in divorce, but the outcome did not harm Walker financially. Inspired by the desire to help women with hair problems, she was well on her way to financial freedom through her manufactured hair goods and various cosmetic preparations.

In 1908, Walker chose a new base of operations for her business. The big and thriving city of Pittsburgh offered the opportunity to reach a wider segment of the African American population. The city also had a complex transportation system and a convenient source of metal for her pressing comb enterprise, an added endeavor. Here is where she established Lelia College to train women in the Walker System, but she ultimately set up her headquarters in Indianapolis in 1910.

Walker filed a patent application for the invention "Hair Drying and Straightening Comb" on February 3, 1913, applying privately as Sarah Walker who lived at 640 North West Street, Indianapolis, but the papers were incomplete, missing some formal requirements. After notification of the deficiencies in a letter dated April 12, 1913, signed by the patent office chief clerk, the application apparently was abandoned because no further record has been found of the issuance of a patent. It is likely that Sarah Walker forsook the patent process for reasons of her own. However, the Mme. C. J. Walker Manufacturing Company of Indianapolis successfully filed for the registration of trademarks. The words "Mme. C. J. Walker" were first used in commerce in 1914, but not until 1917 did the company received is first registered trademark for "The Mme. C. J. Walker Wonderful Hair Grower." On September 26, 1922, the Madam (spellings varied) C. J. Walker Manufacturing Company, Lelia Walker Robinson, president, registered the trademark "Mme. C. J. Walker," continuously in use since 1919 for "toilet preparations of various kind of toilet soaps, comprising complexion soaps and antiseptic soaps." (By the 1942 trademark renewal of the "toilet preparations," the company used the titles "Madam" and "Mme.") On January 13, 1953, the Mme. C. J. Walker Manufacturing Company Inc. of Indianapolis, Indiana, registered the mark "Mme. C. J. Walker's Satin Tress."[32]

Offices of the company were located in many cities. In a program for a Washington, D.C., debutantes' ball in 1948, the local company office took out a half-page advertisement offering greetings to the sponsor and to that year's debutantes. The Madam C. J. Walker Manufacturing Company ad read, "Makers of World-Famous Hair Preparations and Matchless Cosmetics." The promotion further cited the services of the company's Madam C. J. Walker College of Beauty Culture under the "Famous Madam C. J. Walker System." In 1999, the Walker company (now Madame Walker Enterprises Inc., a corporation of Indiana) registered the mark "Mme. C. J. Walker."[33]

Walker traveled extensively to promote her enterprise and continually trained agents who advanced her system worldwide. She even made a visit to the White House in August 1917. A dedicated business promoter and philanthropist, Walker found little time to give herself sorely needed rest. Walker succumbed to kidney failure on May 25, 1919, at her mansion Villa Lewaro on the Hudson River, not far from New York City. She was 52 years old.[34]

The Apex News and Hair Company, established around 1913 by Sarah Spencer Washington, competed with the other black hair-care companies using the well-established practice of selling door-to-door. Sarah, known as "Madame Sarah Spencer Washington," employed a large group of agents, initially doing business in Atlantic City, where she founded the company. Her line of beauty and hair products, marketed under the mark Apex, multiplied, escalating her sales worldwide and placing her in the realm of millionaires.

Washington constructed a manufacturing facility, set up Apex Laboratories, and trained students in the art of hair care at her schools. She further established Apex Publishing. Her line flourished well past the mid-century mark, at its peak with about 40,000 agents extended throughout the nation handling the merchandise. Apex was the premier African American beauty merchandiser on the eastern seaboard.[35] In the same 1948 debutante program mentioned previously, Apex News and Hair Company Incorporated also placed a half-page advertisement citing a medicated scalp cream to improve appearance, sold at Apex Studios and drugstores. The slogan "Millions Use Apex" was prominent. Listed under the "Credits" section in the program was Apex Beauty Products Co., for Hair Styling.[36] Born in Virginia in 1881, Sarah Spencer Washington died in 1953, leaving a daughter to manage the company until it was sold.

For Anthony Overton, doing business as the Overton-Hygienic Manufacturing Company in Chicago became a highly profitable enterprise just after 1900. Overton, born in Monroe, Louisiana, about 1865, received a law degree and spent time as a municipal judge before venturing into the manufacture of goods. He founded the Overton-Hygenic company in Kansas City, Missouri, in 1898, using a large capital of $1,960 first to produce baking powder. Later, he expanded the business to include toilet preparations and established the trade name "De Luxe" to identify face cream, face powder, and talcum powder, first used in commerce in June 1906 and not federally registered until 1923.[37] African American women found them most desirable for the complexion, especially the company's "High-Brown" face powder. Overton's decision to place pictures of girls of color on his talcum powder, hair pomades, and other toiletries was a strategic move guaranteeing success at the market. He was one of the largest black manufacturers in the nation.[38] After relocating the company to Chicago in 1911, Overton produced a line of 52 products, with sales of $117,000. By 1915 the company was capitalized at $286,000 and expanded to producing 62 different items.[39]

His business practices paralleled those of Mme. Walker. At the beginning of the 1920s he was the "country's leading producer of cosmetics for black women, with international sales and distribution extending not only to West Africa and the West Indies but also to Egypt, India, the Philippines, and Japan."[40] He met enormous goals, eschewing personal extravagance in favor of using his money for business development. In 1923 he constructed a facility that housed his cosmetics enterprise and diverse business entities, including the Victory Life Insurance Company; the Douglass National Bank; The Great Northern Realty Company; and publications, consisting of the nationally distributed *Chicago Bee* and the popular rag *Half-Century Magazine*. By the late 1920s, Overton's company was worth about a million dollars, manufacturing over 250 products, including some for other companies.[41]

His bank, operating in 30 states, did not survive the Great Depression. This in turn caused the failure of his insurance company. The fast growth of the bank worked against him. He had desires to be larger than his Chicago competitor, Jesse Binga, who owned the Binga State Bank; however, Binga's bank failed as well. Overton's legendary spare lifestyle, though, did permit his cosmetics enterprise and newspaper to survive for many decades. As of 1986, the trademark registration was not renewed and is considered to be expired.

Beginning with a resource of five dollars, Dr. Julia H. P. Coleman, a licensed pharmacist, founded the Hair Care-Vim Chemical Company in Washington, D.C., in 1911. She produced a composition marketed as "Hair-Vim" and opened the Hair-Vim Vogue and School. Coleman was the earliest African American woman to open a drugstore in the nation.

Coleman, Walker, Malone, Overton, and Washington were the vanguard of the early African American business executives delving in hair commodities of great potential. Coming after the wave to modify African American hair

SOME BLACK-OWNED BEAUTY AND HAIR-CARE ENTERPRISES

Marguerita Ward Cosmetic Company, founded in 1922 in Chicago, resumed manufacturing after World War II

Murray Cosmetic Company, founded by Charles D. Murray in 1926 in Chicago

Rose Meta House of Beauty, established by Rose Morgan along with Olivia Clarke in 1944 in Harlem, New York (Morgan was the wife of the great boxer Joe Louis [Barrow])

Mary Ann Morgan Company, introduced Morganoil in 1948 in Chicago

Soft Sheen Products, established by Edward Garner in 1964, developer of Care-Free Curl

Luster Products, founded by Jory Luster

Pro-Line Corporation, started by Comer Cottrell

Bronner Brothers, founded by Bernard and Nathaniel Bronner

A. W. Curtis Laboratories, established by Austin W. Curtis

Kizure Professional Products, founded by Jerry White

Carol's Daughter, founded by Lisa Price in 1993

Tea and Honey Blends, cofounded by Tiffani Bailey Lash and Tashni-Ann Dubroy in 2009 in Maryland

H.I.M-istry Skincare Inc. established by Darnell Henderson

Moore Unique Skin Care, LLC, developed by Dr. Milton D. Moore

with chemicals, in the 1960s Christina Jenkins of Cleveland, Ohio, brought the notion of hair weaves to the public. Hair weaving consists of permanently attaching commercial hair to live hair for the purpose of enhancing one's coiffure. Jenkins developed the technique and patented it in 1952. She married orchestra leader Duke Jenkins of Malvern, Ohio, who became the president of the black-owned company. Jenkins owned beauty shops in six cities nationwide and an oil well in Louisiana reportedly valued at more than $1 million. She profited handsomely from the invention before unfortunate litigation, the final decision of which in1965 held her patent invalid. Her business enterprise was so prosperous that it compared with the success of Fuller Products, an extraordinary venture of visionary S. B. Fuller, the country's premier black entrepreneur before and after World War II.

Born Samuel B. Fuller on June 4, 1905, in Louisiana, S. B. Fuller started his business in Chicago with door-to-door sales promotion of discarded soap, and he soon expanded into household cleaning and personal care products as well as hair and cosmetic items. Fuller products came about when Fuller purchased a supplier's company at an auction with savings and borrowed money of $150,000.[42] His ventures took him beyond ordinary realms for African Americans. He bought interest in white-owned companies, went into publishing, purchased a franchise, the Fuller Philco Home Appliance Center, and acquired huge real estate holdings. In 1957, the company had $10 million in annual revenue.[43] To his misfortune, racism, discrimination, ill will toward blacks, and a misunderstanding of his philosophy contributed to the downfall of the business. In particular for Fuller Products, a national boycott sent the company into bankruptcy. He was a believer in Booker T. Washington's philosophy of self-help and self-sufficiency. S. B. Fuller was diagnosed with Parkinson's disease in 1976 and passed away on October 24, 1988.[44]

A former employee of Fuller Products became the caretaker of the company's inventory. Joe Louis Dudley Sr., born in Aurora, North Carolina, in 1937, began working as a salesman for Fuller in the summer of 1957 in New York City to obtain tuition money for college. Later, after working as a full-time salesman, he purchased a Fuller distributorship and rose in rank to become president of the company. Dudley acquired the rights to the Fuller Products name in 1984, during which time he was guiding his own enterprise, Dudley Products Company, founded in 1967 in Chicago and later relocated to Greensboro, North Carolina, and then back to Chicago.[45] He and Fuller, his role model and mentor, followed sound principles and beliefs that directed them on a path of success.

During the decline of Fuller Products, Dudley decided to develop his own beauty merchandise. He purchased a small business from a man in Richmond, Virginia, who had produced a line called Rosebud Beauty Products,

Word Mark DUDLEY'S Q+

Goods and Services IC 042. US 100. G & S: COSMETICIAN AND BEAUTY SALON SERVICES. FIRST USE: 19730600. FIRST USE IN COMMERCE: 19730600

Mark Drawing Code (3) DESIGN PLUS WORDS, LETTERS, AND/OR NUMBERS

Design Search Code 26.11.13 - Rectangles (exactly two rectangles); Two rectangles 26.11.21 - Rectangles that are completely or partially shaded

Serial Number 73777183

Filing Date January 27, 1989

Current Filing Basis 1A

Original Filing Basis 1A

Published for Opposition March 13, 1990

Registration Number 1600004

Registration Date June 5, 1990

Owner (REGISTRANT) DUDLEY PRODUCTS, INC. CORPORATION NORTH CAROLINA 1080 OLD GREENSBORO ROAD KERNERSVILLE NORTH CAROLINA 27409

Attorney of Record BURTON S. EHRLICH

Prior Registrations 1286716

Type of Mark SERVICE MARK

Register PRINCIPAL

Affidavit Text SECT 15. SECT 8 (6-YR). SECTION 8(10-YR). SECTION 8(10-YR) 20000811.

Renewal 1ST RENEWAL 20000811

Live/Dead Indicator LIVE

Registered trademark of Dudley's Q+. (U.S. Patent and Trademark Office)

renamed it Dudley's Scalp Special, and packaged it out of his home. Dudley and his wife, Eunice, found retail space at a strip mall and opened Dudley's Beauty Center and Salon.[46] Dudley established a trust partnership with cosmetologists to distribute the Dudley products as an exclusive line with them rather than use retail stores. From that position Dudley persevered, and by 1975 the company had annual sales in excess of $1.5 million. To assist his mentor during a crisis, he invested money in the Fuller company, even buying the Brooklyn, New York, branch where he and Eunice met. By now Dudley was marking his products as "Dudley's Q+," first used in commerce in 1978 and registered in 1984, to identify the goods and services such as shampoos, conditioners, and hair relaxer.[47]

In time the couple built a multibillion-dollar beauty and hair care empire, one of the largest manufacturers and distributors of ethnic hair-care products worldwide. After building new headquarters in Kernersville, North Carolina, Dudley launched the Dudley Cosmetology University (DCU) there in 1989 and built a hotel, DCU Inn, to house the students on campus. The Dudley Beauty School has a global mission to help train others in the field of cosmetology, created to develop a healthy economic base of young, talented entrepreneurs for the world.[48]

Dudley often purchased merchandise for hair-care products from his colleague, Jerry White. White, a prominent innovator of stoves, hot combs, and similar products for hair, established Kizure Products Company Inc. He and his wife, Lucky, persevered for decades through many trials, triumphs, and struggles in California to succeed in the hair-servicing industry. The registered word mark "Kizure" was first used in commerce in 1972.[49]

Demand for the products by women of color, and white women as well, was met by the supply from entrepreneurs who knew that the beauty-care business would result in extremely successful enterprises. When the fashion and modeling world opened up to women of color in the 1960s, one tall, graceful, and elegant model took full advantage of the opportunity and was very lucky. After years of appearances on magazine covers worldwide, the beautiful Naomi Sims became a successful entrepreneur, manufacturing an extensive line of wigs and cosmetics. Before Sims had appeared on the scene, several black models were working in the fashion industry but were restricted to black magazines. In 1964, Donyale Luna became the first black model featured on the cover of *Harper's Bazaar*, but Naomi Sims broke through a barrier. She achieved superstar status, fortune, and glory from modeling and from her successful "Naomi Sims" line of wigs and hairpieces.[50]

Born in Oxford, Mississippi, and later residing in Pittsburgh, Sims lived in foster homes after the breakup of her parents. She graduated from high school and then moved in with her sister in New York City, where she studied merchandising and textile design at the Fashion Institute of Technology. Luckily, when low on capital at age 18, Sims landed a modeling job. Her distinctive runway walk became a signature attribute that put her in great demand throughout her career. Later, at age 24, disillusioned with modeling and with perfect timing, Sims left the field in search of another career at a time when black women were abandoning the native look in favor of an easier approach to hairstyles. Having had problems styling her own hair during her modeling years, she tested wigs made of Caucasian hair but was unsatisfied. She experimented at home with synthetic fibers and became frustrated when manufacturers rejected her ideas. Finally, an import-export company provided Sims with standard research facilities, which drove her to establish a business. She began the "Naomi Sims Collection" of wigs and hairpieces, a name first used in commerce on March 22, 1973.[51] Partnering with the import-export enterprise Metropa Company, which registered the trademark "Naomi Sims" in early 1974, Sims was able to bring forth a line of wigs made with a patented fiber owned by a Japanese firm, having features resembling straightened black hair. The fiber was trademarked "Kanekalon Presselle," registered on April 20, 1976, by Kanegafuchi Kagaku Kogyo Kabushiki Kaisha, for wigs and artificial hair that was first practiced in commerce on March 21, 1973 (one day prior to the use of the word mark "Naomi Sims Collection"). The trademark for these goods and services was renewed in 2006.[52] Through Sims's persistence and teachings about the differences between the hair of African American women and of white women, all skepticism and opposition from white buyers faded, and within one year, sales leveled to $5 million. Competition flourished, but Sims pushed forward even stronger. Her company, now an extremely profitable division of the parent corporation Metropa, had 16 employees in 1979. Initially, she did the lion's share of the work, designing the wigs and advertisements and doing fieldwork to promote the products as well. In the 1980s Sims's merchandise was marketed in 2,000 retail stores in North America and from Great Britain to Africa.[53]

In addition to wigs and hairpieces, Sims branched out into cosmetics and skin care for women of color in 1985, a particular beauty area the white-owned cosmetics companies had failed to notice. Black women wanted products directed to their various skin types. The Naomi Sims line sold in major department stores nationwide.

Given that African American women (including actress Lena Horne, who in 1959 established the Lena Horne Cosmetic Company, based in Oakland, California) dominated this field of endeavor, which gave them a sense of self-worth and pride at a time when their job opportunities had no significant upward mobility, African American males also entered the lucrative business. Some of them were already successful in diverse business enterprises. The giant company Johnson Products, founded by George H. Johnson in 1954,

Word Mark	**FASHION FAIR**
Goods and Services	IC 003. US 001 004 006 050 051 052. G & S: cologne. FIRST USE: 19780401. FIRST USE IN COMMERCE: 19780401
Mark Drawing Code	(5) WORDS, LETTERS, AND/OR NUMBERS IN STYLIZED FORM
Serial Number	78598200
Filing Date	March 30, 2005
Current Filing Basis	1A
Original Filing Basis	1A
Published for Opposition	November 7, 2006
Registration Number	3200502
Registration Date	January 23, 2007
Owner	(REGISTRANT) Johnson Publishing Company, Inc. CORPORATION ILLINOIS 820 South Michigan Avenue Chicago ILLINOIS 60605
Attorney of Record	Leslie Bertagnolli
Prior Registrations	0784137;1015599;1563976;2067130
Description of Mark	The mark consists of stylized words Fashion Fair.
Type of Mark	TRADEMARK
Register	PRINCIPAL
Live/Dead Indicator	LIVE

Registered trademark of Fashion Fair. (U.S. Patent and Trademark Office)

were makers of the ever-popular hair brands "Ultra Wave," "Ultra Sheen," and "Afro-Sheen." Johnson, a former employee of Fuller Products, profited immensely from the 1960s Afro hairstyle worn by a huge majority of African Americans but requiring special upkeep. In later decades, however, the Johnson Products Company suffered a series of missteps that contributed to its decline.[54]

Well recognizing black women's desire and need to be beautiful at a time when the "Black Is Beautiful" mantra of the Civil Rights movement took hold, one giant company in the 1970s picked up on the phenomenon. Entrepreneur and *Ebony* magazine publisher John H. Johnson manufactured Supreme Beauty Products and formulated "Fashion Fair Cosmetics" in 1973 to meet those desires and needs. His Johnson Publishing Company acquired the trademark on "Fashion Fair," but it took five years for the business to find success.[55] After losing millions of dollars in a strategy to reach tony markets, Johnson's "Fashion Fair" finally found a well-suited position there, making the merchandise the largest African American cosmetics line in the world.

The competitive nature of the business was fierce. Foreign companies in addition to white-owned corporations attempted to take 100 percent control of the black-directed skin care and cosmetics market. Ultimately, Johnson Products in 1993 sold the African America cosmetics and skin care manufacturer of "Flori Roberts" to the IVAX Corporation.[56] Even though black-owned beauty care companies were being absorbed by white manufacturers, blacks continued to make innovations in the cosmetics field, finding profitable niches with new products and establishing their own firms.

A great number of businesses organized and established by minorities in the 1900s took full advantage of the protection trademarks, trade names, and trade secrets provided. This kind of federal or state protection was overwhelmingly common in the industry, and rightfully so, because of its immense value. New companies such as Carol's Daughter®, established by Lisa Price, and Tea and Honey Blends™, cofounded by the young entrepreneurial doctoral chemists Tiffani Bailey Lash and Tashni-Ann Dubroy, have taken the leap of faith to venture into the realm of a billion-dollar-a-year industry. A host of entertainers, and sports and media personalities found lucrative markets worldwide for personal clothing, jewelry, accessories, hair, skin, cosmetics, food, appliances, machinery, and other wares, with most of them promoting the products under their own names.

4

Commercialized Concepts: Capital and Enterprises of Today

For wisdom is better than rubies; and all the things that may be desired are not to be compared to it. I, wisdom, dwell with prudence, and find out knowledge of witty inventions.

—*Proverbs 8:11–12*

To convey some idea of the meaningfulness of inventions, a recent analysis is worth consideration. Severinsky and Hirsch propose levels of creativity of inventions to identify their differences and impact on the economy. They define the "value" of an innovation as the total financial benefit derived by all of its users. More than three-fourths of the inventions for the year 2004 fell into two categories: those having "little or no strategic or economic value" and those having a "small value that resides with incremental improvements, the goal of which is to maintain products already on the market."[1] The lowest-valued patents will never be commercialized. The remaining fourth have great significance because they concern improvements that spur an increase in the number of resulting products sold, and they concern improvements that increase profit for each item. A tiny percentage of the remaining fourth includes discoveries that revolutionize existing industries. These are the ones having the highest economic value. African American innovations are found in all levels, and in particular, as noted in chapters 1 and 2, a few concepts developed by people of color revolutionized the existing sugar, shoe, and rail industries. The story is legendary for these highly valuable inventions. Of interest here are the inventors of color who have patents that are commercialized and used to advantage on the open market.

BUSINESS DILEMMA AND COURSE OF ACTION

From about 1960 to the first years of the new millennium, African American ingenuity has significantly impacted the disciplines of mechanical, electrical, and chemical engineering. Although most of their innovations did not impress the economy, others came to the attention of consumers. More business opportunities became available, though, when financing institutions opened their doors to minorities. However, many of the lesser-known inventors individually labored to solve a daily problem only to encounter the difficulties of patenting the invention and then devoting a lifetime searching for venture capital to manufacture and market the merchandise. Although inventor Charles Randolph Beckley's grandfather, Robert Pelham (the famous publisher and editor of the Detroit *Plain-Dealer*), was one of the early renowned black inventors, Beckley is virtually unknown to the general public. Suffering under the weight of making his invention productive, Beckley, a Washington, D.C., attorney, recounts to a radio audience the following:

> I was granted a patent on a folding chair in December 1974. I had considerable difficulty attracting capital, or getting furniture manufacturers interested in this product. So I would think that one of the biggest problems that an inventor faces is really capitalization . . . I have had numerous contacts, but very few of the manufacturers are willing to venture much capital, and the offers I have had that I consider concrete leave just the bare amount for the time and effort I feel that I have devoted to develop this product. So consequently, I am contemplating going my own route. This gets back to the fact I think that it is important that anybody, particularly the small man [inventor], realize that the patent system does protect him as well as others. For instance, I have about 17 years to maybe dillydally around. I mean, if a company does not come up with something that is reasonable, then I do not immediately have to reach a decision, and maybe in a small way begin to develop my own track record in terms of showing other companies the advantage of my product and its marketability.[2]

Beckley's dilemma was not unique just to African American patentees who comprise a small segment of the overall population of patent holders, but was universal for a vast majority of patent holders regardless of ethnicity. But the African American inventor's tenacity transcended migrations, economic upheavals, poverty, the proactive Civil Rights period, racism, and discrimination—all within a context of a hostile environment that would stymie the average soul.

Charles R. Beckley founded Consumer Designs Limited in 1974 in Washington, D.C., to manufacture his wooden household furniture, available in a variety of fabrics and frame colors. The comfortable, convenient, and compact Beckley Chair features adjustable sitting positions. When folded it is stackable and transportable through narrow openings. Utilizing a very modest workforce of several employees, he has estimated annual sales of $71,000, according to the latest company profile.

Another devastating situation for a patentee is having the monopoly that one gets from a patent ignored by someone who is making, using, or selling that invention without permission. Where does it place the small inventor when an individual willfully and wantonly commits an unlawful act? How is he or she going to enforce the patent? Unless the inventor's enterprise is some kind of large company with substantial resources, someone else might try to sell his manufacture. Beckley, for example, will have to call on a lot of resources, such as hiring influential attorneys to help him enforce his property rights. The situation is complicated when it comes to infringement. This has happened too often to the small minority inventor who has invented something out of necessity only to see someone else take advantage of it.

PROFESSIONAL INDEPENDENT INVENTORS IN THE MARKETPLACE

There are two categories of inventors. One, known as the *captive inventor,* is employed by a large company or the government and whose inventiveness is locked in with the corporation or the government by contract. An army of African Americans inventors, trained in engineering, designing, chemistry, and physics, comprise this group. Illustrative in the automotive design arena is the talent of African Americans such as Michael G. Ellis and his wife, Marietta Ellis (a very rare African American combination in automotive design, similar to the unique, rare couple Kenneth W. Hairston and Paula T. Hairston, both adjudicating as judges at the U.S. Patent and Trademark Office, in patents and in trademarks, respectively). The talent of automotive designers Edward T. Welburn Jr. as well as Dennis Moses, Arthur E. Pryde, Walter Battle, and a few others is phenomenal.[3] The immense natural ability of the brilliant industrial designer Charles A. Harrison is found in the wares and commerce of the giant retailer Sears, Roebuck and Company. His prodigious body of work from the time he was hired in 1961 covers more than 700 designs, found worldwide in every household. Two of his noteworthy creative designs include the ubiquitous first-of-its-kind polypropylene trash can (with wheels), designed in 1963, and the 3D View-Master, a plastic photographic slide viewer, successful worldwide.[4]

The second category is the *independent inventor*—one who is not held or attached to a contract. Beyond being possessed with the idea, which has definitive value, and above the contractual relationship between the entity and the inventor, the independent inventor is on his own. A great burden is placed on inventors in this position. They struggle financially and emotionally as well to move the idea from conception to commercialization. Additionally, they are a hidden network, difficult to uncover.

Bayless Builds a Better Mousetrap—with Caution

In a 1981 speech titled "Business Based on Invention," independent black inventor and entrepreneur Robert Gordon Bayless begins with the old saying, "Build a better mousetrap and the world will beat a path to your door." Of the patent process itself that serves to underscore the reality of the promise of opportunity, however, he cautions that "it is *only* a promise of success, *not* a guarantee." Explaining his concern, Bayless says that some of the reasons are obvious enough, stating, "Free enterprise is survival of the fittest," because "Some inventors are better equipped for survival than others by virtue of their education, wealth or family, and corporate or political connections." Beyond obvious distinctions, there are other, more subtle factors at work in the marketplace that tend to equalize everyone's chances. Bayless explains these factors as simple, remorseless reality: first, "The world must be *convinced* that it needs a mouse trap *at all,* much less a better one," and second, "Success is greatly facilitated if you, the inventor, make sure that a path to your door already exists," described as a "well-marked, brightly lit, four-lane blacktop" highway.[5]

Bayless, owner of numerous patents, domestic and foreign, realized the difficult struggle the inventor faces in his need to get from a typical example to proprietary, followed by production, and then to the expected wealth—a struggle that dictated the need for alternative actions.

Born February 18, 1930, in West Mansfield, Ohio, Bayless graduated with a degree in chemistry from Central State University and obtained a master's degree in physical chemistry from the University of Cincinnati. He was a research associate at Antioch College and then a chemist at the U.S. Industrial Chemical Company before joining the National Cash Register Company (NCR) in 1963 in Dayton, Ohio. NCR pioneered the field of microencapsulation, described by Bayless as a combination of science and art in which solids, liquids, and gases are captured in polymer shells (like tiny capsules), often smaller than grains of talcum powder, for control of their use. Bayless authored eight patents during his 10-year tenure there, researching and developing carbonless copy paper, scratch-and-sniff paper, and time-release aspirin. With expertise in polymer chemistry, he left the company in 1972 to start and manage a business based on the unique microencapsulation chemical processes.

In 1973, Bayless, a brilliant scientist, founded the firm Capsulated Systems, Inc. Assisted by his brother and an associate, he incorporated the company at Yellow Springs and years later relocated to Fairborn, both in Ohio. He took a risk because he felt that he could not miss with an enterprise that would conduct research and development in microencapsulation and exploit its commercial benefits. Little did he know that he had a lot to learn about operating a business enterprise. His office, laboratory, and pilot plant were free of pomp but comfortable, located at Antioch College, where he shared space with campus personnel. While working on microencapsulating fish food, which could be the link to fill a vital role in feeding marine animals, Bayless ran into trouble with U.S. Food and Drug Administration requirements. Here he learned his first lesson: In order to be prosperous in business, "One must know how to size and qualify a marketplace and access every external factor, such as federal regulations, that can impact either the market itself" or one's ability to exploit it.[6] However, in attempting to correct the problem, he uncovered unique processes and materials that were acceptable. With this technology, the company received contracts from General Electric and Monsanto and governmental agencies such as the U.S. Air Force and the Department of Agriculture. The company then gave way from manufacturing to operating as a highly skilled research and development laboratory. Contracts appeared on the scene, one after the other.

Bayless developed a technique for microencapsulating gasoline for safe shipping and formulated a method to encapsulate Freon for insulating double-pane windows. He impregnated lumber with a microencapsulated fire retardant for fireproofing homes, encapsulated phosphor particles, and microencapsulated "artificial oranges" with a pesticide that fools, then kills Mediterranean fruit flies. The list goes on. Bayless was nationally and internationally recognized as an authority in this highly specialized field. He is quoted as saying that he has "solved both the Clean Air Act and the Clean Water Act simultaneously."[7]

Earnings were modest during the fledgling years, but sales rose to more than $500,000 in 1982. That same year, however, disappointments came his way. Japanese-owned Canon employed Bayless to come up with a microencapsulated toner for a color copier. This he did under an agreement, but later Canon indicated that the product was inferior. Three years later, he discovered that Canon had secured patents on such a toner and cited the 28 documents Bayless had written.[8]

The firm then implemented an advertising campaign, added capital equipment, and expanded its technical staff. Bayless found that employees are a company's most valued asset, so he treated his 10 full-time employees accordingly to enhance the business's chances of prospering.

During the company's growth period Bayless filed and received dozens more patents. Capsulated Systems Inc. was a business based entirely on inventions. Accordingly, his client base expanded. The firm was active in five major market utilities—consumer products, electronics, paper, graphic arts, and pharmaceuticals. Here is where a *crucial* lesson was learned. Even though the normal business functions of accounting, administration, and the like are assigned to others, the company president and chief executive officer should have an introductory knowledge of these disciplines or have a grasp of sound business practices. It is wise to employ enforceable guidelines and quality-control measures. Additionally, Bayless found that the inventor should not just talk to the attorney of record and certified public account, but must *listen* to them as well. They hold the welfare of the firm in common. He, too, felt that the more things change, the more they stay the same.[9]

After a number of years the company located its corporate headquarters in the Battelle-Kettering Laboratory of Antioch College in Yellow Springs, Ohio. By 1987, Bayless had signed a $380 million, 13-year contract with a Columbus, Ohio, business for working out an encapsulated coating method for film and glass. Another innovation of Capsulated Systems Inc. was approved for the Department of Defense, and a $1 million per year contract with the Department of Agriculture in Mississippi was in the works.[10]

By 1989, the picture for Bayless was not too rosy. At times he suffered setbacks. A large, destructive fire struck his research facility, and his proprietary information was used by others without his consent. He expected lucrative contracts to come in for his film-coat reinforcing bars, his fish food projects, an encapsulated spot remover called Spot-a-Way, and numerous other ingenious microencapsulating concepts, only to find them wishful thinking.

In 1990, Bayless moved to Atlanta, Georgia, and established Bayless Enterprises Inc. for the purpose of seeking suitable markets for his specialized technology. He held the positions of chairman and chief executive officer as well as chief scientist until 1997. During this period Bayless excelled in the field of microencapsulation, developing and inventing techniques applicable to organic chemicals, pigments and dyes, organometallics, inorganic compounds, and various resins, to name just a few. In 1997, he received his Ph.D. from the University of Wexford, and he traveled extensively in the Southeast Asia region from 1998 to 2000. In 2001, Bayless set up ENCAP Technologies, LLC, in Atlanta. As its chairman and CEO, he operates the company under the slogan "Tomorrow's Coating and Microencapsulation Technology Today." In 2009, this talent with a mind never at rest established Petromist Environmental Solutions, LLC. Bayless has outstanding creative ideas ranging from microencapsulation of electroluminescent phosphors (EEL) to a polymeric coating that is impermeable to oxygen and moisture, allowing for the prevention of global corrosion and leading to new ideas for water purification.[11]

Bayless understands that no matter how technically unique and efficient an invention is, it is "not in and of itself a guarantee of success." As many inventive entrepreneurs discover, running a business has its own set of parameters—hard work, sufficiently qualified employees and consultants, serious planning, education, and loads of good fortune.[12]

With drawbacks and problems aside, Bayless gives sage advice to anyone considering starting up an enterprise on his or her invention:

> Don't let your patent act as a death certificate for your invention. Don't let the energy, drive, dedication, and attention to detail you put into creating your invention and working with your attorney to get it protected by patent, die with the patent. To be successful in the business you build based on your invention, you must be willing to give even *more* time, energy, drive, dedication, and attention to detail. If you do, and do it right, well, the world may not *actually* beat a path to your door to get your mousetrap, but, I can tell you this much, *there won't be a mouse in the world that will feel safe!*[13]

The minority entrepreneurial inventor can encounter any number of problems beyond those issues cited by Bayless, who unmistakably faced racism and discrimination. It may be that there is not enough venture capital accessible to the inventor, or perhaps the patent holder does not have enough power of imagination. It could be that he or she, like the inventor of any ethnicity, might run into the classic roadblock from corporate America, which espouses that if the invention is invented other than within their own companies, they are not interested. Further, the inventor's enterprise might be too small for consideration, or he or she lacks skill in selling. There are many scenarios. However, luck plays a big part in the equation for thriving.

Johnson Floods the Toy Market

Lonnie George Johnson, a nuclear engineer and creator of the powerful water gun called the Super Soaker, is a career innovator. In 1989 he established the company Lonnie C. Johnson Engineering to promote his ideas, but in 1991 renamed the firm Johnson Research and Development Company Inc. to sell his invention as well, packaged in modified forms such as a water-powered airplane and a robot. It became an instant international hit with kids as well as playful grownups.

Born October 6, 1949, in Mobile, Alabama, Johnson is the third of six children of David Johnson, a driver for the U.S. Air Force, and Arline Washington Johnson, a nurse's assistant. He completed his secondary school education in his segregated hometown, guided by tolerant and patient parents.[14] Johnson was painfully aware of racial inequities, but that did not deter his curiosity about how things worked. He constantly fiddled with junk. His parents encouraged him to achieve during the early creative years; his mother ingrained in her children the importance of knowledge, emphasizing that what one puts in the brain counts in life.

Likened to a child prodigy, inquisitive young Johnson habitually tinkered with his siblings' toys to see how they functioned. In project after project he monkeyed with old jukeboxes, plastic pipe, compression motors, and explosive rocket fuel, pursuits that occasionally got him into trouble. By this time, thin and wearing eyeglasses, he was dubbed "the professor." As a senior in high school in 1968, he won first place in a national science competition for his ingenuity in making a remote-controlled robot called "Linex" at the University of Alabama Junior Engineering Technical Society Exposition, an unprecedented honor for a student from his locale.[15]

Johnson excelled on the SAT exam and won a mathematics scholarship to Tuskegee University, where he continued his tinkering in between studies and college life. He was an astute and clever intellect, but he was once told that he could not become an engineer because of his inquisitive nature. Lonnie Johnson was awarded an air force ROTC scholarship and graduated with distinction in mechanical engineering in 1973. He received a master of science degree in nuclear engineering two years later.[16]

Johnson had a short stint as a research engineer at the Oak Ridge National Laboratory in 1975 before joining the U.S. Air Force, where he worked for its Weapons Laboratory in Albuquerque, supervising the space nuclear power safety section. Over the ensuing decades, he moved back and forth between engineering for the air force and stints at the NASA Jet Propulsion Laboratory in Pasadena, California. The brilliant engineer enjoyed seeking novel methods to give satellite computer memories their power and delighted at new ways to detect enemy submarines. While working in the aerospace industry, he assisted in designing the spacecraft systems for the Galileo Project to study Jupiter, the Mars Observer, the Voyager mission, and the Cassini mission to Saturn. At one point in his air force career, Johnson, a captain, received a nomination for astronaut training as a space shuttle mission specialist. Throughout his professional career he was given commendation medals and awarded numerous honors for excellence.[17]

During his off-duty hours, in the small military housing unit he shared with his family, Johnson, endowed with a searching mind that never seemed to take a break, busied himself with ideas. He found solace in new thoughts and fresh paths for solving problems, perceiving the questions and the answers—the essence of creativity. Working in Alabama for the air force during the day, the night hours belonged to him and his ideas, much to the chagrin of his wife.

In 1977, fired with ambition, Johnson teamed up with John M. Laterriere on his first patent for a digital distance-measuring instrument, granted March 6, 1979. The following year, as the sole inventor, he obtained two more patents, the first for a variable resistance-type sensor-controlled switch, and the other, when in California, for a smoke-detecting, timer-controlled thermostat.[18]

With those patents in hand he was well on his way to becoming a prolific creative genius and thriving entrepreneur. During these years Johnson, his wife, and their three kids shuttled from state to state with boxes of his junk in tow.

Working on personal time in 1982, the NASA engineer gave birth to the trademarked squirt gun. He was experimenting with heat pumps and wondered how strong a pump he could make by forcing water through a self-made nozzle with a vacuum chamber. A powerful jet of water erupted across the bathroom, flinging the shower curtain aside and drenching the room. This was Johnson's breakthrough moment.

Lonnie Johnson confided in his eldest child, Aneka, then six years old, that he was going to make a "great" water gun. The sudden discovery that kids could pressurize the water by forcing air into the gun mechanism that ejected a high-velocity spray was inspiring. From that day forward, Johnson's creative juices flowed until he made his first power unit. Much to the delight of his daughter and the neighborhood children, the prototype was an instant hit. The history of the toy water gun had begun.

In seeking venture capital for his brainchild Johnson exhaustively pursued investors at trade shows. He had a difficult time getting his other technology sold, so he concentrated on the water gun. It took another seven laborious years for him to get industry respect and recognition by any toy manufacturer. Nonetheless, Johnson filed patent applications and was awarded his first squirt gun patent on May 27, 1986. According to a news article, "[T]he lowest point [in his life] came in 1987, when Johnson left the air force with the understanding that an investment capital firm would contract to develop some of his ideas. At the last minute, the firm backed out, demanding that he first pay $8,000."[19] The predicament left the family without an income or a home, and, most unfortunately, with a lawsuit when he tried to retreat from the agreement. The Jet Propulsion Laboratory rehired him, happy at his return.

Strong in heart with a firm belief in himself, Johnson set his own path and in 1991 moved the family to Atlanta, Georgia. He was fortunate that year when an executive saw the Super Soaker at a New York trade show. Licensed at the time to Larami Corporation, a small Philadelphia company, the water gun invention began a meteoric climb. Johnson's fortitude, resilience, and perseverance paid off.

The first water gun, priced at $10, sold very well; however, sales escalated after Johnny Carson experimented with it on his *Tonight* show, and nationally televised commercials touted it.

The phenomenal success of the Super Soaker with its "Wetter is better" slogan was well worth the chance for Lonnie Johnson to leave the NASA Jet

Propulsion Laboratory in 1991 for the last time and devote full-time work to the novel innovation. It was one of the 10 top-selling toys of the year, with sales of 10 million units. This success of the commodity won the young entrepreneur's company the "Small Business of the Year" award from the Cobb County, Georgia, Chamber of Commerce. The unit number then doubled the following year, generating more than $200 million in retail sales. For the next 10 years sales rose close to $1 billion.[20]

In the mid-1990s, Larami became a subsidiary of the giant toy manufacturer Hasbro Corporation. Due to Johnson's intellectual property rights, the Super Soaker maintains a competitive edge in the toy industry around the planet. From another license agreement with Hasbro, Johnson designed, engineered, and developed a soft foam dart gun, trademarked NERF, which has become a popular staple toy of the summer. Johnson's research company ventured into the field of toy rocketry and air power technology with Estes Air Rockets.[21]

Capitalizing on the victory of the squirt gun, the brilliant entrepreneur and businessman initiated some years later two other Atlanta-based companies, Excellatron Solid State, LLC, and Johnson Electro-Mechanical Systems, LLC,

Lonnie G. Johnson, displaying his Super Soaker squirt gun for NIPLA national secretary Pat Sluby. (From the Patricia Carter Ives Sluby Collection)

established to develop leading-edge technology from consumer products and toys to environmentally friendly alternative methods of power. The former enterprise specializes in solid-state tin film lithium rechargeable batteries—technology originating at Oak Ridge National Laboratory—while the latter company produces ideas that have the potential to change the global market. After years of effort, the Johnson companies have been awarded contracts from NASA as well as from the U.S. Department of Energy. Another of the Johnson group of companies, Johnson Real Estate Investments, LLC, is involved with the community in outreach programs and has a vested interest in stimulating economic growth in Atlanta's disadvantaged enclave.[22]

Lonnie Johnson's outstanding achievement has not gone unnoticed. Many works chronicle his career. In addition to publishing in technical journals, he makes television appearances, including the Oprah Winfrey show and segments of *Science Times* broadcast on the National Geographic Channel. The Hasbro Corporation inducted him into their Inventor Hall of Fame in 2000, and the following year Tuskegee University bestowed upon him an honorary doctorate of science. With his first marriage dissolved, Johnson married Linda Moore in 2002 and had another daughter.[23]

The inventor holds more than one hundred U.S. patents and pending patent applications, including a number of foreign patents as well, the rights of which are owned by the Johnson companies. Among his other concepts, Johnson patented an electrochemical conversion system, a magnetic propulsion toy system, a thin lithium film battery, and hair-curler drying apparatus. Johnson's bent to invent is prolific, placing him on the roll with other idolized super inventors who have revolutionized industries.

ORDINARY PEOPLE—BEAUTIFUL MINDS

So many ordinary persons with beautiful creative minds have come up with brilliant concepts. The captive inventors who work under contractual agreements number in the hundreds. Among that number are women inventors who made their appearance in this category within the last three or four decades, thus joining the black men who surfaced as early as the 1940s. For example, there are captive black women creative thinkers at Dow Chemical Company, International Business Machines Corporation, Johnson Products Company, and Monsanto Agricultural Company and in the federal sector and at various universities as well.

The independent inventor comprises a large segment of patent holders. These men and women wholeheartedly endeavor in the marketplace, true believers of the free enterprise system. Some inventors experience a modest profit, some are more financially comfortable, but many end up with a negative bottom line, only to regroup in tough situations. These economic experiences are commonplace for risk-taking entrepreneurs but particularly irksome for African Americans.

The creative skill of Sharon B. Duncan surfaced just at the end of the last millennium when she was shopping for shoes. Duncan, a native Washingtonian with a degree in economics from Barnard College and an MBA from the Wharton School of Finance, came up with a feasible idea for a shoe size scanner. As she was looking at shoe displays and waiting in line to pay for her selection, she thought about the problems that arise when a clerk has to spend time searching the stockroom to look for the customer's shoe size, only to find that the specific size is not available. The potential buyer can get frustrated, and a sale may be lost. Duncan knew that there had to be a better way to buy shoes. She figured out a different path for sales clerks and customers to find out whether shoe display models are currently in stock in a given size and color. Armed with business know-how and a specialty in information systems, she found a solution to the time-consuming task of manually searching the stockroom shelves, thus freeing up store clerks' time for assisting customers. She developed a scanner device with a base unit that links with the store's computerized inventory system for use by customers and clerks in shoe stores and applied for a patent in 2000 on her automated shoe size scanner system. In 2002, she was awarded the coveted grant. Duncan set up Duncan Technologies Solutions, LLC to protect the patented invention, and then sold the full patent rights to Symbol Technologies, the largest bar-coding company in the nation. The three foreign patents received on the innovation were also sold to the company.[24]

In 2005, Duncan patented a vertically stacked utensil holder for containing multiple spoons, forks, and spatulas during cooking. Exactly one year later, she acquired another patent in the field of luggage carriers. Wheeled hand-carts and such mechanisms for transporting luggage have been known in a variety of configurations; however, Duncan devised a small, unique wheeled carrier for a book bag or backpack. She left the marketing of her inventions to skilled specialists rather than tackling the field herself, a more comfortable position for her. While Duncan journeyed through the complexities of patenting and commercializing her products, she is in the percentile of the favored.

For the executive vice president of Quantum Technology Consultants Inc. inventor Clyde G. Bethea modeled his enterprise as a consultant company located in Franklin Park, New Jersey. Owner of more than 30 domestic patents and more than 100 worldwide, Bethea is a giant talent in the field of lasers, imaging, quantum electronics, and more. He conceived the Quantum well infrared photo detector camera (QWIP), and high-speed tunable communications lasers as well. His ingenious concepts are useful to both industry and the federal government. In particular, entities such as the Jet Propulsion

Laboratory, National Aeronautics and Space Administration (NASA), and the U.S. Air Force have great interest in his work. The consultant enterprise works under contract with universities based on grants the institutions receive. Assisting professors and Ph.D. graduate students on their thesis projects are important projects for Quantum. Bethea will work for private companies but does not pursue them.[25]

After receiving a degree in electronics technology from New York Technical College, Bethea went to work at the Research Division of AT&T Bell Laboratories (later Lucent Technologies) in Murray Hill, New Jersey, from 1970 to 2005. He was a Distinguished Member of the Technical Staff. His research extended over wide areas of endeavor, covering advanced laser imaging physics, nonlinear optics, high-speed optics and electronics, and advanced thermal dynamics of semiconductors and other network systems. Bethea was the first to design numerous techniques and critical systems and is working in a research reliability group, performing research on optical laser transmission procedures and advanced wireless communications. He was awarded the Black Engineer of the Year Award in 1989 and was inducted into the Space Foundation Hall of Fame in 2001.[26]

Trailblazer John F. Dove was one of the earliest African Americans to arrive in Rome, New York. He moved there at age 20 to work at Rome Air Development Center when it opened its doors in 1955. He is the inventor of the technology that created the compact disk (CD) for storing information.

Dove served in the U.S. Army as an X-ray technician after graduating in science and mathematics from Columbia University. At the center (now the Air Force Research Laboratory) he solved difficult technological problems that baffled his colleagues. His supervisor and peers did not trust his genius because of his young age and because they did not think an African American could be that intelligent. Dove found out that electronic beams could be used to record and store information. The army division chief denigrated him for being "ignorant of science" when told of Dove's discovery. Plugging along nevertheless, John Dove secured a patent on the technology titled "Data Storage and Retrieval System" on December 28, 1965, the precursor to the compact disk. A technological revolution was taking place, creating a "seemingly insatiable demand for recording, storage, readout, and display of data of all types and forms."[27]

After a 28-year career with the Air Force Lab, Dove retired in 1983, moving into private enterprises. He founded Dove Electronics Inc. in Rome, one of whose products was a wind shear detector formulated for the Federal Aviation Administration. Seven years later he established Dove Photonics, Inc. A business alliance also was formed with Syracuse University to research a fiber optic amplifier to transmit computer data and video by way of fiber optic lines, a faster way using light. Moreover, Dove was put on retainer by huge global companies for his vast knowledge of optics and the compact disk. To assist minority citizens of the community, he established a real estate business, thus achieving another distinction—the first African American real estate agent in Rome. He was a civic-minded resident who advocated for the community at large, serving on many organizations' boards. John F. Dove, born in rural North Carolina, died on January 16, 2004, of a bacterial infection. He was 79 years of age.[28]

The extraordinary creativity of Reverend Johnny G. Allen Sr. continues to surface well into his advanced years. Allen, one of seven children, born on May 1, 1924, in Edison, Georgia, possesses more than 30 patents, obtained over the last five decades, mostly for designs of garbage can holders and refuse bag supports. Several of his utility patents, acquired in 1990 and 1991, are directed toward retention ring assemblies for supporting refuse bags. A World War II veteran, the prolific inventor was the pastor of Macedonia Missionary Church at Fort Gaines, Georgia, for 49 years before retiring. When floods damaged the church, he rebuilt it using his brick masonry expertise. To earn additional income to finance his inventions and to pay for his patent attorney's services, he operated a grocery store near his home in Albany, Georgia, and returned, on and off, to laying brick.[29]

Allen's creativity started in 1947 "from a dream," and by 1955, a "revelation" came through to him. He had noticed, and was annoyed by, the amount of trash strewn in neighborhoods, caused, in part, by dogs knocking trash cans to the ground, sending the lids everywhere. The trash was an enormous eyesore, so, using his God-given talents to solve the dilemma, in the 1960s he began designing garbage can holders and racks. He then he established the Allen Rack and Manufacturing Company to market his inventions and improvements.[30]

Coming from humble beginnings, Allen, whose grandfather was a former slave, lived on a farm in southwest Georgia, where his parents cultivated cotton, corn, and peanuts and raised hogs and chickens. He was born in the same house as his dad but did not go to school much because help was needed on the farm, which supported the family. Later, Allen served in the army, receiving his training at Fort Lee, Virginia.[31]

Allen began with a simple idea that grew into multiple improvements. The inventor was always reaching for a better product. His patent attorney, who initially put him off, worked for the family's attorney but then rethought Allen's concept and commented, "More money is made from simple ideas than from sophisticated ones." The first garbage can holders were sold off the back of Allen's truck to many white customers and a few African Americans. Says Allen, "My simple ideas brought me money," and with this financial gain, "I paid my lawyer."[32] A work team consisting of Allen, his son, and a friend built the mechanism. After paying the two, Allen had enough money to move to the next step. Concrete blocks were needed on which to place the cans, so he filled that need. From the axiom "one need creates another," Allen achieved success, although modestly.[33]

In 1979, Allen became the earliest African American granted a contract in Albany, Georgia. He had made a bid to the city for supplying garbage can holders. The mayor "said he would buy some for the city," indicated the inventor, because his garbage can holder "was the best."[34] His first paycheck resulted from the purchase of two hundred holders, but collecting the money was not easy.

In a cleanup initiative, a bank in Albany supplied 1,500 trash cans and holders to the local African American community. Allen's holders were used but he was paid for only 700 units. To move his enterprise along Allen obtained a small business loan to establish a manufacturing plant for the invention. It took 20 months to receive one-third benefit out of the loan. However, ideas continued to unfold, especially when city orders came to have residents bag all leaves, followed by the law to recycle waste. His floating ring assembly for supporting refuse bags spurred more improvements, all of which he patented. The latest development concerns a concept to fill and then close sandbags in an orderly series of actions. Allen has the Albany State University office of business development assist him as a minority businessman. Initiating a community effort, Reverend Allen set up the Helping Hands activity to make separation and bagging less effortless for recycling centers.[35]

MEDICAL SCIENCE

Independent inventor Frances Christian Gaskin established a firm in Albany, New York, in her name after discovering new products to protect the skin and hair of people. Gaskin, a clinical nurse for more than 30 years, earned a doctorate from Fordham University for research on melanin. Frances Christian Gaskin Inc. an outgrowth of her dissertation, brought to market the first patented melanin-based sun-care and hair-care products in the United States. The company successfully manufactured novel items to shield people of color from harmful UV sun rays. As a by-product of her first patent, received in 1989, Gaskin's progressive business initially persevered against all comers. Though having an impressive inventory of products such as shampoos, conditioners, and hair balm in addition to skin lotions, crèmes, and ointments, her firm eventually encountered economic upturns and downturns, some brought on by business naivety and lack of savvy.

With belief in herself and a strong will to succeed, Gaskin continued to develop new and useful compositions and methods for protecting the skin and strengthening hair. Between 1989 and 1997 she was awarded four domestic patents and an Australian patent grant as well. At present her products

Melanin Plus™
cream rinse product
developed and
distributed by Frances C.
Gaskin, Ph.D.
(Courtesy Frances C.
Gaskin, Ph.D.)

are sold in stores on Martha's Vineyard, where she has a home, and through direct mail.[36]

Inventor Johnnie R. Jackson was destined for prosperity; he wanted to be the best in everything, from picking cotton at six years of age to becoming the top student at every level of his education. Jackson, born in Crawford, Texas, graduated cum laude with a B.S. in premedicine from Prairie View A&M University in 1960. In 1971, he received an M.S. degree, summa cum laude, in computer and management information systems, accomplished in nine months, and then in 1976 completed his Ph.D. requirements, summa cum laude, in another nine months, both at American University. This achievement made him the first African American to attain a doctorate in computer systems and management information systems. Jackson also became the first African American and the youngest, at age 29, to head the management information systems at the Walter Reed Army Center in Washington, D.C. Jackson is now a retired lieutenant colonel in the Army Medical Service Corps.[37]

A passionate researcher and innovator, Jackson is credited with conceiving and played a major role in developing and implementing the Department of Defense's TRI-service medical information system. He helped design the military's electronic health record system that enables healthcare providers to access data about beneficiaries' conditions, prescriptions, diagnostic tests, and other information necessary to provide quality care.

Jackson first invented a portable clinical electronic medical records system, and then originated a system and method for portable medical records data flash cards, for which he filed a patent application in 2008. This innovation has the ability to integrate computer-based technologies with medicine. In his system, a patient's entire electronic health record is downloaded to a desktop without the need for converting the sophisticated, complex hospital information system records. Major diseases such as diabetes and other debilitating diseases can be managed by this cutting-edge technology. Further, it can help reduce deaths due to drug contraindications and can establish a paperless environment for small, rural medical clinics and outpatient providers as well as possibly transform the nation's severely abused Medicare and Medicaid systems.[38]

As founder and president of Diabetics Informatics Inc. the inventor set up a small business venture to provide verified services and, additionally, established Biotechnology and Environmental Services (BITES) Inc. to augment his pioneering and trailblazing efforts.

Jackson's fervor for how to improve healthcare by way of information technology is well expressed in his book *Genocide of Americans—the Healthcare Tsunamis*. The basic emphasis is on the "effects of diabetes mellitus on the human body." America, in his words, has "broken-down healthcare delivery systems" that contribute to "genocide of Americans." Jackson was a pioneer in health informatics and telemedicine for the military. He was a captain at age 25, promoted to major at 29, and achieved the rank of lieutenant colonel at 34. A highly decorated Vietnam service-connected disabled veteran, Jackson was awarded the Legion of Merit, the Bronze Star Service Medal, and a host of other awards during his illustrious military career.[39]

The teamwork of inventors James A. Gary and Samuel Merrill resulted in a seven-year journey to patent fruition. Persistence, patience, and perseverance paid off for the inventors, who worked their way through school by assisting the pathologist in performing autopsies in the morgue at Suburban Hospital in Bethesda, Maryland. Gary was attending Bowie State College, reaching toward a degree in public administration and further toward his goal to become a hospital administrator, and Merrill was a graduate pathology student at Howard University. The experience of working in the medical field for about 20 years provided the foundation for their innovative procedure to remove the brain.

Gary and Merrill, working together in 1978, were responsible for the expensive labor-intensive and time-consuming process of removing the brain, then preparing it for autopsy. Using the manual instrument of choice was slow and tedious. Should they pick up the pace, the device would overheat. With expert knowledge, and believing that there was a better, faster, and safer way to achieve the end result without damage to brain tissue or cosmetic damage to the head, the pair solved the problem by developing an apparatus with an automatic depth-control cutting tool that has speed adjustability, meaning it cuts only bone. Further, it is mounted on a carrier. Minus the ring support, the instrument is also useful manually. Also saving precious time, the tool is designed to be sensitive to soft brain tissue in addition to the spread of bone dust that can have deleterious consequences in the work environment, particularly if communicable diseases are involved.[40]

James A. Gary was born in Edenborn, Pennsylvania, in 1940, a son of a coal miner. During his 20 years in the U.S. Navy, he received medic training as a hospital corpsman and for eight years was stationed on Capitol Hill in Washington, D.C., at the dispensary for members of Congress working at the pharmacy unit. After discharge, Gary worked from 1978 to 1990 at Suburban Hospital in the morgue and in other departments to learn and develop hospital administration skills. For five years, he was the administrator of operations for the Affiliated Santé Group of Silver Spring, Maryland. In 1995, he relocated to Atlanta, Georgia, to become the clinical director of Family Practice Center, and then director of Ambulatory Care Centers at the Morehouse School of Medicine. In 2001, Gary moved to Florida to become chief executive officer of the Madison County Memorial Hospital, and is now retired, living in Palm Coast, Florida.[41]

Samuel Merrill Jr. was born in Laurel, Mississippi, and graduated in biochemistry in 1961 from Fisk University. From there he went into the U.S. Army, became a medic, and afterward moved to Los Angeles, where he worked for the Veterans Administration. For a time Merrill was employed at Dow Chemicals between residency in Los Angeles and Denver. He received a master's degree in neuroanatomy from Howard University, and then completed his Ph.D. requirements in brain development and nutritional science at the University of Maryland. He retired from the Public Health Service's office of research integrity in 2007 and now shuttles between his homes in Maryland and Florida.[42]

After applying for a patent in 1988, Gary and Merrill received the grant in 1992 and proceeded to organize the company S & J Scientific Association Inc. to promote the highly specialized product. They took the instrument to trade shows in Pittsburgh and in Pasadena, California, and have been interviewed on television, trying to market the invention.

In 2002, the inventors suffered an unfortunate incident. Along with other items, the prototype was stolen from its storage unit. A company potentially wanted to help take the apparatus to market, but they needed the prototype to move forward. Even after diligent searching, the costly instrument was never recovered. The inventors continue to press forward from this setback, operating the business from Maryland and Florida and aiming at markets such as municipal morgues, medical schools, hospitals, medical examiners, and veterinary practices. Gary and Merrill estimate the value of the product, once manufactured, to be about $10,000. The team faces many challenges, including, in part, the attitude from others in the specialized field who question their ability to conceive the invention. Undaunted by this negative energy and the general financial difficulties from the manufacturing community, Merrill and Gary seek venture capital to work on a new outcome for the instrument. Several companies have expressed an interest in the unique invention, but negotiations have not been fruitful. Nonetheless, with a positive attitude, they look forward to mass production of the specialized product.[43]

Finding a niche in the skin-care business was a cinch for the Aberdeen, Maryland–born dermatologist Milton Donald Moore Jr., a pharmacy undergraduate of Xavier University and a 1980 graduate of Meharry Medical College School of Medicine. Giving particular attention to facial skin problems, Dr. Moore has received numerous patents on shaving preparations and devices, the first awarded in 1987 for a razor bump tool, which is used to lift trapped (ingrown) hairs with a curved and tapered blade. His wide array of products, trademarked "Moore Unique," includes a shaving system comprising the tool; an antibacterial shaver's wash; a shaving solution to hydrate, lubricate, and moisturize the skin; a razor rash relief; and toner cream to ease pigmentation and smooth skin texture.[44]

A patented shaving preparation is specific for aid in the prevention and treatment of the bothersome condition called pseudofolliculitis barbae (PFB), which can lead to a painful rash resulting from ingrown hairs, and on occasion scarring. The affliction is common among African American males who shave coarse or curly hair, although males of other ethnic groups can suffer as well. To enhance knowledge of the problem, Moore began an educational awareness initiative to inform men about how to address the debilitating skin condition to enhance their personal grooming. In fact, the condition became an issue in the workforce with regard to dress codes that forbid employees to wear beards. Men with PFB grow them to ease pain and suffering.

Dr. Moore organized Moore Unique Skin Care, LLC, to promote his skin product line, useful for men and for women who shave the face, legs, or underarms. The very profitable business, situated in Houston, Texas, supplies a Razor Rash Relief and Eventone Cream, among other items, to nationwide drugstore chains and select national outlets.[45] In early 2007, the company launched the Pseudofolliculitis Barbae Educational Awareness Initiative to help inform men on how to address the skin condition to enhance their appearance. Dr. Moore's new discoveries, for which he has applied for patents, include a design for a markedly different razor, a "GlipperGlide" shaving solution, and a novel gel shaving product with "superior lubrication." The "Moore Unique" trademark, registered for dermatological and health spa medications and ointments, was first used in commerce in 1994.

VENTRILOQUIST AND ENTERTAINER

Arthur Oliver Takeall Jr., a professional ventriloquist and entertainer of radio fame in Las Vegas and numerous other cities, hailed from Annapolis, Maryland. Born January 7, 1947, he came up with the jingle "You got the right one baby, Uh Huh," having first use in commerce in 1984, according to his 1997 U.S. registered service mark for entertainment, namely, live performances in the nature of a ventriloquist act. He also obtained a federal copyright for the popular song, written as a love song.

Takeall sent the jingle to Pepsico Inc. in 1989, when he was seeking funds to begin an educational program with his dummy, "Scooter." In 1992, at age 45, he filed a lawsuit against Pepsico Inc. for using his song; however, a federal court judge dismissed the action, ruling in a summary judgment against his claim because he lacked proof that the giant soft drink company had known of his version before using it. The slogan became famous as the signature song of Ray Charles for Diet Pepsi.

He received numerous honors and awards and created "Common Sense," an educational effort of great merit. He graduated from Wiley H. Bates High School and furthered his education through the University of Maryland extension courses while serving in the U.S. Air Force. Arthur O. Takeall Jr. passed away on March 20, 2009. He donated his body to science.

Source: Friend, Clarence Ross of Annapolis, Md., personal interview, June 18, 2009.

THE ENTERTAINER

The entertainment field harbors a multitude of individuals with creative talent who develop and design such elements as sets, wardrobes, and play boards, just to name a few. There are talents of wide magnitude and skill who achieve fame as world-renowned performers in their genre. However, little information about the performers who have genius in the field of inventions is known. The invention titled "Method and Means for Creating Anti-Gravity Illusion" is the brainchild of the late pop singer Michael Joseph Jackson.

Michael Jackson, a musical child prodigy with a gift for singing and performing mature dance routines, was creative in an arena generally unknown to his fans and the general public. On October 26, 1993, Jackson and two other inventors conceived a "system for engaging shoes with a hitch means to permit a person standing on a stage surface to lean forward beyond his or her center of gravity." The shoes have "a specially designed heel slot which can be detachably engaged with the hitch member." The wearer of the shoe simply slides the foot forward to make contact with the hitch member. In essence, this new shoe design gave Jackson and other dancers the impression of

United States Patent [19]

Jackson et al.

[11] Patent Number: **5,255,452**

[45] Date of Patent: **Oct. 26, 1993**

[54] **METHOD AND MEANS FOR CREATING ANTI-GRAVITY ILLUSION**

[75] Inventors: **Michael J. Jackson**, Los Angeles; **Michael L. Bush; Dennis Tompkins,** both of Hollywood, Calif.

[73] Assignee: **Triumph International, Inc.,** Los Angeles, Calif.

[21] Appl. No.: **905,479**

[22] Filed: **Jun. 29, 1992**

[51] Int. Cl.⁵ A43B 5/00; A43B 3/00
[52] U.S. Cl. 36/113; 36/1; 36/136; 36/80; 36/132
[58] Field of Search 36/1, 80, 103, 113, 36/114, 131, 132, 136; 482/70, 71, 105

[56] **References Cited**

U.S. PATENT DOCUMENTS

1,059,284	4/1913	Dennis	36/114
2,114,790	4/1938	Venables	36/132
2,473,099	6/1949	Hatch	36/1
3,889,399	6/1975	Emrich	36/1
4,445,287	5/1984	Garcia	36/114
4,538,480	9/1985	Trindle	36/131
4,645,466	2/1987	Ellis	36/132
4,762,019	8/1988	Beyl	36/131
4,882,858	11/1989	Signori	36/131
5,042,173	8/1991	Blizzard et al.	36/113

Primary Examiner—Steven N. Meyers
Assistant Examiner—M. Denise Patterson
Attorney, Agent, or Firm—Drucker & Sommers

[57] **ABSTRACT**

A system for allowing a shoe wearer to lean forwardly beyond his center of gravity by virtue of wearing a specially designed pair of shoes which will engage with a hitch member movably projectable through a stage surface. The shoes have a specially designed heel slot which can be detachably engaged with the hitch member by simply sliding the shoe wearer's foot forward, thereby engaging with the hitch member.

13 Claims, 4 Drawing Sheets

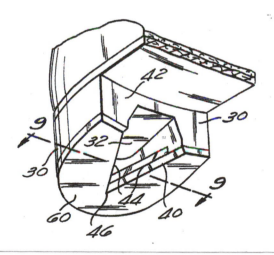

Method and Means for Creating Anti-Gravity Illusion, patented invention of Michael J. Jackson. (U.S. Patent and Trademark Office)

defying gravity. By so doing the performers deliver an interesting visual effect, which Jackson utilized in his music video "Smooth Criminal."[46]

The inventors applied for a patent on June 29, 1992, and received the grant on October 26, 1993. The patent disclosure acknowledges the identity of one of the inventors as a "professional entertainer" who " has incorporated dance steps in his recorded video performance." When the patent was issued, it was assigned to Triumph International Inc. of Los Angeles. It is not readily known if Michael Jackson pursued any business activity with the company; however, by 2005 the patent expired due to nonpayment of fees to maintain it during its 17-year time limitation. As a consequence, the document entered into the public domain.[47]

Jackson was born August 29, 1958, in Gary, Indiana, the seventh of nine children. Michael and his brother Marlon joined three other brothers in the band called the Jackson Brothers in 1964. At age eight Michael and his brother Jermaine became lead singers of the group renamed the Jackson 5.[48] Singer Gladys Knight discovered the group and repeatedly tried to get the attention of Motown Records founder Berry Gordy.[49] In July 1965, they auditioned for him.[50] In 1971 Michael began a solo career, and between 1976 and 1984 he was the lead composer of songs for the brothers' group, at that point renamed the Jacksons. Their first four records went to number one on the charts, unprecedented. Originally signed with Motown Records, the group left the company in 1975 and signed with Epic. Jackson's musical career soared to greatness over the decades. His second album, *Thriller*, issued by Epic, became undeniably the world's largest-selling album of all time, catapulting Jackson into a rare realm of performers. The immensely successful artist won eight Grammys in a single night. He was a very astute businessman with a keen sense of know-how. Jackson negotiated with Sony Music Entertainment over the album *Invincible* but later departed after a label dispute. He released the album himself in 2001. Commercially successful, it had a worldwide distribution of more than 10 million copies.[51] He was inducted into the Rock and Roll Hall of Fame twice because of his art. His music catalog is enviable.

Michael Jackson, an eccentric but brilliant artist and creative genius, passed away suddenly on June 25, 2009, at age 50 after being a part of the entertainment industry since age 6. After several days of rehearsing to begin his comeback for the "This Is It" 50-show extravaganza in London, scheduled to begin July 13, 2009, the King of Pop succumbed to an apparent overdose of drugs at his rented mansion in Los Angeles. He had many trademarks that punctuated his lifestyle—his signature Moonwalk dance step, the white sequined glove, and white socks worn always with black shoes. A public memorial was held on July 7, 2009, at the Staples Center in Los Angeles.[52]

SWEET SUCCESS

The energy, determination, and fortitude of Michele Hoskins, owner and founder of Michele Foods Inc. is meritorious. Now with numerous trademarks to protect her company's products, Hoskins has parlayed a secret recipe into a multibillion-dollar enterprise.

The Chicago native, former schoolteacher, and single mother had a vision and her great-great-grandmother's recipe for honey creme syrup that traditionally was passed on only to the third daughter of each generation. Hoskins was an only daughter; however, she herself had three daughters. With this fact, she convinced her mother after eight years to give her the syrup recipe for Keisha, her third daughter. Hoskins performed a balancing act between raising three young children and managing part-time jobs, all while struggling through difficult divorce proceedings. She wanted to be in charge of her destiny; however, poverty almost weakened her resolve. Nonetheless, during the 1980s, the rising visibility in society of the successful, independent woman encouraged Hoskins to embrace the idea of going into business, and in 1984, when she was about 30, she decided to become an entrepreneur.[53]

Armed with the secret recipe, no business experience, and her mom's support, Hoskins launched Michele Foods Inc. in the early 1990s, but her crucial lack of business acumen was almost fatal to her enterprise. She made several business arrangements that, in time, turned sour. With her naïveté in business practice, she experienced one setback after another. These missteps began to affect her attitude and spirit.

After learning of resources afforded by the Woman's Business Development Center in Chicago, Hoskins found sorely needed direction. The advice supplied by the center's leadership proved indispensable, guiding her toward a workable business plan. In time, from perseverance, passion, and good fortune, she reached her goal. Blood, sweat, and tears were shed along the way. The secret syrup concoction, initially called Supreme Products, turned rancid on the shelves within a short length of time. The product, now named Michele's Honey Creme Syrup, had to be rendered chemically stable to remain on the shelves of retail stores. After professional intervention from food experts, Hoskins's pancake syrup became a reality, ready for wide distribution to places near and far.

In 1993, Hoskins was diagnosed with a huge brain tumor. The news could not have come at a worse time—she was in the throes of a massive change in her nine-year-old syrup manufacturing enterprise. Surviving ordeals, Hoskins embraced changes that took place in her life and saw it as bringing to her "life's greatest gifts." She envisioned a way to transform her life and create her own way. The rough journey ended with sweet success.[54]

Hoskins, a gifted entrepreneur, expresses the entrepreneur's spirit in terms of knowing the problem and having the answer—the essence of creativity. She speaks of this spirit as the force "that continues to build companies from the ground up." She writes in her book *Sweet Expectations*, "This is the spirit in which I always deal with my problems, big or small. Sometimes the big ones have seemed as if they could doom my operation. But it depends on your perspective."[55]

FORGING AHEAD IN THE SPIRIT

Vision and foresight—the spirit that nudged many African American inventors to forge ahead—moved them in a direction normally seen as risky business. Risk takers such as Randall S. Marshall, conceiver of a system to substantially reduce the odds in lottery games, and John Pelham Beckley, inventor of a portable electric furnace and founder of the "Melting Pot" enterprise to promote the apparatus, concentrate on the goal of building a successful enterprise. Husband and wife Reginal and Michelle Payne, inventors of a device to fill buckets called "The Bucket Philler" and originators of Payne Family Enterprises (PFE), journey into this risk-taking realm of manufacturing, selling, and distributing the invention with different and diverse results. Inclusive in the broad field of design are African American graphic, industrial, clothing, stage, interior, and architectural designers who focus on a certain aesthetic look, many of whom independently initiate enterprises protected by patents and/or trademarks. Ruane Jeter of California, industrial designer and inventor of varied containers, founded Ruje Designs, while inventor Brothella Quick of Evanston, Illinois, markets her design of pocketed underwear under the name "PUG-C" in Chicago, from the initial investment of $100,000 for manufacture, distribution, and advertisement, to turn a profit.[56]

Patentees such as James H. Pickett Jr., who established "Picket Creations" as his trademark, and Dannie Byers, who introduced the "Mini-Dozer" as his mark in the trade, are finding ways to exploit their innovations. These aspiring entrepreneurs applied for patent protection, received it, and are heading to the marketplace with the inventions that they hope will bring great reward. However, complications have interrupted the pace, but they nonetheless press on. Many factors affect the commercialization of the product.

Some businesses are easier than others to penetrate and therefore have a need for new ideas. One has to thoroughly research market needs to find the right nexus for an innovation. Just having a patent does not guarantee success or make an inventor rich and famous. Nor does it mean that the invention is superior; contrarily, it indicates only that a patented invention is *significantly* different and distinctive enough to merit the grant by standards set forth in patent law. The patent holder has to remember that exclusive patent rights do come to an end—they are no longer in force after the expiration date. It is during this critical, limited time frame when the inventor finds the patent valuable, and it is during this period that the patent owner struggles to recover his or her investment before the innovation enters the public domain.

Critical also is the ability to protect a patented concept from infringers. New ideas that catch on in the market are magnets for others to copy them without permission. Large companies and corporations spend enormous energy and considerable amounts of money protecting their intellectual property; how-

NORRIS A. DODSON SR.: ARLINGTON EMBALMING PRODUCTS FINDING A NICHE

During a tumultuous time when black men and women suffered severe racism and discrimination, Norris Augustus Dodson Sr. took a chance and started his own chemical establishment at his home at 2253 8th Street NW, Washington, D.C. A Canadian-born pharmacist and chemist who could not find employment after graduate training at the University of Michigan, Dodson began manufacturing embalming fluids under the name Arlington Embalming Products in 1924, becoming the earliest African American to traverse that highly specialized realm. This unusual step provided Dodson a modest income for him and his family. Dodson supplied funeral homes in the vicinity and then nationwide under the name Norris A. Dodson, Incorporated. His two sons, Louis Dodson, a chemist, and Norris Jr., carried on the business, which they eventually sold in 1992 (the year their father died) to brothers Geary and Phillip Powell of Washington, D.C., who renamed the company Arlington Chemical Company. Before this time, a second African American embalming company, called Bondol Laboratories, founded in 1938 by Charles Latimar, was on the scene, based in Madison, Arkansas.

There are about 10 companies in the nation selling embalming fluids, and of that number only two were black owned until a few years ago, when the Powells purchased Latimar's laboratories, making them the single largest minority-owned embalming company in the United States. All of their products are manufactured at the main plant in Tuxedo, Maryland, and then shipped nationwide as well as to the Caribbean, the West Coast of African, and South America.

Sources: Norris A. Dodson III; and Geary Powell and Phillip Powell, owners of Arlington Chemical Company, 2313 51st Place, Tuxedo, Maryland.

ever, the average patentee at the marketplace with profitable products has to be forever vigilant for look-alike products that cut into any profits. After all, the basic purpose of an invention is for the owner to make money from the idea, and having a patent gives the owner "exclusive rights to his or her invention," as dictated in Article I, Section 8 of the federal Constitution.

Chicago inventor Calvin Flowers took his 1998 patented telephone jack security device to a manufacturer that produced 10,000 units of his invention. After approaching the nationwide enterprise Walgreen's, the device was placed at specific stores in Illinois, and by 2001, the device was advertised nationally at the chain. With many commercially successful products, closely similar items often appear of the market, and Flowers's phone jack was no exception. Within 12 months, he found his patented component being mass-produced and cheaply priced by a huge conglomerate. Taking appropriate measures, Flowers promptly filed a lawsuit and forced the company to quit manufacture of the poorer-quality, imitation merchandise, which blocked both incoming and outgoing calls by a certain rotating lock mechanism.[57] Eventually the infringement lawsuit was settled out of court.[58] Flowers's patented concept was vulnerable at the development and marketing stages. Protecting an invention

---

United States Patent [19]

Jeter

[11] Patent Number: **Des. 289,249**

[45] Date of Patent: ** Apr. 14, 1987

[54] **TOASTER**

[76] Inventor: **Ruane Jeter,** 1779 Alvira St., Los Angeles, Calif. 90035

[**] Term: **14 Years**

[21] Appl. No.: **591,578**

[22] Filed: **Mar. 20, 1984**

[52] **U.S. Cl.** **D7/330; D7/328**

[58] **Field of Search** D7/330, 328, 329; 99/385

[56] **References Cited**

U.S. PATENT DOCUMENTS

D. 151,113   9/1948   Yaeger D7/330
D. 176,275 12/1955   May D7/330
D. 218,209   7/1970   Shalvoy D7/330
2,838,989   6/1958   Clark et al. .... 99/385 X

3,169,469 2/1965 Parr .... 99/385 X

Primary Examiner—Bernard Ansher
Assistant Examiner—Linda Titolo
Attorney, Agent, or Firm—Joseph E. Baker

[57] **CLAIM**

The ornamental design for a toaster, as shown and described.

DESCRIPTION

FIG. 1 is a top front and right side perspective view of a toaster, showing my new design;
FIG. 2 is a right side elevational view thereof, the left side being a mirror image thereof;
FIG. 3 is a top plan view thereof;
FIG. 4 is a front elevational view thereof; and
FIG. 5 is a rear elevational view thereof.
The bottom of the toaster is plain and unornamented.

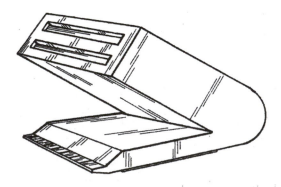

Toaster, patented design of Ruane Jeter. (U.S. Patent and Trademark Office)

**Ruane Jeter. (From the Patricia
Carter Ives Sluby Collection)**

from infringers is a struggle for an independent inventor with limited financial resources. The path to success for Flowers was not easy.

Flowers encouraged his family and friends to back the cost of his quest to acquire a patent by investing in his fledgling enterprise Tel-Lock Inc. but then many business turns brought various problems. To help novice inventors traverse the steps of product development and avoid pitfalls, Flowers in 2003 founded the nonprofit organization Chicago 1st Black Inventors/Entrepreneurs.[59]

Across the country, a number of programs were initiated to assist minority companies in bridging the technology divide. One in particular is the NASA Glenn Garrett Morgan Commercialization Initiative, launched in 1998 in Cleveland and originally guided by program manager Gail Wright of Battelle-GLITeC. It promoted the slogan "Helping Small Business Achieve a Competitive Advantage through NASA Technology." The companies selected to participate in the initiative were characterized as on the "threshold" of success but suffering from barriers that NASA resources could "help overcome." Small, minority-owned, and women-owned firms entered the program as companies "that are able to embrace and utilize innovative technology," placing them in a better position to succeed. NASA set up six regional technology transfer facilities to further the initiative.[60] Several African American technology and manufacturing companies who were better able to take advantage of NASA technology participated, with varying degrees of success. The program fosters growth, partnerships, assistance with procurement, working capital, marketing, improved business practices, and commercialization. Of particular mention here are those enterprises associated with acquired patents.

Dr. Harold J. Gulley of Cleveland patented a nontoxic organic substitute for chromate coatings that has been greeted enthusiastically as the industry standard. His company, Bi-K Corporation, developed a conversion coating or concentrate that inhibits metallic corrosion on metallic surfaces exposed to atmospheric environments. The environmentally safe specialty product is useful for industrial users of steel, such as the aircraft and automotive industries, which need nontoxic, durable, noncorrosive materials. In 1987, Gulley received a patent on an improved additive composition with corrosion-inhibitive and scale-preventive properties to avoid the buildup of scale and other substances on the inside walls of cooling systems.

Bi-K partnered with Clark-Atlanta University, a historically black university, to test and evaluate the company's conversion coating, for which agreement Bi-K received $50,000 of a $200,000 Partnership award from NASA Glenn Research Center. Dr. Gulley, president of the company, directed and observed the tests and carried out comparisons with chromate processes such that the end product, a chromate-free system, could be marketed to large chemical suppliers. The coatings of Bi-K were found superior to the state-of-the-art commercial coatings for select applications. To provide safe environments for children, the nontoxic product has application also for playground equipment made from alternative metals.[61]

Inventor Levi T. Thompson Jr. is chief technology officer of his company, T/J Technologies Inc. cofounded with his wife, Maria Thompson, who is president of the firm. From 1998 to 2000, the company was a Garrett Morgan Commercialization Initiative participant and won three of its assistance awards for a grand total of $130,000. The company, based in Ann Arbor, Michigan, excelled in engineering, design, and marketing of its ultra-capacitor technology. Its mission is to design, improve, and make advanced materials and instruments for electrochemical energy storage and conversion that include lithium batteries, fuel cells, and gas sensors in addition to ultra-capacitors, for which Thompson developed a unique class of materials.

Large worldwide enterprises have recognized T/J Technologies' patent record and expertise. Thompson's company owns the majority of his impressive patent portfolio, which covers the last several decades. Because ultra-capacitors store energy and deliver short, high-power pulses quickly, they are useful for cellular phones, portable computers, electric vehicles, and other commercially available electronics products. Says T/J Technologies president Maria Thompson, "The Garrett Morgan Initiative has helped us find the right people, brought in outstanding groups, and did a lot of the legwork."[62] With the initiative helping them focus on what is important, it facilitated advancement of the commercialization process.

Patented manufactures, that is, machines, products, and processes, provide the consumer with novel, or better, or cheaper products or some combination thereof; however, a revolutionary change, whether imaginatively creative or scientific, brings about a state of deep-seated ill will. Why? Any change in the status quo is followed by disorder because it is a natural instinct for humankind to protect its familiar way of life. When Jan Matzeliger invented the revolutionary automatic shoe lasting machine—a final step in shoe construction—the shoe industry workers revolted. The apparatus was a threat to their livelihood, eroding their status and income. At that period shoe lasting was already a threatened skill, so consequently Matzeliger's mechanism virtually eliminated the art. Very few individual, independent inventors are able to influence an entire industry, much less alter its course. Modern history teaches us about a few African American inventors of influence.

5

Epilogue

The American innovator of color at the marketplace leaves an impressive legacy for future generations. Through educational achievement and scientific prowess at the hands of technical wizards and risk takers, it continues as we witness the birth and growth of new black enterprises in a multitude of fields. From inventing to patenting and then selling, patience, strength, and an enormous desire to take charge of one's own destiny are elements of motivated entrepreneurs, many of whom are self-inspired. Today, African American businesspersons, instructors, scholars, and scientists labor to educate future entrepreneurs and innovators through a variety of educational, spiritual, and scientific programs, and by way of strategies put forth by professional associations and civic groups as well. They are dedicated to move beyond what their forebears gained.

Sustained by a passion, fueled with persistence, these inventive entrepreneurs persevered and believed in themselves and in the American dream. Their business acumen in the economic realm sharpened at every turn, giving them an education worth the cost. Undoubtedly, the contributions of black Americans have added to the nation's and to the world's economies, not only by dint of revolutionizing industries but also by their prowess and craftsmanship. The accomplishments of past and present inventors and pioneers serve as a pathfinder for future engineers and scientists. Driven and highly motivated, inventive entrepreneurs believe in a system that can reward them. Factors that may have been limited in the past, such as environment, geographical area, and personal interests, are easily surmountable in today's

Typed Drawing

Word Mark	**BLACK ENTERPRISE**
Goods and Services	IC 016. US 038. G & S: BUSINESS MAGAZINE OF GENERAL INTEREST TO THE BLACK COMMUNITY AND OTHERS. FIRST USE: 19700713. FIRST USE IN COMMERCE: 19700713
Mark Drawing Code	(1) TYPED DRAWING
Serial Number	73046663
Filing Date	March 14, 1975
Current Filing Basis	1A
Original Filing Basis	1A
Registration Number	1032295
Registration Date	February 3, 1976
Owner	(REGISTRANT) EARL G. GRAVES PUBLISHING CO., INC. CORPORATION NEW YORK 130 FIFTH AVENUE NEW YORK NEW YORK 10011
Assignment Recorded	ASSIGNMENT RECORDED
Attorney of Record	Elizabeth A. Corradino, Esq.
Type of Mark	TRADEMARK
Register	PRINCIPAL
Affidavit Text	SECT 15. SECT 8 (6-YR). SECTION 8(10-YR) 20060303.
Renewal	2ND RENEWAL 20060303
Live/Dead Indicator	LIVE

Registered trademark of *Black Enterprise* magazine. (U.S. Patent and Trademark Office)

electronic climate where inventors can thrive and think independently, productively, and creatively. Mainstream minority journals such as *Black Enterprise* and other similar business magazines are vehicles that bring to the black community and others subjects of general interest to help foster ingenuity, entrepreneurship, innovation, and excellence. Their clarion call helps forward economic empowerment.

Given established and well-proven business advantages, franchising opportunities are lures for minorities who are well suited to handle the ticklish responsibilities of operations and management. For those who desire to exploit this field of endeavor by building on sound reasoning, it is highly worthy of the effort as industries and new types of businesses emerge.

I desire that this work on the entrepreneurial spirit of inventive African Americans will encourage supporters; silence doubters; put new inspiration into politicians, professionals, ministers, scientists, teachers, lawyers, businesspersons, technologists, and the average citizen; and fill every youth studying in the classrooms of our great nation with *hope.* Opportunities abound. Whatever anyone can invent can be improved upon by another.

Appendix

ROSTER OF AFRICAN AMERICAN PATENTEES

Utility and Design Grants from 1821

The listed African American inventors have solely owned patent grants and/or grants that are jointly owned. A number of the inventors cited have numerous U.S. patents, and foreign grants as well, which are not presented herein. Patent numbers beginning with "Re." refer to those patents that have been reissued under a special ruling. The patents identified "Des" before the number are design patent grants. The document number preceding "SIR" refers to an invention issued under a special U.S. Statutory Invention Registration procedure. Patent numbers followed by an "X" designate those patents granted before the year 1836.

Name	Invention	Number	Issue Date
Abbott, Liston	Cancelling Cross Modulation in Two Color TV Signals	4,264,919	1981 Apr 28
Abbott, Liston	TV Privacy System Using Gray Sync	4,454,544	1984 Jun 12
Abbott, Liston, et al.	System for Transmitting Two Color TV Signals	4,179,703	1979 Dec 18
Abbott, Liston, et al.	Reducing Video Crosstalk in a Data Carrier	5,909,253	1999 Jun 1
Abbott, Liston, et al.	Recovering Data from a Vestigial Sideband	6,046,775	2000 Apr 4
Abbott, Liston, et al.	System for Passing Two Color TV Signals	4,120,001	1978 Oct 10
Ables, Charles A.	Electric Bow for the Electric Bass Guitar	4,526,082	1985 Jul 2
Abraham, Kwesi E., et al.	Uniform Media Tensioning of Print Media During Transport in Laser Printer	5,417,413	1995 May 23
Abraham, Kwesi E., et al.	Apparatus and Method to Handle Power Supply Failures for a Peripheral Device	6,996,746	2006 Feb 7
Abraham, Kwesi E., et al.	Internet Print Device Font Distribution Method and Web Site	6,889,202	2005 May 3
Abraham, Kwesi E., et al.	Creating Operating System Fonts from Printer Font Metrics	7,075,665	2006 Jul 11
Abrams, William B.	Hame Attachment	450,550	1891 Apr 14
Adae-Amoakoh, Sylvia, et al.	Photographic Developing Composition and Use Thereof in the Processing of Photographic Elements	5,503,966	1996 Apr 2
Adae-Amoakoh, Sylvia, et al.	Photographic Developing Composition and Use Thereof in the Processing of Photographic Elements	5,792,598	1998 Aug 11
Adae-Amoakoh, Sylvia, et al.	Capacitor Laminate for Use in Printed Circuit Board as an Interconnector	6,370,012	2002 Apr 2
Adae-Amoakoh, Sylvia, et al.	Method of Making a Parallel Capacitor Laminate	6,524,352	2003 Feb 25

Name	Title	Number	Date
Adae-Amoakoh, Sylvia, et al.	Economical High Density Chip Carrier	6,753,612	2004 Jun 22
Adae-Amoakoh, Sylvia, et al.	Economical High Density Chip Carrier	6,998,290	2006 Feb 14
Adams, Christopher P.	Method for Performing Amplification of Nucleic Acid with Two Primers Bound to a Single Solid Support	5,641,658	1997 Jun 24
Adams, James Sloan	Propelling Means for Aeroplanes	1,356,329	1920 Oct 19
Aire,Christopher	Watch	Des508,420	2005 Aug 16
Albert, Albert P.	Cotton Picking Apparatus	851,475	1907 Apr 23
Albert, Albert P.	Cotton Picking Apparatus	1,031,902	1912 Jul 9
Alcorn, George Edward, et al.	Method for Forming Dense Dry Etched Metallurgy	4,172,004	1979 Oct 23
Alcorn, George Edward, et al	Hardened Photoresist Master Image Mask	4,201,800	1980 May 6
Alcorn, George Edward, et al	Dense Dry Etched Multi-level Metallurgy	4,289,834	1981 Sep 15
Alcorn, George Edward, et al.	Cold Drink Vending Machine with Window Front Panel	5,392,953	1995 Feb 28
Alcorn, George Edward, et al.	Imaging X-ray Spectrometer	4,472,728	1984 Sep 18
Alcorn, George Edward, et al.	GaAs Schottky Barrier Photo-Responsive Device	4,543,442	1985 Sep 24
Alcorn, George Edward, et al.	Method of Fabricating an Imaging X-ray Spectrometer	4,618,380	1986 Oct 21
Alexander, Benjamin H., et al.	Process for Preparation of D-Glucosaccharic Acid	2,472,168	1949 Jun 7
Alexander, Benjamin H., et al.	6-Bromopiperonyl and 6-Chloropiperonyl Esters	2,886,485	1959 May 12
Alexander, Benjamin H., et al.	Process for Preparing Mixed Piperonyl Acetals of Acetaldehyde	3,070,607	1962 Dec 25
Alexander, Eugene D.	Geographic Cultural and Economic Board Game	5,292,133	1994 Mar 8
Alexander, Nathaniel	Folding Chair	997,108	1911 Jul 4
Alexander, Ralph W.	Corn Planter Check Rower	256,610	1882 Apr 18

(Continued)

Name	Invention	Number	Issue Date
Alexander, Winser Edward	System for Enhancing Fine Detail in Thermal Photographs	3,541,333	1970 Nov 17
Alfonso, Pedro Marcos, et al.	Front Panel of Computer	Des370,475	1996 Jun 4
Alfonso, Pedro Marcos, et al.	Printer Operator Panel	Des537,479	2007 Feb 27
Alfonso, Pedro Marcos, et al.	Printer Housing	Des558,822	2008 Jan 1
Allain, Joseph L. Jr.	Portable Life Monitor, Medical Instrument	4,350,164	1982 Sep 21
Allen, Charles William	Self-Leveling Table	613,436	1898 Nov 1
Allen, Floyd	Telemeter for Battery	3,919,642	1975 Nov 11
Allen, Harrison Jr, et al,	Apparatus for Igniting Solid Propellants	3,173,251	1965 Mar 16
Allen, James B.	Clothes Line Support	551,105	1895 Dec 10
Allen, James Matthew	Remote Control Apparatus	2,085,624	1937 Jun 29
Allen, John H.	Computer Generated Image Simulator	4,303,394	1981 Dec 1
Allen, John H.	High Speed Digital to Analog Converter Circuit	4,342,984	1982 Aug 3
Allen, John S.	Package Tie	1,093,096	1914 Apr 14
Allen, Johnny G. Sr.	Mobile Garbage Can Holder	Des246,848	1978 Jan 3
Allen, Johnny G. Sr,	Pedestal Type Garbage Can Holder	Des248,364	1978 Jul 4
Allen, Johnny G. Sr.	Pedestal Type Garbage Can Holder	Des252,441	1979 Jul 24
Allen, Johnny G. Sr.	Retention Ring	4,948,075	1990 Aug 14
Allen, Johnny G. Sr.	Ring Assemblies for Supporting Refuse Bags	5,033,703	1991 Jul 23
Allen, Johnny G. Sr.	Garbage Can Rack	Des320,104	1991 Sep 17
Allen, Tanya R.	Undergarment with Pocket	5,325,543	1994 Jul 5
Alleyne, Ernest P.	Obstetrical Instrument	2,323,183	1943 Jun 29

Author	Title	Number	Date
Ambrose, Ronald R., et al.	Thermosetting High Solids Solvent-Based Polyester Polyol Coating	4,535,132	1985 Aug 13
Ambrose, Ronald R., et al.	Thermosetting High Solids Solvent-Based Polyester-Urethane	4,540,766	1985 Sep 10
Ambrose, Ronald R., et al.	High Solids Polyester Polyols and Resinous Polyols	4,540,771	1985 Sep 10
Ambrose, Ronald R., et al.	High Solids Polyurethane Polyols and Coating	4,543,405	1985 Sep 24
Ambrose, Ronald R., et al.	Color Plus Clear Application of High Solids Thermosetting Coating Composition Containing Epoxy-Functional Polyurethanes	4,699,814	1987 Oct 13
Ambrose, Ronald R., et al.	Color Plus Clear Application of Thermosetting High Solids Coating Composition of Hydroxy-Functional Epoxies & Anhydrides	4,732,790	1988 Mar 22
Ambrose, Ronald R., et al.	Epoxy-Functional Polyurethanes and High Solids Thermosetting Coating	4,749,743	1988 Jun 7
Ammons, Virgie M.	Fireplace Damper Actuating Tool	3,908,633	1975 Sep 30
Amoah, John P.	Shoe	Des351,714	1994 Oct 25
Amos, Carl Raymond	Method and Apparatus for Manipulating Phenomenon	5,369,511	1994 Nov 29
Amos, Carl Raymond	Automatic Instant Money Transfer Machine	6,554,184	2003 Apr 29
Anderson, Alan, et al.	Zodiac Designer Jeans	4,513,454	1985 Apr 30
Anderson, Vance J.	Safety Streetcar Fender	1,102,563	1914 Jul 7
Anthony, John A.	System for Conserving Energy and Washing Agents in a Dishwasher	4,357,176	1982 Nov 2
Armstead, Kenneth W., et al.	Pop-up Artificial Christmas Tree	4,847,123	1989 Jul 11

(Continued)

Name	Invention	Number	Issue Date
Artis, Derrick L.	Contact Lens Case with Automatic Counter	5,699,900	1997 Dec 23
Ashe, Ira S.	Mouthpiece for Telephone Transmitter	772,310	1904 Oct 11
Ashbourne, Alexander P.	Improvement in Processes for Preparing Coconut for Domestic Use	163,962	1875 Jun 1
Ashbourne, Alexander P.	Improvement in Processes of Treating Coconut	194,287	1877 Aug 21
Ashbourne, Alexander P.	Biscuit Cutters	170,460	1875 Nov 30
Ashbourne, Alexander P.	Refining Coconut Oil	230,518	1880 Jul 27
Ashley, Chiquita Mickens	Container	Des412,081	1999 Jul 20
Askew, Ben	Cotton Chopper	1,174,538	1916 Mar 7
Asom, Moses T.	Semiconductor Devices Based on Optical Transitions between Quasibound Energy Levels	5,386,126	1995 Jan 31
Auguste, Donna M.	Method and Apparatus for Training a Recognizer	5,680,480	1997 Oct 21
Auguste, Donna M.	Method and Apparatus for Reformatting Paragraphs on a Computer Screen	6,032,163	2000 Feb 29
Austin, Theodore Dunbar	Desensitization of Liquid Explosives	3,116,188	1963 Dec 31
Austin, Theodore Dunbar	Radar Reflecting Electrolytes	4,638,316	1987 Jan 20
Bagley, Joseph C.	Combined Shovel	1,451,195	1923 Apr 10
Bagley, Joseph C.	Wall Tie	2,262,130	1941 Nov 11
Bailey, Byron H.	Preparation of Liquid Liniment	4,582,706	1986 Apr 15
Bailey, Clarence R.	Automatic Switch	982,410	1911 Jan 24
Bailey, Leonard C.	Combined Truss and Bandage	825,545	1883 Sep 25
Bailey, Leonard C.	Folding Bed	629,286	1899 Jul 18

Bailey, Ronald Irwin	Swivel Electrical Receptacle	5,967,836	1999 Oct 19
Bailey, Samuel G.	Talking Marionette with Theatre	4,690,655	1987 Sep 1
Bailiff, Charles Orren	Shampoo Head Rest	612,008	1898 Oct 11
Bailis, William	Ladder Scaffold-Supports	218,154	1879 Aug 5
Baker, Bertram F.	Automatic Cashier	1,582,659	1926 Apr 27
Baker, David	Railway Signal Apparatus	1,054,267	1913 Feb 25
Baker, David	Railway Signal Apparatus	1,620,054	1927 Mar 8
Baker, Franklin Wallace	Antitheft Steering Wheel Resistor	Des350,274	1994 Sep 6
Baker, Hailey L.	Heater Device Control	4,629,114	1986 Dec 16
Baker, Jackson R.	Car Brake	314,417	1885 Mar 24
Ballow, William J.	Combined Hat Rack and Table	601,422	1898 Mar 29
Bankhead, Charles A.	Assembled Composition Printing	3,097,594	1963 Jul 16
Banks, Charles M.	Hydraulic Jack	1,758,640	1930 May 13
Banks, Charles M.	Jack	1,774,693	1930 Sep 2
Banks, Charles M.	Release Valve	1,893,757	1933 Jan 10
Barnes, George A. E.	Sign	Des29,193	1898 Aug 9
Barnes, Ned E.	Sand Band for Wagon	702,109	1905 Jun 13
Barnes, Ned E.	Rail and Tie Brace	815,059	1906 Mar 13
Barnes, Ned E.	Hot Box Cooler and Oiler	899,939	1908 Sept 29
Barnes, Ned E.	Indicator or Bulletin	969,592	1910 Sep 6
Barnes, Ned E.	Tie Plate for Railway	1,180,467	1916 Apr 25

(Continued)

Name	Invention	Number	Issue Date
Barnes, Ned E.	Rail Brace	1,446,957	1923 Feb 27
Barnes, Ned E.	Tie Plate and Joint Brace	1,655,305	1928 Jan 3
Barnes, Ned E.	Pole, Post, and Tree Protector	1,673,729	1928 Jun 12
Barnes, Ned E., et al.	Automatic Film Mover	1,124,879	1915 Jan 12
Barnes, Sharon, J.	Process and Apparatus for Contactless Measurement of Sample Temperature	4,988,211	1991 Jan 29
Barnett, Sharon B.	Shoe Size Scanner System	6,343,276	2002 Jan 29
Barnwell, Irving	Air Valve Guard for Radiators	2,476,578	1949 Jul 19
Baron, Neville A.	Method and Apparatus for Sterilizing and Storing Contact Lenses	4,063,890	1997 Dec 20
Baron, Neville A.	Apparatus and Process for Recurving the Cornea of an Eye	4,461,294	1984 Jul 24
Baron, Neville A.	Process for Recurving the Cornea of an Eye	4,712,543	1987 Dec 15
Baron, Neville A.	Ophthalmic Liquid Sunglasses	4,765,977	1988 Aug 23
Barton, Lyndon O.	Dual Timer Device	4,236,242	1980 Dec 9
Barton, Lyndon O.	Timing Device	4,238,846	1980 Dec 9
Bath, Patricia E.	Apparatus for Ablating and Removing Cataract Lenses	4,744,360	1988 May 17
Bath, Patricia E.	Method and Apparatus, Ablating and Removing Cataract Lenses	5,843,071	1998 Dec 1
Bath, Patricia E.	Laser Apparatus for Surgery for Cataractous Lenses	5,919,186	1999 Jul 6
Bath, Patricia E.	Pulsed Ultrasound Method for Cataractous Lenses	6,083,192	2000 Jul 4
Bath, Patricia E.	Combination Ultrasound and Laser Method and Apparatus for Removing Cataract Lenses	6,544,254	2003 Apr 8

Battle, James	Variable Resistance Resistor Assembly	3,691,503	1972 Sep 12
Bauer, James A.	Coin Changer Mechanism	3,490,571	1970 Jan 20
Bayless, Robert Gordon	Solid Microgobules Containing Dispersed Materials	3,922,373	1975 Nov 25
Bayless, Robert Gordon	Process of Feeding Larval Marine Animals	4,073,946	1978 Feb 14
Bayless, Robert Gordon	Method of Producing Microcapsules and Product	4,107,071	1978 Aug 15
Bayless, Robert Gordon, et al.	Encapsulation Process and Its Product	3,565,818	1971 Feb 23
Bayless, Robert Gordon, et al.	Encapsulation Process and Its Product	3,574,133	1971 Apr 6
Bayless, Robert Gordon, et al.	Pressure-Sensitive Record Sheet and Coating Composition	3,576,660	1971 Apr 27
Bayless, Robert Gordon, et al.	Process of Forming Minute Capsules	3,674,704	1972 Jul 4
Bayless, Robert Gordon, et al.	Capsule Wall Treating Process	3,726,803	1973 Apr 10
Bayless, Robert Gordon, et al.	Capsule Manufacture	3,755,190	1973 Aug 28
Bayless, Robert Gordon, et al.	Continuous Encapsulation and Device	3,816,331	1974 Jun 11
Bayless, Robert Gordon, et al.	Tobacco-Substitute Smoking Material	4,195,645	1980 Apr 1
Bayless, Robert Gordon, et al.	Hydrolyzed Ethylene Vinyl Acetate Encapsulating Coating	4,377,621	1983 Mar 22
Bayless, Robert Gordon	Microencapsulated Particles and Process for Manufacturing Same	6,562,460	2003 May 13
Bayless, Robert Gordon	Microencapsulated Particles and Process for Manufacturing Same	6,833,191	2004 Dec 21
Bayless, Robert Gordon	Moisture Barrier Resins	6,899,958	2005 May 31
Bayless, Robert Gordon	Microencapsulated Particles and Process for Manufacturing Same	7,297,404	2007 Nov 20
Bayless, William E. & Frank B.	Blackboard Eraser	1,214,411	1917 Jan 30

(Continued)

Name	Invention	Number	Issue Date
Baylis, Robert M.	Aerial Toy	2,105,579	1938 Jan 18
Baylor, Sandra Johnson, et al.	Optimum Write-back Strategy for Directory-based Cache Coherence Protocols	5,313,609	1994 May 17
Baylor, Sandra Johnson, et al.	Using Virtual Disks for Disk System Checkpointing	5,634,096	1997 May 27
Baylor, Sandra Johnson, et al.	Parallel Network Communications Protocol Using Token Passing	5,742,812	1998 Apr 21
Baylor, Sandra Johnson, et al.	Invalidation Bus Optimization for Multiprocessors Using Directory-Based Cache Coherence Protocols	5,778,437	1998 Jul 7
Baylor, Sandra Johnson, et al.	Cache Coherence Protocol for Reducing the Effects of False Sharing in Non-bus-based Shared-memory Multiprocessors	5,822,763	1998 Oct 13
Baylor, Sandra Johnson, et al.	Efficient Method for Providing Fault Tolerance Against Double Device Failures in Multiple Device Systems	5,862,158	1999 Jan 19
Baylor, Sandra Johnson, et al.	Home Node Migration for Distributed Shared Memory Systems	5,893,922	1999 Apr 13
Baylor, Sandra Johnson, et al.	Cache Coherence for Lazy Entry Consistency in Lockup-free Caches	6,094,709	2000 Jul 25
Baylor, Sandra Johnson, et al.	Hierarchical Bus Simple COMA Architecture for Shared Memory Multiprocessors Having a Bus Directly Interconnecting	6,148,375	2000 Nov 14
Baylor, Sandra Johnson, et al.	Method for Providing Virtual Atomicity in Multiprocessor Environment Having Access to Multilevel Caches	6,175,899	2001 Jan 16

Name	Title	Number	Date
Baylor, Sandra Johnson	Method and System for Dynamically Changing Page Types in Unified Scalable Shared-memory Architectures	6,360,302	2002 Mar 19
Baylor, Sandra Johnson, et al.	Hardware-assisted Method for Scheduling Threads Using Data Cache Locality	6,938,252	2005 Aug 30
Bean, Lloyd F.	Multiple Layer Migration Imaging System	3,966,465	1976 Jun 29
Bean, Lloyd F.	Multiple Layer Migration Imaging System	3,982,939	1976 Sep 28
Bean, Lloyd F.	Single Component Color Development System	4,057,340	1977 Nov 8
Bean, Lloyd F.	Multi-Reflection Scanner	5,136,415	1992 Aug 4
Bean, Lloyd F.	Single Pass Duplexing Method and Apparatus	6,345,167	2002 Feb 5
Bean, Lloyd F., et al.	Toner Combination for Carrierless Development	4,142,981	1979 Mar 6
Bean, Lloyd F., et al.	Tribo Induction Toner Combination	4,457,996	1984 Jul 4
Beard, Andrew Jackson	Double Plow	240,642	1881 Apr 26
Beard, Andrew Jackson	Plow or Cultivator	347,220	1886 Aug 10
Beard, Andrew Jackson	Rotary Engine	478,271	1892 Jul 5
Beard, Andrew Jackson	Car Coupling	594,059	1897 Nov 23
Becket, George E.	Letter Box	483,525	1892 Oct 4
Beckley, Charles Randolph	Folding Chair	3,856,345	1974 Dec 24
Beckley, Charles Randolph	Folding Seat	4,006,910	1977 Feb 8
Beckley, Charles Randolph	Folding Furniture Piece	4,046,417	1977 Sep 6
Beckley, Charles Randolph	Furniture Structure and Joint	4,079,995	1978 Mar 21
Beckley, Charles Randolph	Knockdown Furniture Structure	4,146,269	1979 Mar 27

(Continued)

Name	Invention	Number	Issue Date
Beckley, John Pelham	Vertical Lifted Portable Electric Furnace and Method	5,539,183	1996 Jul 23
Beckley, John Pelham	Vertical Lifted Portable Electric Furnace and Method	5,585,023	1996 Dec 17
Beckley, John Pelham	Vertical Lifted Portable Electric Furnace and Method	5,783,802	1998 Jul 21
Becoat, Billie J.	Kit for Converting Bicycle to Dual Wheel Driven Cycle	4,895,385	1990 Jan 23
Becoat, Billie J.	Kit for Converting Bicycle to Dual Wheel Driven Cycle	5,004,258	1991 Apr 2
Becoat, Billie J.	Dual Wheel Driven Bicycle	5,116,070	1992 May 26
Belcher, Paul Eugene, et al.	Remote AC Power Control with Control Pulses	4,328,482	1982 May 4
Bell, Landrow	Locomotive Smoke Stack	115,153	1871 May 23
Bell, Landrow	Dough Kneaders	133,823	1872 Dec 10
Benjamin, Alfred	Stainless Steel Scouring Pads	3,039,125	1962 Jun 19
Benjamin, Lyde W.	Broom Moisteners and Bridles	497,747	1893 May 16
Benjamin, Miriam E.	Gong and Signal Chair for Hotels	386,289	1888 Jul 17
Bennett, George	Central Air Uptake Attachment	4,850,266	1989 Jul 25
Bennett, Herbert Glenn	Fire Retardant Coating Composition	4,229,329	1980 Oct 21
Benton, James W.	Lever Derrick	658,939	1900 Oct 2
Berman, Bertha F.	Bed Sheet Construction	2,462,156	1949 Feb 22
Berman, Bertha F.	Fitted Bed Sheet Construction	2,907,055	1959 Oct 6
Berman, Bertha F.	Table Cover	3,557,856	1971 Jan 26
Bernard, Francis S.	Motion Detection Apparatus as for an Interlace	5,027,201	1991 Jun 25
Bernard, Francis S., et al.	Apparatus for Generating Scaled Weighting Coefficients	4,494,214	1985 Jan 15
Bernard, Francis S., et al.	Interstitial Signal Generating System	4,731,648	1988 Mar 15

Author	Title	Number	Date
Best, Lester Jr., et al.	Syringe Holder with Retractable Needle Assembly	5,360,409	1994 Nov 1
Bethea, Clyde George, et al	Modulation-doped Photodetector	4,739,385	1988 Apr 19
Bethea, Clyde George, et al.	Thin Film Liquid Waveguide Converter	3,935,472	1976 Jan 27
Bethea, Clyde George, et al.	Photodetector with Graded Bandgap Region	4,599,632	1986 Jul 8
Bethea, Clyde George, et al.	Infrared-Radiation Detector Device	4,894,526	1990 Jan 16
Bethea, Clyde George, et al.	Device Including a Radiation Sensor	4,942,442	1990 Jul 17
Bethea, Clyde George, et al.	Quantum-Well Radiation-Interactive Device, and Methods	5,023,685	1991 Jun 11
Bethea, Clyde George, et al.	Making a Semiconductor Device Including Infrared Imaging, and Apparatus for Use in Imagir-g	5,396,068	1995 Mar 7
Bethea, Clyde George, et al.	Laser-Transmitter for Reduced SBS	5,991,061	1999 Nov 23
Bethea, Clyde George, et al.	Laser-Transmitter for Reduced Signal Distortion	5,991,323	1999 Nov 23
Bethea, Clyde George, et al.	Sub-carrier Multiplexing in Broadband Optica. Networks	6,081,361	2000 Jun 27
Bethea, Clyde George, et al.	Broadband Tunable Semiconductor Laser Source	6,108,362	2000 Aug 22
Bethea, Clyde George, et al.	WDM System for Reduced SBS	6,166,837	2000 Dec 26
Bethea, Clyde George, et al.	Optical System for Reduced SBS	6,331,908	2001 Dec 18
Bethea, Clyde George, et al.	Method and Apparatus for Suppressing Interference	6,564,038	2003 May 13
Binga, M[oses] William	Street-Sprinkling Apparatus	217,843	1879 Jul 22
Bishop, Alfred A. et al.	Nuclear Reactor with Self-Orificing Radial Blanket	4,077,835	1978 Mar 7
Black, Keith L.	Method for Selective Opening of Abnormal Brain Tissue Capillaries	5,527,778	1996 Jun 18
Black, Keith L., et al.	Enhanced Opening of Abnormal Brain Tissue Capillaries	6,043,223	2000 Mar 28

(Continued)

Name	Invention	Number	Issue Date
Black, Keith L., et al.	Method for Inducing Selective Cell Death of Malignant Cells by Activation of Calcium-Activated Potassium Channels	7,211,561	2007 May 1
Blackburn, Albert B.	Railway Signal	376,362	1888 Jan 10
Blackburn, Albert B.	Spring Seat for Chairs	380,420	1888 Apr 3
Blackburn, Albert B.	Cash Carrier	391,577	1888 Oct 23
Blackburn, Charles M., et al.	Electronic Counting Apparatus	3,618,819	1971 Nov 9
Blair, Connie D.	Enclosure for Curling Iron and Similar Device	5,062,529	1971 Nov 5
Blair, Henry	Seed Planter	8447X	1834 Oct 14
Blair, Henry	Cotton Planter	15	1836 Aug 31
Blair, Joseph N.	Propeller	2,105,963	1938 Jan 18
Blanton, John W.	Hydromechanical Rate-Damped Servo System	3,101,650	1963 Aug 27
Blauntia, Volono Hopi, et al.	Window	2,093,161	1937 Sep 14
Blenman, Orman L.	Variable Pressure Fuel Generator and Method	4,054,423	1977 Oct 18
Blue, Lockrum	Hand Corn Shelling Device	298,937	1884 May 20
Bluford, Guion S. Sr. et al.	Artillery Ammunition Training Round	2,541,025	1951 Feb 13
Bolling, Yvonne	Doorbell Actuated Air Freshener	4,570,824	1986 Feb 18
Bondu, David M.	Golf Tee	3,907,289	1975 Sep 23
Booker, Louis Fred	Rubber Scrap, Knife	Des30,404	1899 Mar 28
Booker, Peachy	Flying Landing Platform	3,003,717	1961 Oct 10
Boone, Sarah	Ironing Board	473,653	1892 Apr 26

Name	Title	Number	Date
Boston, Russell E., et al.	Thermosetting Compositions Comprising Acrylic Polymers	4,864,000	1989 Sep 5
Boston, Russell E., et al.	Coatings for the Protection of Products in Light-transmitting Containers	5,085,903	1992 Feb 4
Boston, Russell E., et al.	Coatings and Method for Coloring Light-transmitting Containers	5,182,148	1993 Jan 26
Bowman, Henry A.	Method of Making Flags	469,395	1892 Feb 23
Boyd, Henry, III, et al.	Syringe Holder with Retractable Needle Assembly	5,360,409	1994 Nov 1
Boyd, Robert N.	Dental Filling Composition of a Coefficient of Thermal Expansion Approximating that of Natural Tooth Enamel	3,503,128	1970 Mar 31
Boykins, Otis F.	Wire Type Precision Resistor	2,891,227	1959 Jun 16
Boykins, Otis F.	Electrical Resistor	2,972,726	1961 Feb 21
Boykins, Otis F.	Electrical Capacitor and Method of Making	3,191,108	1965 Jun 22
Boykins, Otis F.	Electrical Resistance Element and Method of Making	3,271,193	1966 Sep 6
Boykins, Otis F.	Method of Making a Thin Film Capacitor	3,348,971	1967 Oct 24
Boykins, Otis F.	Thin Film Capacitor	3,394,290	1968 Jul 23
Bradberry, Henrietta	Bed Rack	2,320,027	1943 May 25
Bradberry, Henrietta	Torpedo Discharge Means	2,390,688	1945 Dec 11
Bradley, Alex	File	1,709,654	1929 Apr 16
Bradley, John E.	Viscous Blower Drive	4,020,634	1977 May 3
Bradley, John E., et al.	Detection of Catalytic Converter Operability by Light-Off Time Determination	5,419,122	1995 May 30

(Continued)

Name	Invention	Number	Issue Date
Bradley, John E., et al.	Active Adaptive Bias for Closed Loop Air/Fuel Control System	6,604,357	2003 Aug 12
Bragg, Robert M.	Safety Flow Valve	2,834,377	1958 May 13
Braxton, Kenneth Jerome	Security System for Centralized Monitoring and Selective Reporting	4,141,006	1979 Feb 20
Briscoe, James R.	Building Blocks with Sides Converging Upwardly	3,376,682	1968 Apr 9
Brittain, Thomas H.	Level	940,671	1909 Nov 23
Broadnax, Sean H.	Hanging Rack for Beef Jerky	5,996,820	1998 Dec 7
Brooks, Charles B.	Punch	507,672	1893 Oct 31
Brooks, Charles B.	Street Sweeper	556,711	1896 Mar 17
Brooks, Charles B.	Dust Proof Bag for Street Sweepers	560,154	1896 May 12
Brooks, Charles B., et al.	Street Sweepers	558,719	1896 Apr 21
Brooks, Eddie L.	Gear Reduction Multiplier	5,913,938	1999 Jun 22
Brooks, Eddie L.	Gear Ratio Multiplier	6,244,126	2001 Jun 12
Brooks, James M.	Envelope Moistener	1,092,688	1914 Apr 7
Brooks, John S.	Internal Combustion Engine Spark Timing Control Including Peak Combustion Sensor	4,481,925	1984 Nov 13
Brooks, Phil	Disposable Syringe	3,802,434	1974 Apr 9
Brooks, Robert Roosevelt	Line Blanking Apparatus for Bar Generating Equipment	3,334,178	1967 Aug 1
Brooks, Robert Roosevelt	Preset Sensitivity and Amplification Control System	3,518,371	1970 Jun 30
Brooks, Robert Roosevelt	Vertical and Horizontal Aperture Equalization	3,546,372	1970 Dec 8

Brookins, Andrew J.	Train Control Signal	1,486,946	1924 Mar 18
Brookins, Andrew J.	Application Valve for Automatic Train Control Apparatus	1,483,276	1924 Feb 12
Brown, Albert L., et al.	Home Security System	3,482,037	1969 Dec 2
Brown, Charles W., et al.	Water Closets for Railway Cars	147,363	1874 Feb 10
Brown, Firmin Charles	Self-feeding Attachment for Furnaces	1,719,258	1929 Jul 2
Brown, Henry	Receptacle for Storing and Preserving Papers	352,036	1886 Nov 2
Brown, Henry T.	Combined Isomerization and Cracking Process	3,000,995	1961 Sep 19
Brown, Henry T.	Reactivating Hydroforming Catalysts	3,407,135	1968 Oct 22
Brown, Jacob Theodore	Specimen Collection Kit for Mailing	4,949,840	1990 Aug 21
Brown, Lincoln F.	Bridle Bit	484,994	1892 Oct 25
Brown, Marie V. B., et al.	Home Security System	3,482,037	1969 Dec 2
Brown, Oscar E.	Horseshoe	481,271	1892 Aug 23
Brown, Paul L.	Spinnable Stringless Top	3,523,386	1970 Aug 11
Brown, Paul L.	Gyroscopic Top	3,945,146	1976 Mar 23
Brown, Paul L.	Spinnable Object on a Length-Adjustable Tether	4,086,722	1978 May 2
Brown, Paul L., et al.	Gyro Top	Des322,100	1991 Dec 3
Brown, Paul L., et al.	Spinning Musical Toy Top	Des331,082	1992 Nov 17
Brown, Ronald L.	Antenna Orientation Assembly	5,764,194	1998 Jun 9
Brown, William H. Jr., et al.	Air-Sea Rescue Device with Rotation Collar	3,444,569	1969 May 20
Browne, Hugh M.	Sewer or Other Trap	426,429	1890 Apr 29
Browne, Hugh M.	Damper Regulator	886,183	1908 Apr 28

(Continued)

Name	Invention	Number	Issue Date
Bryan, Joseph D.	Scrubbing Brush	1,041,011	1912 Oct 15
Buchanan, Relva C.	Chemical Analysis	3,558,332	1971 Jan 26
Buchanan, Relva C.	Dielectric Glasses	3,928,051	1975 Dec 23
Buchanan, Relva C.	Low Temperature Densifcation of PZT Ceramics	4,283,228	1981 Aug 11
Buchanan, Relva C.	Low Temperature Densification of PZT Ceramics	4,303,447	1981 Dec 1
Buchanan, Relva C., et al.	Temperature Stable Ceramic Dielectric Compositions	H987,SIR	1991 Nov 5
Bundy, Robert F.	Signal Generator	2,922,924	1960 Jan 26
Bundy, William Oliver Jr., et al.	Electrical Switch	2,283,534	1942 May 19
Burgess, Cheryl	Methods of Administering a Material into a Patient for Dermal Enhancement	7,637,900	2009 Dec 29
Burgin, Paul	Head Lamp Rim Remover	1,788,507	1931 Jan 13
Burkins, Eugene	Breech Loading Cannon	649,433	1900 May 15
Burnham, Gerald O.	Direction Coded Digital Stroke Generator	3,938,130	1976 Feb 10
Burr, John Albert	Lawn Mower	624,749	1899 May 9
Burr, William F.	Switching Device for Railways	636,197	1899 Oct 31
Burrell, Dennis	Quarter Wave Gap Coupled Tunable Strip Antenna	5,420,596	1995 May 30
Burton, Andrew F.	Infusion of Liquids into Tissue	4,159,720	1979 Jul 3
Burton, Gus	Emergency Landing Runway	2,315,002	1944 Jun 13
Burton, Gus	Airplane Mail Loading and Unloading Device	2,369,133	1945 Feb 13
Burwell, Wilson	Boot or Shoe	638,043	1899 Nov 28
Butcher, James W. Jr.	Truck Handle Clamp	1,020,961	1912 Mar 26
Butler, Francis Edward	Audible Underwater Signal	2,803,807	1957 Aug 30

Butler, Francis Edward	Drill Mine	2,912,929	1959 Nov 17
Butler, Francis Edward	Watertight Electrical Connector	2,991,441	1961 Jul 4
Butler, Francis Edward	Detachable Practice Mine Selector	3,086,464	1963 Apr 23
Butler, Richard A.	Train Alarm	584,540	1897 Jun 15
Butts, John W.	Luggage Carrier	634,611	1899 Oct 10
Byers, Dannie R.	Manual Dozer	6,219,944	2001 Apr 24
Byrd, Turner Jr.	Improvement for Holders of Reins for Horses	123,328	1872 Feb 6
Byrd, Turner Jr.	Apparatus for Detaching Horses from Carriages	124,790	1872 Mar 19
Byrd, Turner Jr.	Improvement in Neck Yokes for Wagons	126,181	1872 Apr 30
Byrd, Turner Jr.	Improvement in Car Couplings	157,370	1874 Dec 1
Cadet, Gardy	Acoustic Analysis of Gas Mixtures	5,392,635	1995 Feb 28
Cadet, Gardy	Process for the Manufacture of Devices	5,427,659	1995 Jun 27
Cadet, Gardy	Process and Apparatus for Generating Precursor Gases Used in the Manufacture of Semiconductor Devices	5,474,659	1995 Dec 12
Cadet, Gardy	Electrochemical Generation of Silane	5,510,007	1996 Apr 23
Cadet, Gardy	Acoustic Analysis of Gas Mixtures	5,625,140	1997 Apr 29
Cadet, Gardy	Plasma Etch End Point Detection Process	5,877,407	1999 Mar 2
Caliver, Ambrose	Work Cabinet	1,568,498	1926 Jan 5
Cambridge, Alonzo C.	Cigar Maker's Board	704,235	1902 Jul 8
Campbell, Peter R.	Screw Press	213,871	1879 Apr 1
Campbell, Robert Leon	Valve Gear for Steam Engines	728,364	1903 May 19

(Continued)

Name	Invention	Number	Issue Date
Campbell, William S.	Self Setting Animal Trap	246,369	1881 Aug 30
Cannon, Thomas C. Jr.	Remote Controlled Vehicle Systems	3,926,434	1975 Dec 16
Cargill, Benjamin F.	Invalid Cot	629,658	1899 Jul 25
Carrington, Alfred C.	Aerodynamic Device	4,433,819	1984 Feb 28
Carrington, Alfred C.	Aerodynamic Device	5,072,892	1991 Dec 17
Carrington, Thomas A.	Ranges	180,323	1876 Jul 25
Carruthers, George R.	Image Converter for Detecting Electromagnetic Radiation	3,478,216	1969 Nov 11
Carswell, Phillip A.	Secure Cryptographic Logic Arrangement	5,365,591	1994 Nov 15
Carter, Charles H.	Automatic Fish Cleaner	1,394,711	1921 Oct 25
Carter, Iula A.	Nursery Chair	2,923,950	1960 Feb 9
Carter, James M. Jr., et al.	Selective Programming Control System for Tuning and Recording	3,681,541	1972 Aug 1
Carter, John L., et al.	Equivalent High-Power Pulsed Microwave Transmitter	3,078,424	1963 Feb 19
Carter, John L., et al.	Technique for Shaping Crystalline Spheres	3,103,770	1963 Sep 17
Carter, John L., et al.	Electron Discharge Device	3,112,426	1963 Nov 26
Carter, John L., et al.	Ferrite Power Limiter Duplexer	3,183,457	1965 May 11
Carter, John L., et al.	Waveguide Power Limiter	3,629,735	1971 Dec 2
Carter, John L., et al.	Power Dividing and Combining Techniques for Microware Amplifiers	3,928,806	1975 Dec 23
Carter, John L., et al.	Passive Microwave Power Distribution Systems	3,953,853	1976 Apr 27
Carter, John L., et al.	Passive Microwave Power Distribution Systems	3,969,693	1976 Jul 13

Carter, John L., et al.	Power Divider and Power Combiner	3,986,147	1976 Oct 12
Carter, John L., et al.	Power Dividing and Combining Techniques for Microwave Amplifiers	4,028,632	1977 Jun 7
Carter, John L., et al.	Constant Current Charging Circuits for High Energy Modulators	4,090,140	1978 May 16
Carter, John L. et al.	Distributed Pulse Forming Network	4,612,455	1986 Sep 16
Carter, Thomas J.	Apparatus for Water Penetration Testing of Sole Leather	3,028,755	1962 Apr 10
Carter, William C.	Umbrella Stand	323,397	1885 Aug 4
Carver, George Washington	Cosmetic and Process of Producing	1,522,176	1925 Jan 6
Carver, George Washington	Paint and Stain and Process of Producing	1,541,478	1925 Jun 9
Carver, George Washington	Process of Producing Paints and Stains	1,632,365	1927 Jun 14
Cashaw, Allen, et al.	Operating Room Gown and Drape Fabric with Improved Repellent Properties	4,705,712	1987 Nov 10
Cassell, Oscar Robert	Bedstead Extension	990,107	1911 Apr 18
Cassell, Oscar Robert`	Flying Machine	1,024,766	1912 Apr 30
Cassell, Oscar Robert	Angle Indicator	1,038,291	1912 Sep 10
Cassell, Oscar Robert	Bedstead Extension	1,105,487	1914 Jul 28
Cassell, Oscar Robert	Flying Machine	1,406,344	1922 Feb 14
Cato, Elaine	Convertible Brassiere	6,547,636	2003 Apr 15
Cavell, Winston W., et al.	Smoke Tracer Composition	2,823,105	1958 Feb 11
Cavell, Winston W., et al.	Spotter-Tracer Projectile	3,013,495	1961 Dec 19
Cavell, Winston W., et al.	Electrically Initiated Spotter Tracer Bullet	3,101,045	1963 Aug 20

(Continued)

Name	Invention	Number	Issue Date
Certain, Jerry M.	Parcel Carrier for Bicycles	639,708	1899 Dec 26
Chapman, Coit Timothy	Cotton Planter and Fertilizer Distributor	423,311	1890 Mar 11
Chapman, Gilbert B.	Integrated Utility/Camper Shell for a Pick-up Truck	5,421,633	1995 Jun 6
Chappelle, Emmet W.	Light Detection Instrument	3,520,660	1970 Jul 14
Chappelle, Emmet W., et al.	Method of Detecting and Counting Bacteria in Body Fluids	3,745,090	1973 Jul 10
Chappelle, Emmet W., et al.	Method of Detecting and Counting Bacteria	3,971,703	1976 Jul 27
Chappelle, Emmet W.	Rapid, Quantitative Determination of Bacteria	4,385,113	1983 May 24
Cheetham, Margaret	Toy	1,998,270	1935 Apr 16
Cherry, Matthew A.	Velocipede	382,351	1888 May 8
Cherry, Matthew A.	Street Car Fender	532,908	1895 Jan 1
Chriss, Henry T.	Footwear Additive Made from Recycled Materials	5,346,934	1994 Sep 13
Christian, John B.	Ion-Incorporation of Polar Solids as Lubrication Stabilizers	3,201,347	1965 Aug 17
Christian, John B.	Multipurpose Grease Composition	3,314,889	1967 Apr 18
Christian, John B.	Evaporation Loss Determination Apparatus and Method	3,360,985	1968 Jan 2
Christian, John B.	Grease Composition for Use at High Temperature and High Speed Applications	3,518,189	1970 Jun 30
Christian, John B.	Grease Composition	3,525,690	1970 Aug 25
Christian, John B.	Grease Composition for Vacuum and High Temperature Applications	3,536,621	1970 Oct 27
Christian, John B.	Grease Compositions of Fluorocarbon Polyethers Thickened with Polyfluoro-Phenylene Polymers	3,536,624	1970 Oct 27

Christian, John B.	Grease Composition	3,563,894	1971 Feb 16
Christian, John B.	Grease Compositions of Polyol Aliphatic Esters	3,622,512	1971 Nov 23
Christian, John B.	Grease Composition Comprising Polyfluoroalkyl-Polysiloxane	3,642,626	1972 Feb 15
Christian, John B.	Grease Composition of Perfluoroolefin Epoxide Polyethers	3,658,709	1972 Apr 25
Christian, John B.	Grease Composition	3,725,273	1973 Apr 3
Christian, John B.	Polyfluoroalkyl-Dimethyl Poly-siloxane/Polyol Aliphatic Ester Greases	3,814,689	1974 Jun 4
Christian, John B.	Fluorine-containing Benzimidazoles	4,269,348	1981 May 12
Christian, John B.	Polyfluoroalkylether Substituted Phenyl Phosphines	4,454,349	1984 Jun 12
Christmas, Charles T.	Hand Power Attachment for Sewing Machines	226,492	1880 Apr 13
Christmas, Charles T.	Baling Press	228,036	1880 May 25
Christmas, Charles T.	Bale Band Tightener	231,273	1880 Aug 17
Chubb, Lewis W.	Electrolytic Apparatus	1,324,797	1919 Dec 16
Church, Titus S.	Carpet Beating Machine	302,237	1884 Jul 29
Clare, Obadian B.	Trestle	390,753	1888 Oct 9
Clark, Ceffus, Jr.	Trash Container	4,823,979	1989 Apr 25
Clark, Erastus	Nut Lock	308,876	1884 Dec 9
Clark, Joan	Medicine Tray	Des283,249	1986 Apr 1
Clark, Samuel A. Jr.	Protective Metal Cap for Plastic Fuze Radomes	3,780,661	1973 Dec 25
Clark, Samuel A. Jr., et al.	Protective Metal Shield for Plastic Fuze Radomes	3,971,024	1976 Jul 20

(Continued)

123

Name	Invention	Number	Issue Date
Clark, Wardell F.	Cart for Pots, Pans	Des285,852	1986 Sep 23
Clarke, Charles R.	Kwanzaa Unity Tree	Des441,688	2001 May 8
Clarke, Robert E.	Agricultural Implement	726,642	1903 Apr 28
Clay, Boston	Button Making Machine	1,105,757	1914 Aug 4
Clay, Percy	Signal Lantern	1,035,420	1912 Aug 13
Clemens, Tony	Vehicle Running-Gear	1,174,392	1916 Mar 7
Coates, Robert	Overboot for Horses	473,295	1892 Apr 19
Cobb, James W.	Method and System for Attaching a Pocket to a Portion of a Garmet	3,670,675	1972 Jun 20
Cobb, Melvin	Electrical Power Conservation Circuit	4,687,947	1987 Aug 18
Cobbs, William N.	Locomotive Headlight	1,780,865	1930 Nov 4
Colbert, Douglas W.	Pallet Construction	4,145,975	1979 Mar 27
Coles, James J.	Cap and Collar Case	1,577,632	1926 Mar 23
Coles, Leander M.	Mortician's Table	3,799,543	1974 Mar 26
Collic, Edward H. Sr.	Clamp and Hook Arrangement and Attachment	4,261,280	1981 Apr 14
Collins, Cap B.	Portable Electric Light	2,105,719	1938 Jan 18
Collins, Phillip	Bubble Machine	4,775,348	1988 Oct 4
Connor-Ward, Dannette V. et al.	Method for Soybean Transformation	5,416,011	1995 May 16
Connor-Ward, Dannette V. et al.	Method for Soybean Transformation	5,569,834	1996 Oct 29
Connor-Ward, Dannette V. et al.	Method for Soybean Transformation	5,824,877	1998 Oct 20

Connor-Ward, Dannette V. et al.	Efficiency Soybean Transformation Protocol	5,914,451	1999 Jun 22
Connor-Ward, Dannette V. et al.	Method for Transforming Soybeans	5,959,179	1999 Sep 28
Cook, Bertha, et al.	Multicharacter Doll	4,921,459	1990 May 1
Cook, George	Automatic Fishing Device	625,829	1899 May 30
Coolidge, Joseph Sidney	Harness Attachment	392,908	1888 Nov 13
Cooper, Albert R.	Shoemaker's Jack	631,519	1899 Aug 22
Cooper, James	Elevator Safety Device	536,605	1895 Apr 2
Cooper, James	Elevator Safety Device	590,257	1897 Sep 21
Cooper, John Richard	Two-Stage Phosgenation	3,234,253	1966 Feb 8
Cooper, John Richard	Process for Isolating a Fluorene-Containing Polymer	3,536,683	1970 Oct 27
Cooper, John Richard	Separation of Distillable Isocyanates	3,694,323	1972 Sep 26
Cooper, Jonas	Shutter and Fastening	276,563	1883 May 1
Cooper, Walter	Polymerization by Contact with Materials	3,532,680	1970 Oct 6
Cooper, Walter	Polymerizable Composition	3,551,153	1970 Dec 29
Cornwell, Phillip W.	Draft Regulator	390,284	1888 Oct 2
Cornwell, Phillip W.	Draft Regulator	491,082	1893 Feb 7
Cosby, Thomas L.	Rotary Machine	3,456,594	1969 Jul 22
Cosby, Thomas L.	Closed Cycle Energy Conversion System	3,826,092	1974 Jul 30
Cosgrove, William Francis	Automatic Stop Plug for Gas and Oil Pipes	314,993	1885 Mar 17
Cotton, Donald J.	Vertical Liquid Electrode in Electrolytic Cells	4,040,932	1977 Aug 9
Cotton, Donald J.	Capillary Liquid Fuel Nuclear Reactor	4,327,443	1982 Apr 27

(Continued)

Name	Invention	Number	Issue Date
Covington, Joseph C.	Snow Chain	4,265,399	1981 May 5
Cowans, Beatrice L., et al.	Embroidered Fruit Bowl Wall Hanging	4,016,314	1977 Apr 5
Cowings, Patricia S.	Autogenic-Feedback Training Exercise (AFTE) Method and System	5,694,939	1997 Dec 9
Cox, David Wesley Jr.	Manual Tool for Preparing Tube Ends for Jointure	4,899,409	1990 Feb 13
Cox, Elbert L., et al.	Presettable Bistable Circuits	3,334,245	1967 Aug 1
Craig, Arthur U.	Cushion Support for Vehicles	1,258,748	1918 Mar 12
Cralle, Alfred L.	Ice Cream Mold	576,395	1897 Feb 2
Crawford, Dale K.	Remote Controlled Movable Fan	5,256,039	1993 Oct 26
Crawford, Samuel T.	Boat Propeller	929,564	1909 Jul 27
Crawford, Samuel T.	Comb	1,381,804	1921 Jun 14
Creamer, Henry	Steam Feed Water Trap	313,854	1885 Mar 17
Creamer, Henry	Steam Feed Water Trap	358,964	1887 Mar 8
Creamer, Henry	Steam Trap	376,586	1888 Jan 17
Creamer, Henry	Steam Trap and Feeder	394,463	1888 Dec 11
Crenshaw, Benjamin A.	Signaling Device	1,836,705	1931 Dec 15
Chrichlow, Henry B.	Petroleum Extraction from Hydrocarbons Formations	7,621,326	2009 Nov 24
Crichton, Francis D.	Flag Staff	1,855,824	1932 Apr 26
Crichton, Francis D.	Picture Frame	2,354,183	1944 Jul 25
Croslin, Michael E.	Method and Apparatus for Performing Non-Invasive Blood Pressure and Pulse	4,271,844	1981 Jun 9

Name	Title	Number	Date
Croslin, Michael E.	Method and Apparatus for Performing Non-Invasive Blood Pressure and Pulse	4,326,537	1982 Apr 27
Croslin, Michael E.	Method and Apparatus for Performing Non-Invasive Blood Pressure and Pulse	4,338,949	1982 Jul 13
Croslin, Michael E.	Method and Apparatus for Performing Non-Invasive Blood Pressure and Pulse	4,407,297	1983 Oct 4
Crossley, Frank A.	Titanium Base Alloy	2,798,807	1957 Jul 9
Crossley, Frank A.	Grain Refinement of Beryllium with Tungsten Carbide and Titanium Diboride	3,117,001	1964 Jan 9
Crossley, Frank A.	Grain Refinement of Titanium Alloys	4,420,460	1983 Dec 13
Crosthwaite, David N. Jr.	Thermostatic Steam Trap	1,315,596	1919 Sep 9
Crosthwaite, David N. Jr.	Apparatus for Returning Water to Boilers	1,353,457	1920 Sep 21
Crosthwaite, David N. Jr.	Method and Apparatus for Setting Thermostats	1,661,323	1928 Mar 6
Crosthwaite, David N. Jr.	Differential Vacuum Pump	1,755,430	1930 Apr 22
Crosthwaite, David N. Jr.	Steam Trap	1,797,258	1931 Mar 24
Crosthwaite, David N. Jr.	Automatic Discharge Valve	1,871,044	1932 Aug 9
Crosthwaite, David N. Jr.	Freezing Temperature Indicator	1,874,911	1932 Aug 30
Crosthwaite, David N. Jr.	Refrigerating Method and Apparatus	1,874,912	1932 Aug 30
Crosthwaite, David N. Jr.	Exhausting Mechanism	1,893,883	1933 Jan 10
Crosthwaite, David N. Jr.	Bucket Trap	1,930,224	1933 Oct 10
Crosthwaite, David N. Jr.	Vacuum Pump	1,946,524	1934 Feb 13
Crosthwaite, David N. Jr.	Method of Steam Heating from Central Station Mains	1,963,735	1934 Jun 19

(Continued)

Name	Invention	Number	Issue Date
Crosthwaite, David N. Jr.	Refrigeration and Apparatus and Process	1,972,704	1934 Sep 4
Crosthwaite, David N. Jr.	Refrigeration and Apparatus and Process	1,972,705	1934 Sep 4
Crosthwaite, David N. Jr.	Steam Heating System	1,977,303	1934 Oct 16
Crosthwaite, David N. Jr.	Steam Heating Apparatus	1,977,304	1934 Oct 16
Crosthwaite, David N. Jr.	Vacuum Heating System	1,986,391	1935 Jan 1
Crosthwaite, David N. Jr.	Remote Control Proportional Movement Motor	2,007,240	1935 Jul 9
Crosthwaite, David N. Jr., et al.	Heating	2,064,197	1936 Dec 15
Crosthwaite, David N. Jr.	Effective Temperature Thermostat	2,086,258	1937 Jul 6
Crosthwaite, David N. Jr., et al.	Effective Temperature Control Apparatus	2,094,738	1937 Oct 5
Crosthwaite, David N. Jr.	Exhaustive Method and Apparatus	2,096,226	1937 Oct 19
Crosthwaite, David N. Jr.	One Pipe Heating System Regulating Plate	2,102,197	1937 Dec 14
Crosthwaite, David N. Jr.	Regulating Radiator Valve	2,114,139	1938 Apr 12
Crosthwaite, David N. Jr., et al.	Generating Mixed Fluid Heating Medium	2,169,683	1939 Aug 15
Crosthwaite, David N. Jr., et al	Heat Balancer	2,185,500	1940 Jan 2
Crosthwaite, David N. Jr., et al.	Unit Heater and Air Conditioner	2,205,716	1940 Jun 25
Crosthwaite, David N. Jr., et al.	Unit Heater and Air Conditioner	2,263,074	1941 Nov 18
Crosthwaite, David N. Jr., et al.	Resistance Type Temperature Controlling System	2,362,977	1944 Nov 21
Crosthwaite, David N. Jr., et al.	Discharge Valve	2,275,132	1942 Mar 3
Crosthwaite, David N. Jr., et al.	Window Thermostat	2,346,560	1944 Apr 11
Crosthwaite, David N. Jr.	Balanced Resistance Type Temperature Control	2,431,790	1944 Dec 2

Crumble, James H.	Bicycle Driving Mechanism	2,277,391	1942 Mar 24
Crumble, James H.	Vehicle	2,384,728	1945 Sep 11
Crumble, James H.	Float Operated Mechanism	2,384,536	1945 Sep 11
Crumble, James H.	Fluid Power Machine	2,461,037	1949 Feb 8
Crumble, James H.	Manually Energized and Spring Operated Bicycle	2,638,359	1953 May 12
Curtis, William Childs	Airborne Moving-Target Indicator Radar System	4,034,373	1977 Jul 5
Dacons, Joseph Carl	Process for the Manufacture of Nitroform	3,125,606	1964 Mar 17
Dacons, Joseph Carl	Dodecanitroquaterphenyl	3,450,778	1969 Jun 17
Dacons, Joseph Carl	Recrystallization of Hexanitrostilbene	4,260,847	1981 Apr 7
Dale, Josie	Bed Sham with Pockets	Des471,049	2003 Mar 4
Dale, Josie	Bedside Organizer	6,848,132	2005 Feb 1
Dammond, William Hunter	Signalling System	747,949	1903 Dec 29
Dammond, William Hunter	Safety System for Operating Railroads	823,513	1906 Jun 19
Darkins, John Thomas	Ventilator	534,322	1895 Feb 19
Davidson, Shelby J.	Paper Rewind Mechanism for Adding Machines	884,721	1908 Apr 14
Davidson, Sidney N.	Pants Presser	1,088,329	1914 Feb 24
Davidson, Sidney N.	Body Lifter	2,607,103	1952 Aug 19
Davis, Israel D.	Tonic	351,829	1886 Nov 2
Davis, Mack C.	Combined Floor Wiper and Scourer Apparatus	3,484,888	1969 Dec 23
Davis, Stephen H.	Load Weighing and Totaling Device for Cranes, Hoists	2,324,769	1943 Jul 20
Davis, Stephen S.	Flexible Walled Wind Tunnel Nozzel	2,933,922	1960 Apr 26

(Continued)

Name	Invention	Number	Issue Date
Davis, William D.	Riding Saddles	568,939	1896 Oct 6
Davis, William R. Jr.	Library Table	208,378	1878 Sep 24
Davis, William R. Jr.	Game Table	362,611	1887 May 10
Dean, Mark E., et al.	Color Video Display System Having Programmable Border Color	4,437,092	1984 Mar 13
Dean, Mark E., et al.	Composite Video Color Signal Generation from Digital Color Signals	4,442,428	1984 Apr 10
Dean, Mark E., et al.	Microcomputer System with Bus Control Means for Peripheral Processing Devices	4,528,626	1985 Jul 9
Dean, Mark E., et al.	Refresh Generator System for Dynamic Memory	4,575,826	1986 Mar 11
Dean, Mark E., et al.	Data Processing System	4,598,356	1986 Jul 1
Dean, Mark E., et al.	Computer System Including a Page Mode Memory	5,034,917	1991 Jul 23
Dean, Mark E., et al.	Method and Apparatus for Selectively Posting Write Cycles	5,045,998	1991 Sep 3
Dean, Mark E., et al.	Bidirectional Buffer with Latch and Parity Capability	5,107,507	1992 Apr 21
Dean, Mark E., et al.	Control of Pipelined Operation in a Microcomputer System	5,125,084	1992 Jun 23
Dean, Mark E., et al.	System Bus Preempt for 80886 When Running in an 80386/82385 Microcomputer System with Arbitration	5,129,090	1992 Jul 7
Dean, Mark E., et al.	Microprocessor Hold and Lock Circuitry	5,170,481	1992 Dec 8
Dean, Mark E., et al.	Delayed Cache Write Enable Circuit for a Dual Bus Microcomputer System	5,175,826	1992 Dec 29
Dean, Mark E., et al.	Data Processing Apparatus for Selectively Posting Write Cycles	5,327,545	1994 Jul 5

Name	Invention	Patent No.	Date
Dean, Mark E., et al.	Connecting a Short Word Length Non-volatile Memory to a Long Word Length Address Data Multiplexed Bus	5,448,521	1995 Sep 5
Dean, Mark E., et al.	Microcomputer System Employing Address Offset Mechanism	5,450,559	1995 Sep 12
Dean, Mark E.	System and Method for Perfecting Information	5,544,342	1996 Aug 6
Dean, Mark E., et al.	Non-contiguous Mapping of I/O Addresses to Use Page Protection of a Process	5,548,746	1996 Aug 20
Dean, Mark E.	Self-Time Processor with Dynamic Clock Generator	5,553,276	1996 Sep 3
Dean, Mark E., et al.	Method and System for Reading from M-byte Memory	5,603,041	1997 Feb 11
DeCosta, John, et al.	Dynamic Position Locating System	4,340,777	1982 Jul 20
DeCosta, John, et al.	Mounting Arrangement for Position Locating System	4,355,202	1982 Oct 19
Dedmon, Robert	Combined Sleigh and Boat	1,716,230	1929 Jun 4
Deenkley, Kenneth J.	3-D Viewing Glasses	4,810,057	1989 Mar 7
Deitz, William A.	Improvement in Shoes	64,205	1867 Apr 30
DeLeon, Mary Jones	Improvement in Cooking Apparatus	140,253	1873 Jun 24
Delfyett, Peter J. Jr., et al.	Method and Apparatus for Generating Ultrashort Light Pulses	4,972,423	1990 Nov 20
Delfyett, Peter J. Jr., et al.	Optical Pulse-Shaping Device and Method	5,166,818	1992 Nov 24
Delfyett, Peter J. Jr., et al.	Broadband Absorber Having Multiple Quantum Wells	5,265,107	1993 Nov 23
Delfyett, Peter J. Jr.	Self Starting Femtosecond Ti Sapphire Laser with Intracavity	5,434,873	1995 Jul 18

(Continued)

Name	Invention	Number	Issue Date
Delfyett, Peter J. Jr.	Mode Locked Laser Diode in a High Power Solid State Regenerative Amplifier and Mount Mechanism	5,469,454	1995 Nov 21
Delfyett, Peter J. Jr., et al.	High Speed Pulse Slicer/Demultiplexer with Gain for Use in Solid State Regenerative Amplifier System	5,546,415	1996 Aug 13
Delfyett, Peter J. Jr.	Mode Locked Laser Diode in a High Power Solid State Regenerative Amplifier and Mount Mechanism	5,652,753	1997 Jul 29
Delfyett, Peter J. Jr., et al.	Three Dimensional Optional Imaging Colposcopy	5,921,926	1999 Jul 13
Delfyett, Peter J. Jr., et al.	Optical Disk Readout Method Using Optical Coherence Tomography and Spectral Interferometry	6,072,765	2000 Jun 6
Delfyett, Peter J. Jr., et al.	Three Dimensional Optical Imaging Colposcopy	6,141,577	2000 Oct 31
Delfyett, Peter J. Jr., et al.	Multiwavelength Modelocked Semiconductor Diode Laser	6,256,328	2001 Jul 3
Delfyett, Peter J. Jr., et al.	Hybrid WDM-TDM Optical Communication and Data Link	6,314,115	2001 Nov 6
Delfyett, Peter J. Jr., et al.	Hybrid WDM-TDM Optical Communication and Data Link	6,647,031	2003 Nov 11
Deloatch, Essex	Motor Control System for Self-Serving Table	1,466,890	1923 Sep 4
Denson, Costel D.	Particulate Filled Coating Composition of Hydroxyl Polyester Cured with Pyromellitic Acid and Anhydride	3,205,192	1965 Sep 7
Denson, Costel D.	Apparatus for Measuring the Thickness of a Liquid Draining from a Vertically Disposed Surface	3,569,722	1971 Mar 9
Dent, Anthony L., et al.	Rehydrated Silica Gel Dentifrice Abrasive	4,346,071	1982 Aug 24
Dent, Anthony L., et al.	Toothpaste Containing pH-adjusted Zeolite	4,349,533	1982 Sep 14
Dent, Benjamin A.	Procedure Entry for a Data Processor Employing a Stack	3,548,384	1970 Dec 15

Dickenson, Robert C.	Trolley Guard	1,314,130	1919 Aug 26
Dickerson, Leary	Oyster Punching Machine	2,444,635	1948 Jul 6
Dickinson, Joseph Hunter	Reed-Organ	624,192	1899 May 2
Dickinson, Joseph Hunter	Pedal-Housing for Pianos	770,563	1904 Sep 30
Dickinson, Joseph H.	Music Sheetfed Controlling Mechanism	772,225	1904 Oct 11
Dickinson, Joseph H.	Means for Controlling Tension, Musical Players	780,411	1905 Jan 17
Dickinson, Joseph H.	Mechanical Musical Apparatus	819,985	1906 May 8
Dickinson, Joseph H.	Puppet-Valve	886,357	1908 May 5
Dickinson, Joseph H.	Adjustable Tracker for Pneumatic Playing Attachments	915,942	1909 Mar 23
Dickinson, Joseph H.	Player-Piano	1,028,996	1912 Jun 11
Dickinson, Joseph H.	Phonograph and the Like	1,242,155	1917 Oct 9
Dickinson, Joseph H.	Phonograph	1,252,411	1918 Jan 8
Dickinson, Joseph H.	Brake	1,253,475	1918 Jan 15
Dickinson, Joseph H.	Talking-Machine	1,279,522	1918 Sep 24
Dickinson, Joseph H.	Record-Repeating Device for Phonographs	1,300,135	1919 Apr 8
Dickinson, Joseph H.	Combined Talking-Machine and Piano	1,314,578	1919 Sep 2
Dickinson, Joseph H.	Automatic Musical Instrument	1,359,040	1920 Nov 16
Dickinson, Joseph H.	Rewind Device for Phonographs	1,359,802	1921 Nov 1
Dickinson, Joseph H.	Motor Drive for Phonographs	1,405,572	1922 Feb 7
Dickinson, Joseph H.	Automatic Musical Instrument	1,444,832	1923 Feb 13
Dickinson, Joseph H.	Sound Box for Sound Reproducing Machines	1,446,886	1923 Feb 27

(Continued)

Name	Invention	Number	Issue Date
Dickinson, Joseph H.	Multiple Record Magazine Phonograph	1,448,733	1923 Mar 20
Dickinson, Joseph H.	Player Piano and the Like	1,502,618	1924 Jul 22
Dickinson, Joseph H.	Automatic Musical Instrument	1,547,645	1925 Jul 28
Dickinson, Joseph H.	Automatic Piano	1,732,879	1929 Oct 22
Dickinson, Joseph H.	Automatic Piano	1,734,717	1929 Nov 5
Dickinson, Joseph H.	Music Roll Magazine	1,808,808	1931 Jun 9
Dickinson, Samuel L.	Player Piano	1,059,123	1913 Apr 15
Dickinson, Samuel L.	Recording Attachment for Pianos	1,126,724	1915 Feb 2
Dickinson, Samuel L.	Apparatus for Use in Making Music Sheets	1,126,725	1915 Feb 2
Diggs, Thomas M.	Small Portable Universal Spark Plug Cleaner	3,604,156	1971 Sep 14
Diggs, Thomas M.	Centrifugal Clutch	3,656,599	1972 Apr 18
Diggs, Thomas M.	Plural Motor Drive Including a Servo Control System	3,911,336	1975 Oct 7
Diuguid, Lincoln Isaiah	Burning Efficiency Enhancement Method	4,539,015	1985 Sep 3
Dixon, Irma G., et al.	Underarm Perspiration Pad	2,911,647	1959 Nov 10
Dixon, James	Car-Coupling	471,843	1892 Mar 29
Dixon, Samuel Jr.	Gyromagnetic Waveguide Power Limiter	3,131,366	1964 Apr 28
Dixon, Samuel Jr.	Microwave Power Limiter Utilizing a Planar Ferrite Sphere	3,319,191	1967 May 9
Dixon, Samuel Jr.	Microwave Power Limiter Comprising Abutting Semiconductor and Ferrite	3,426,299	1969 Feb 4
Dixon, Samuel Jr.	RF Power Limiter Comprising Irradiated Semiconductor Block	3,465,266	1969 Sep 2

Inventor	Title	Patent Number	Date
Dixon, Samuel Jr.	Ferrite Power Limiter Comprising Synchronously Tuned, Resonant Cavities	3,609,404	1975 Sep 16
Dixon, Samuel Jr.	Low Level Broadband Limiter Having Ferrite Rod Extending through Dielectric Resonators	4,027,256	1977 May 31
Dixon, Samuel Jr.	Electronically Tuned Gunn Oscillator and Mixer	4,342,009	1982 Jul 27
Dixon, Samuel Jr., et al.	Dielectric Waveguide Power Limiter	4,342,010	1982 Jul 27
Dixon, Samuel Jr.	Millimeter- Wave Power Limiter	4,344,047	1982 Aug 10
Dixon, Samuel Jr., et al.	Single Device for Measurement of Infrared or Millimeter Wave Radiation	4,509,009	1985 Apr 9
Dixon, Samuel Jr.	Millimeter Wave Signal Limiter	4,511,865	1985 Aug 16
Dixon, Samuel Jr.	Millimeter Wave Image Guide Band Reject Filter and Mixer Circuit	4,545,073	1985 Oct 1
Dixon, Samuel Jr., et al.	Three Diode Balanced Mixer	4,554,680	1985 Nov 19
Dixon, Samuel Jr., et al.	Monolithic Planar Doped Barrier Subharmonic Mixer	4,563,773	1986 Jan 7
Dixon, Samuel Jr. et al.	Dual Gunn Diode Self-Oscillating Mixer	4,573,213	1986 Feb 25
Dixon, Samuel Jr., et al.	Monolithic Planar Doped Barrier Limiter	4,654,609	1987 Mar 31
Dorcas, Lewis B.	Combination Stove, Wood, Gas, or Coal	868,417	1907 Oct 15
Dorman, Linneaus Cuthbert, et al.	3,5 Dihalo-4-Cyanoalkoxy Phenols	3,468,926	1969 Sep 23
Dorman, Linneaus Cuthbert, et al.	Absorbents for Airborne Formaldehyde	4,517,111	1985 May 14
Dorman, Linneaus Cuthbert, et al.	Composite of Unsintered Calcium Phosphates	4,636,526	1987 Jan 13
Dorman, Linneaus Cuthbert, et al.	Composite of Unsintered Calcium Phosphates	4,698,375	1987 Oct 6
Dorman, Linneaus Cuthbert, et al.	Composite of Unsintered Calcium Phosphates	4,843,604	1989 Jun 27

(Continued)

Name	Invention	Number	Issue Date
Dorsey, Osbourn	Improvement in Door-Holding Device	210,764	1878 Dec 10
Dorticus, Clatonia Joaquin	Device for Applying Coloring Liquids to Sides of Soles or Heels of Shoes	535,820	1895 Mar 19
Dorticus, Clatonia Joaquin	Machine for Embossing Photos	537,442	1895 Apr 16
Dorticus, Clatonia Joaquin	Photographic Print Washer	537,968	1895 Apr 23
Dorticus, Clatonia Joaquin	Hose Leak Stop	629,315	1899 Jul 18
Douglas, Fred J.	Valve Block	1,087,354	1914 Feb 17
Douglas, Herman Sr.	Child's Toilet Training Pants	4,909,804	1990 Mar 20
Douglass, William	Self-Binding Harvester	789,010	1905 May 2
Douglass, William	Band Twister	789,120	1905 May 2
Douglass, William	Carrier Chain	789,122	1905 May 2
Downing, Gertrude E., et al.	Reciprocating Corner and Baseboard Cleaning Auxiliary	3,715,772	1973 Feb 13
Downing, Philip Bell	Street Railway Switch	430,118	1890 Jun 17
Downing, Philip Bell	Street Letter Box	462,092	1891 Oct 27
Downing, Philip Bell	Letter Box	462,093	1891 Oct 27
Downing, Philip Bell	Envelope Moistener	1,243,595	1917 Oct 16
Downing, Philip Bell	Desk Appliance	1,269,584	1918 Jun 18
Downing, Philip Bell	Combined Writing Tablet and Copyholder	1,538,629	1925 May 19
Doyle, James	Serving Apparatus for Dining Rooms	659,057	1900 Oct 2
Doyle, James	Automatic Serving System	1,019,137	1912 Mar 5
Doyle, James	Server for Automatic Serving System	1,098,788	1914 Jun 10

Name	Title	Number	Date
Dozier, Willie L., et al.	Selective Programming Control System for Tuning and Recording	3,681,541	1972 Aug 1
Dugger, Cortland Otis	Method for Growing Oxide Single Crystals	3,595,803	1971 Jul 27
Dugger, Cortland Otis	Solid-State Laser Produced by Chemical Reaction between a Germinate and Oxide Dopant	3,624,547	1971 Nov 30
Dugger, Cortland Otis	Aluminum Nitride Single Crystal Growth from a Molten Mixture with Calcium Nitride	3,933,573	1976 Jan 20
DuLaney, James W., et al.	Electronic Ballast for Discharge Lamps	6,650,067	2003 Nov 18
DuLaney, James W., et al.	Adaptive Index Reference Position Qualification	6,950,270	2005 Sep 27
Duncan, Sharon B. Barnett	Vertical Utensil Holder	6,948,626	2005 Sep 27
Duncan, Sharon B. Barnett	Compact Carrier	7,111,851	2006 Sep 26
Dunkley, Kenneth J.	Three-Dimensional Viewing Glasses	4,810,057	1989 Mar 7
Dunnington, James Henry	Horse Detatcher	578,979	1897 Mar 16
Dyer, Ben Elwood	Ball Bearing Fuel Mixer	1,614,665	1927 Jan 18
Dyer, Henry H.	Pipe, Cigar Holder, and the Like	1,090,036	1914 Mar 10
Eaton, Harold Jr., et al.	Detection System for Monitoring Gaseous Components in Air	3,617,734	1971 Nov 2
Eaton, Harold Jr., et al.	Method of Removing Deposits on Refrigeration System Surfaces	4,124,408	1978 Nov 7
Edelin, Benedict F.	Pneumatic Toy Pistol	1,441,975	1923 Jan 9
Edmonds, Joseph	Utility Carrier	4,790,559	1988 Dec 13
Edmonds, Thomas Henry	Separating Screens	586,724	1897 Jul 20
Edmonds, Willie L.	Collapsible Fishing Gear and Load Bearing Carriage	4,749,209	1988 Jun 7

(Continued)

Name	Invention	Number	Issue Date
Elcock, John	Brick Kiln	767,637	1904 Aug 16
Elcock, John	Kiln	1,329,830	1920 Feb 3
Elder, Clarence L.	Timing Device	3,165,188	1965 Jan 12
Elder, Clarence L.	Non-Capsizeable Container	3,367,525	1968 Feb 6
Elder, Clarence L.	Sweepstake Programmer	3,556,531	1971 Jan 19
Elder, Clarence L.	Bidirectional Monitoring and Control System	4,000,400	1976 Dec 28
Elkins, Thomas	Dining, Ironing Table and Quilting Frame Combined	100,020	1870 Feb 22
Elkins, Thomas	Chamber Commode	122,518	1872 Jan 9
Elkins, Thomas	Refrigerating Apparatus	221,222	1879 Nov 4
Ellis, Michael G.	Vehicle Headlight	Des550,382	2007 Sep 4
Ellis, Michael G.	Vehicle Grille	Des561,655	2008 Feb 12
Ellis, Michael G.	Vehicle Bumper	Des561,662	2008 Feb 12
Ellis, Michael G.	Vehicle Hood	Des562,199	2008 Feb 19
Ellis, Michael G.	Vehicle Headlamp	Des569,017	2008 May 13
Ellis, Michael G.	Vehicle Fender	Des601,934	2009 Oct 13
Emile, Philip E.	Transistorized Gating Circuit	2,982,868	1961 May 2
Emile, Philip E.	Transistorized Multivibrator Circuit	3,005,963	1961 Nov 24
Engram, Robert L.	Shock Falsing Inhibitor Circuit for a Plural Tone Receiver	3,806,938	1974 Apr 23
Evans, James C., et al	Airplane Appliance	1,749,858	1930 Mar 11
Evans, Monica	Notebook Construction	5,213,369	1993 May 25

Ezekwe, Michael O.	Feed Compositions Comprising Purslane Leaves and Methods of Using Thereof	5,688,508	1997 Nov 18
Evans, John H.	Convertible Settee and Bed	591,095	1897 Oct 5
Faison, Charles Rudolph	Perspiration Absorbent Arm Band	6,243,867	2001 Jun 12
Falkner, Henry	Ventilated Shoe	426,495	1890 Apr 29
Farmer, Gilbert, et al.	Preferential Multihole Combustor Liner	6,513,331	2003 Feb 4
Farmer, Gilbert, et al.	Combustor Liner and Method for Making Thereof	6,651,437	2003 Nov 25
Ferrell, Frank J.	Steam Trap	420,993	1890 Feb 11
Ferrell, Frank J.	Apparatus for Melting Snow	428,670	1890 May 27
Ferrell, Frank J.	Valve	428,671	1890 May 27
Ferrell, Frank J.	Valve	450,451	1891 Apr 14
Ferrell, Frank J.	Valve	462,762	1891 Nov 10
Ferrell, Frank J.	Valve	467,796	1892 Jan 26
Ferrell, Frank J.	Valve	468,242	1892 Feb 2
Ferrell, Frank J.	Valve, Gate, or Similar Device	468,334	1892 Feb 9
Ferrell, Frank J.	Valve	490,227	1893 Jan 17
Ferrell, Frank J.	Valve	501,497	1893 Jul 18
Figgures, Abraham F.	Trench Diggs	1,366,253	1921 Jan 18
Fisher, David A. Jr.	Improvement in Joiner's Clamp	162,281	1875 Apr 20
Fisher, David A. Jr.	Improvement in Furniture Caster	174,794	1876 Mar 14
Fitzgibbon, Chester Manfield	Method and Machine for Making Bamboo Veneer and Products Thereof	3,643,710	1972 Feb 22

(Continued)

Name	Invention	Number	Issue Date
Fitzgibbon, Chester Manfield	Component Type Building Construction System	4,165,591	1979 Aug 28
Flemmings, Robert F. Jr.	Guitar	338,727	1886 Mar 30
Fletcher, Sylvester J.	Refuse Container	Des310,744	1886 Mar 30
Flipper, Henry Ossian	Tent	615,544	1898 Dec 6
Florence, Saulia O.	Mail Box	2,164,855	1939 Jul 4
Flowers, Calvin	Telephone Jack Security Device	5,774,543	1998 Jun 30
Flowers, Danny J.	Body Mountable Carrier	5,433,359	1995 Jul 18
Flowers, Thomas	Boring Tool	4,419,032	1983 Dec 6
Flowers, Thomas	Apparatus for Installing Conduit	4,527,775	1985 Jul 9
Ford, Curtis A.	Method of and Apparatus for Testing Internal Combustion Engines	4,702,620	1987 Oct 27
Ford, Curtis A.	Method and Apparatus for Identifying Faults in Internal Combustion Systems	6,389,889	2002 May 21
Ford, David E., et al.	Control Circuit	3,081,427	1963 Mar 12
Ford, David E., et al.	IR Compensation for Direct Current Motor Control	3,320,507	1967 May 16
Ford, David E., et al.	Three Terminal Solid State Pilot Light	4,464,605	1984 Aug 7
Forbes, Dennis A.	Card Game	Des91,996	1934 Apr 17
Foy, Frank E.	Wheel of Black History Game	5,100,140	1992 Mar 31
Frame, George L., et al.	Genealogy Apparatus	4,201,386	1980 May 6
Francis, Dawn E.	Organic Fertilizer and Production Thereof	4,957,543	1990 Sep 18
Frazier, Orville Z.	Humidifier for Internal Combustion Engines	1,542,999	1925 Jun 23

Freelain, Kenneth W.	Water Pipe	4,268,610	1987 Jul 28
Freeman, Louis W.	Cuff of Trousers	1,805,577	1931 May 19
Frye, Clara C.	Surgical Appliance	847,758	1907 Mar 19
Frye, Irvin S.	Adjustable Shackle	3,468,123	1969 Sep 23
Gamell, Joseph A.	Power Generating System	3,800,528	1974 Apr 2
Gamell, Joseph A.	Ignition System for Engine	3,861,371	1975 Jan 21
Gamell, Joseph A.	Internal Combustion Engine Having Coaxially Mounted Compression Combustion Chamber, and Turbine	3,886,732	1975 Jun 3
Gamell, Joseph A.	Radiant Heat Boiler	3,906,188	1975 Sep 16
Gamell, Joseph A.	Combined Supercharger and Carburetion System	3,935,847	1976 Feb 3
Gamell, Joseph A.	Supercharger System for Internal Combustion Engine	3,935,848	1976 Feb 3
Gamell, Joseph A.	System for Utilizing Waste Heat of an Internal Combustion Engine	3,948,053	1976 Apr 6
Gamell, Joseph A.	System for Utilizing Waste Heat of an Internal Combustion Engine	3,948,235	1976 Apr 6
Gamell, Joseph A.	Power Generating System	3,967,914	1976 Jul 6
Gamell, Joseph A.	Internal Combustion System	4,003,672	1977 Jan 18
Gamell, Joseph A.	Rotary Motor	4,232,991	1980 Nov 11
Gamell, Joseph A.	Turbo-electric Power Plant and Process	4,293,777	1981 Oct 6
Gamell, Joseph A.	Air Compressing System and Process	4,307,574	1981 Dec 29
Gamell, Joseph A.	Turbo-Flywheel-Powered Vehicle	4,336,856	1982 Jul 29
Gamell, Joseph A.	Pressure Fluid Motor	4,378,195	1983 Mar 29

(Continued)

Name	Invention	Number	Issue Date
Gamell, Joseph A.	Turbine Generator	5,118,961	1992 Jun 6
Gant, Virgil A.	Method for Treating Hair	2,643,375	1953 Jun 23
Gant, Virgil A.	Hair Treating Composition and Method of Use	2,750,947	1956 Jun 19
Gant, Virgil A.	Ammonium Polysiloxanolate Hair Treating Composition	2,787,274	1957 Apr 2
Garner, Albert Y.	Novel Phosphonyl Polymers	3,127,357	1964 Mar 30
Garner, Albert Y.	Process for Making Flame Retardant Material	3,955,029	1976 May 4
Garner, Albert Y.	Flame Retardant	3,989,702	1976 Nov 2
Garrett, Gloster J., et al.	Vehicle Wheel	1,055,029	1913 Mar 4
Garrett, Herbert C., et al.	Vehicle Wheel	1,055,029	1913 Mar 4
Garrett, Robert Wesley	Taxicab Cruising Lamp	Des153,871	1948 May 24
Gary, Alvin C.	Parking Mirrors for Automobiles	2,264,690	1941 Dec 2
Gary, Alvin C,	Pliers	2,268,282	1941 Dec 30
Gary, James A. Sr., et al.	Autopsy Apparatus	5,160,340	1992 Nov 3
Gaskin, Frances Christian	Sun Protectant Composition and Method	4,806,344	1989 Feb 21
Gaskin, Frances Christian	Compositions and Method of Strengthening Hair	5,006,331	1991 Apr 9
Gaskin, Frances Christian	Compositions and Method for Protecting the Skin from UV-Rays	5,256,403	1993 Oct 26
Gaskin, Frances Christian	Methods and Composition for Reducing Pyrimidine Photo-products	5,629,314	1997 May 13
Gatling, Jean M.	Adjustable Garment Hanger	4,905,877	1990 Mar 6
Gay, Eddie C.	Cathode for a Secondary Electrochemical Cell	3,907,589	1975 Sep 23

142

Name	Title	Number	Date
Gay, Eddie C.	Method of Preparing Electrodes	3,933,520	1976 Jan 20
Gay, Eddie C.	Compartmented Electrode Structure	4,029,860	1977 Jun 14
Gibson, John	Locomotive Body	Des118,370	1940 Jan 2
Gier, Joseph T., et al.	Thermoelectric Heat Flow	2,493,651	1950 Jan 3
Gier, Joseph T., et al.	Black Body Reflectometer	3,216,310	1965 Nov 9
Gill, Vincent A.	Quick Disconnect Valve Coupling	2,948,553	1960 Aug 9
Gilliard, Joseph	Car Park	2,771,200	1956 Nov 20
Gilmore, John T. Jr.	Method of Displaying Descriptive Data Representing a Candidate as a Plurality of Lines on an Output Device	5,606,653	1997 Feb 25
Gizaw, Daniel	Permanent Magnet Brushless DC Motor Having Reduced Cogging	5,250,867	1993 Oct 5
Gloster, Clay S.	Method and Apparatus for High Precision Weighted Random Pattern Generation	5,043,988	1991 Aug 27
Goffney, Janice F., et al.	Racquet with Reinforced Throat	4,906,002	1990 Mar 6
Goffney, Lawrence J. Jr., et al.	Scalp Massaging Implement	4,308,860	1982 Jan 5
Goffney, Lawrence J. Jr., et al.	Self-Generated Lighted Hubcap	4,893,877	1990 Jan 16
Golding, Russell J. Sr.	Motor Vehicle Camper	4,279,440	1981 Jul 21
Goldsberry, Ronald E.	Ultraviolet and Thermally Stable Polymer Compositions	3,965,096	1976 Jun 22
Goldson, Alfred L. and Amy R.	Parent-Child Bonding Bib	4,776,546	1988 Oct 11
Goode, Sarah E.	Cabinet Bed	322,177	1885 Jul 14
Gordon, William S.	Berth Ladder for Sleeping Cars	1,887,301	1932 Nov 8

(Continued)

Name	Invention	Number	Issue Date
Gourdine, Meredith C.	Electrogasdynamic Method and Apparatus for Detecting Properties of Particulate Matter	3,449,667	1969 Jun 10
Gourdine, Meredith C.	Electrogasdynamic Systems	3,452,225	1969 Jun 24
Gourdine, Meredith C.	Electrogasdynamic Systems	3,519,855	1970 Jul 7
Gourdine, Meredith C.	Electrogasdynamic Generating Systems	3,551,710	1970 Dec 29
Gourdine, Meredith C.	Electrogasdynamic Precipitator	3,558,286	1971 Jan 26
Gourdine, Meredith C.	Electrogasdynamic Systems Adapted for Circuit Breaking	3,562,585	1971 Feb 9
Gourdine, Meredith C.	Improved Acoustic Image Reproduction System	3,573,845	1971 Apr 6
Gourdine, Meredith C., et al.	Turbulence Inducing Electrogasdynamic Precipitator	3,581,468	1971 Jun 1
Gourdine, Meredith C.	Electrogasdynamic Systems and Methods	3,582,694	1971 Jun 1
Gourdine, Meredith C., et al.	Electrogasdynamic Particle Disposition System	3,585,060	1971 Jun 15
Gourdine, Meredith C.	Alternating Current Systems	3,585,420	1971 Jun 15
Gourdine, Meredith C.	Copying System Using Electrogasdynamics	3,592,541	1971 Jul 13
Gourdine, Meredith C.	Image Reproduction Using Electrogasdynamics	3,606,531	1971 Sep 20
Gourdine, Meredith C.	Electrogasdynamic Converter with Resisting Channel	3,612,923	1971 Oct 12
Gourdine, Meredith C., et al.	Electrostatic Painting Method and Apparatus	3,613,993	1971 Oct 19
Gourdine, Meredith C., et al	Electrogasdynamics Precipitator Utilizing Retarding Fields	3,650,092	1972 Mar 21
Gourdine, Meredith C.	Method and Apparatus for Electrogasdynamic Coating	3,673,463	1972 Jun 27
Gourdine, Meredith C., et al.	Electrostatic Precipitator System	3,704,572	1972 Dec 5
Gourdine, Meredith C., et al.	Electrostatic Mass Per Unit Volume Dust Monitor	3,718,029	1973 Feb 27
Gourdine, Meredith C.	Apparatus for Suppressing Airborne Particles	3,757,491	1973 Sep 11

Name	Title	Number	Date
Gourdine, Meredith C.	Methods for Electrogasdynamic Coating	3,853,580	1974 Dec 19
Gourdine, Meredith C.	Electrogasdynamic Production Line Coating System	3,991,710	1976 Nov 16
Gourdine, Meredith C.	Electrogasdynamic Coating System	4,433,033	1984 Feb 21
Gourdine, Meredith C.	Electrogasdynamic Coating System	4,498,631	1985 Feb 12
Gourdine, Meredith C.	Method and Apparatus for Improved Cooling of Hot Materials	4,555,909	1985 Dec 3
Gourdine, Meredith C.	Electrogasdynamic Coating System	4,574,092	1986 Mar 4
Gourdine, Meredith C.	Method for Airport Fog Precipitation	4,671,805	1987 Jun 9
Gourdine, Meredith C.	Apparatus and Method for Cooling Heat Generating Electronic Compounds in a Cabinet	5,297,005	1994 Mar 22
Gourdine, Meredith C.	Apparatus and Method for Cooling Heat Generating Electronic Compounds in a Cabinet	5,422,787	1995 Jun 6
Gousouland, Henry P.	Water Heating Apparatus	1,178,445	1916 Apr 4
Gousouland, Henry P.	Water Heating Apparatus	1,198,344	1916 Sep 12
Graham, Lonzell	Liquid Laundering Detergent and Softener	3,984,356	1976 Oct 5
Graham, Lonzell, et al.	Moisturizing Body Soap and Shampoo	5,658,868	1997 Aug 19
Graham, Lonzell	Settled Solids Process of Preparing Polyester Copolymer Resin	5,789,479	1998 Aug 4
Graham, Lonzell	Continuous Process of Preparing Polyester Copolymer Resin	5,891,982	1999 Apr 6
Grant, George F.	Golf Tee	638,920	1899 Dec 12
Grant, William S.	Curtain Support	565,075	1896 Aug 4
Graves, Kurt M.	Infant Walker	4,773,639	1988 Sep 27

(Continued)

Name	Invention	Number	Issue Date
Gray, Maurice T.	Racquet with Reinforced Throat	4,906,002	1990 Mar 6
Gray, Robert H.	Bailing Press	525,203	1894 Aug 28
Gray, Robert H.	Cistern Cleaner	537,151	1895 Apr 9
Green, Harry James Jr.	Method of Making a Striated Support for Filaments	3,548,045	1970 Dec 15
Green, Harry James Jr.	Substrate for Mounting Filaments	3,584,130	1971 Jun 8
Green, Harry James Jr.	Method for Sealing Microelectronic Device Packages	3,648,357	1972 Mar 14
Green, James P.	Health Food Composition	4,806,354	1989 Feb 21
Greene, Bettye W., et al.	Stable Latexes Containing Phosphorus Surface Groups	4,506,057	1985 Mar 19
Greene, Bettye W., et al.	Composite Sheet Prepared with Stable Latexes Containing Phosphorus Surface Groups	4,609,434	1986 Sep 2
Greene, Bettye W., et al.	Latex Based Adhesive Prepared by Emulsion Polymerization	4,968,740	1990 Nov 6
Greene, Ervin G.	Guard for Downspouts	1,930,354	1933 Oct 10
Greene, Frank S. Jr.	Use of Faulty Storage Circuits by Position Coding	3,654,610	1972 Apr 4
Gregg, Clarence	Machine Gun	1,277,307	1918 Aug 27
Gregory, James	Motor	361,937	1887 Apr 26
Grenon, Henry	Razor Stropping Device	554,867	1896 Feb 18
Griffin, Bessie V.	Portable Receptacle Support	2,550,554	1951 Apr 24
Griffin, Michael D.	Progressive Throttle Positioning System	4,476,068	1984 Oct 9
Griffin, Michael D.	Throttle Return Spring Assembly	4,576,068	1984 Oct 9
Griffin, Thomas Walker	Pool Table Attachment	626,902	1899 Jun 13
Grimes, Herman L.	Airplane	2,137,486	1938 Nov 22

Name	Title	Patent No.	Date
Groves, Thomas Conrad	Hydraulic Timing Device	3,822,544	1974 Jul 9
Gulley, Harold J.	Coolant Additive with Corrosion Inhibitive and Scale Preventive Properties	4,711,735	1987 Dec 8
Gulley, Harold J.	Organic-Aqueous Composition and Process Forming Corrosion-Resistant Coatings on Metal Surfaces	5,330,588	1994 Jul 19
Gunn, Selim W.	Shoe	641,642	1900 Jan 16
Gurley, Clyde Edward, et al.	Automatic Telephone Alarm Apparatus	3,505,476	1970 Apr 7
Gurley, Clyde Edward, et al.	Programmable External Dial Operating Device	3,505,483	1970 Apr 7
Haines, James Henry	Portable Shampooing Basin	590,833	1897 Sep 28
Hale, Ernest E. III	Well Pipe Top Cap	5,184,608	1993 Feb 9
Hale, William	Aeroplane	1,563,278	1925 Nov 24
Hale, William	Motor Vehicle	1,672,212	1928 Jun 5
Haley, Vincent L.	Bottle	Des413,067	1999 Aug 24
Haley, Vincent L., et al.	Workbench	Des394,761	1998 Jun 2
Hall, Andrew	Garment with Indicia	4,991,233	1991 Feb 12
Hall, Lloyd Arthur, et al.	Asphalt Emulsion and Manufacture	1,882,834	1932 Oct 18
Hall, Lloyd Arthur, et al.	Protective Coating	1,914,351	1933 Jun 13
Hall, Lloyd Arthur, et al.	Solid Seasoning Composition Containing Capsicum and Chloride	1,995,119	1935 Mar 19
Hall, Lloyd Arthur, et al.	Nonbleaching Solid Seasoning Composition	1,995,120	1935 Mar 19
Hall, Lloyd Arthur, et al.	Stabilized Solid Seasoning Composition	1,995,121	1935 Mar 19
Hall, Lloyd Arthur	Vitamin Concentrate	2,022,464	1935 Nov 26

(Continued)

Name	Invention	Number	Issue Date
Hall, Lloyd Arthur, et al.	Solid Seasoning Composition Containing Lecithin	2,032,612	1936 Mar 3
Hall, Lloyd Arthur	Manufacture of Bleached Pepper Products	2,097,405	1937 Oct 26
Hall, Lloyd Arthur, et al.	Sterilizing Foodstuffs	2,107,697	1938 Feb 8
Hall, Lloyd Arthur	Curing of Meats and the Like	2,117,478	1938 May 17
Hall, Lloyd Arthur, et al.	Alkaline Detergent Compound	2,142,870	1939 Jan 3
Hall, Lloyd Arthur, et al.	Homogeneous Alkaline Detergents and Producing Same	2,142,871	1939 Jan 3
Hall, Lloyd Arthur, et al.	Edible Dusting Powder	2,144,371	1939 Jan 17
Hall, Lloyd Arthur	Stabilized Nitrite Salt Compound	2,145,417	1939 Jan 31
Hall, Lloyd Arthur, et al.	Inhibited Detergent Composition	2,155,045	1939 Apr 18
Hall, Lloyd Arthur, et al.	Inhibited Detergent Composition	2,155,046	1939 Apr 18
Hall, Lloyd Arthur, et al.	Composition of Matter	2,171,428	1939 Aug 29
Hall, Lloyd Arthur, et al.	Sterilization Process	2,189,947	1940 Feb 13
Hall, Lloyd Arthur, et al.	Sterilization of Pancreatin	2,189,948	1940 Feb 13
Hall, Lloyd Arthur, et al.	Sterilizing Colloid Materials	2,189,949	1940 Feb 13
Hall, Lloyd Arthur	Protein Composition of Matter	2,251,334	1941 Aug 5
Hall, Lloyd Arthur, et al.	Seasoning Material Derived from Red Peppers and the Derivatives	2,260,897	1941 Oct 28
Hall, Lloyd Arthur, et al.	Sterilization Process	Re.22,284	1943 Mar 9
Hall, Lloyd Arthur	Yeast Food	2,321,673	1943 Jun 15
Hall, Lloyd Arthur	Puncture-Sealing Composition and Manufacture	2,357,650	1944 Sep 5

Author	Title	Number	Date
Hall, Lloyd Arthur	Manufacture of Nitrogen-Fortified Whey Concentrate	2,363,730	1944 Nov 28
Hall, Lloyd Arthur	Capsicum-Containing Seasoning Composition	2,385,412	1945 Sep 25
Hall, Lloyd Arthur	Production of Protein Hydrosylate Flavoring Material	2,414,299	1947 Jan 14
Hall, Lloyd Arthur	Manufacture of Stable Dry Papain Composition	2,464,200	1949 Mar 15
Hall, Lloyd Arthur, et al.	Antioxidant	2,464,927	1949 Mar 22
Hall, Lloyd Arthur	Phospholipoid Carrier for Antioxidant	2,464,928	1949 Mar 22
Hall, Lloyd Arthur	Gelatin-Base Coating for Food	2,477,742	1949 Aug 2
Hall, Lloyd Arthur	Synergistic Antioxidant and Methods of Preparing the Same	2,493,288	1950 Jan 3
Hall, Lloyd Arthur	Antioxidant	2,500,543	1950 Mar 14
Hall, Lloyd Arthur	Synergistic Antioxidant	2,511,802	1950 Jun 13
Hall, Lloyd Arthur	Antioxidant Flakes	2,511,803	1950 Jun 13
Hall, Lloyd Arthur	Antioxidant Salt	2,511,804	1950 Jun 13
Hall, Lloyd Arthur	Synergistic Antioxidant Containing Amino Acids	2,518,233	1950 Aug 8
Hall, Lloyd Arthur	Antioxidant	Re.23,329	1951 Jan 16
Hall, Lloyd Arthur	Production of Protein Hydrosylate	2,536,171	1951 Feb 2
Hall, Lloyd Arthur	Curing Process for Bacon	2,553,533	1951 May 15
Hall, Lloyd Arthur	Spice Extraction and Product	2,571,867	1951 Oct 16
Hall, Lloyd Arthur	Spice Extract and Product	2,571,948	1951 Oct 16
Hall, Lloyd Arthur	Manufacture of Meat-Curing Composition	2,668,770	1954 Feb 9
Hall, Lloyd Arthur	Stable Curing Salt Composition and Manufacture	2,669,771	1954 Feb 9
Hall, Lloyd Arthur	Synergistic Antioxidants Containing Antioxidant Acids	2,677,616	1954 May 4

(Continued)

Name	Invention	Number	Issue Date
Hall, Lloyd Arthur	Antioxidant Composition	2,758,931	1956 Aug 14
Hall, Lloyd Arthur	Reaction Product of Poly-oxyethylene Derivative	2,761,784	1956 Sep 14
Hall, Lloyd Arthur, et al.	Meat-Curing Composition	2,770,548	1956 Nov 13
Hall, Lloyd Arthur	Meat-Curing Composition	2,770,549	1956 Nov 13
Hall, Lloyd Arthur, et al.	Meat-Curing Composition	2,770,550	1956 Nov 13
Hall, Lloyd Arthur, et al.	Meat-Curing Composition	2,770,551	1956 Nov 13
Hall, Lloyd Arthur	Antioxidant Material and Use of Said Material in Treating Meats	2,772,169	1956 Nov 27
Hall, Lloyd Arthur	Antioxidant Composition	2,772,170	1956 Nov 27
Hall, Lloyd Arthur	Fatty Monoglyceride Citrate and Antioxidant Containing Same	2,813,032	1957 Nov 12
Hall, Lloyd Arthur, et al.	Method of Preserving Fresh Pork Trimmings	2,845,358	1958 Jul 29
Hall, Lloyd Arthur	Sterilization of Hospital and Physician's Supplies	2,938,766	1960 May 31
Hall, Lloyd Arthur	Antioxidant Composition	2,981,628	1961 Apr 25
Hall, Norman R.	Convertible Mat and Carrying Bag Combination	4,375,111	1983 Mar 1
Hall, Virginia E., et al.	Embroidered Fruit Bowl Wall Hanging	4,016,314	1977 Apr 5
Hammond, Benjamin F.	Inhibition of Plaque-Forming Bacteria	4,579,736	1986 Apr 1
Hammonds, Julia Terry	Apparatus for Holding Yarn Skeins	572,985	1896 Dec 15
Hannah, Marc R.	Pixel Mapping Apparatus for Color Graphics	4,772,881	1988 Sep 20
Hannah, Marc R.	Interleaved Pipeline Parallel Processing Architecture	4,789,721	1988 Dec 6
Hannah, Marc R.	Method for Updating Piplined, Single Port Z-Buffer	4,951,232	1990 Aug 21

Hannah, Marc R.	Method and Apparatus for Clearing a Region of Z-Buffer	5,038,297	1991 Aug 6
Hannah, Marc R.	Integrated Apparatus for Displaying a Plurality of Modes of Color Information on a Computer Output Display	5,847,700	1998 Dec 8
Harbin, Lawrence	Screen Saver for Exhibiting Artists and Artworks	5,680,535	1997 Oct 21
Hardin, Joanna, et al.	Keyboard Stand	5,188,321	1993 Feb 23
Harding, Felix Hadley	Extension Banquet Table	614,468	1898 Nov 22
Harney, Michael C.	Lantern or Lamp	303,844	1884 Aug 19
Harper, David	Mobile Utility Rack	Des187,654	1960 Apr 12
Harper, David	Bookcase	Des190,500	1961 Jun 6
Harper, Solomon	Electric Hair Treating Implement	1,663,078	1928 Mar 20
Harper, Solomon	Electrical Hair Treating Implement	1,772,002	1930 Aug 5
Harper, Solomon	Thermostatic Controlled Hair Curlers, Bombs, and Irons	2,648,757	1953 Aug 11
Harper, Solomon	Thermostatic Controlled Fur and Material Dressing Equipment	2,711,095	1955 Jun 21
Harper, Solomon	Mercury Switch-Indicator Thermostat Controlled Electric Hair Treating Implement	2,748,782	1956 Jun 5
Harris, Betty Wright	Spot Test for TATB	4,618,452	1986 Oct 21
Harris, Charles F.	Coin Changer and Control Device	2,269,936	1942 Jan 13
Harris, Don Navarro, et al.	Inhibition of Blood Platelet Aggregation	4,051,236	1977 Sep 27
Harris, Don Navarro, et al.	Inhibition of Thromboxane Synthetase Formation and A-rachidonic Acid-inducted Platelet Aggregation etc.	4,243,671	1977 Jan 6
Harris, Edward L.	Apparatus for Handling Corrosive Acid Substances	2,756,129	1956 Jul 24

(Continued)

Name	Invention	Number	Issue Date
Harrison, Charles A., et al.	Sewing Machine Carrying Case	Des224,815	1972 Sep 19
Harrison, Charles A., et al.	Sewing Machine	Des225,574	1972 Dec 19
Harrison, Charles A., et al.	Lighting Fixture	Des252,772	1979 Aug 28
Harrison, Charles A., et al.	Housing for Hand Vacuum and the Like	Des261,851	1981 Nov 17
Harrison, Emmett Scott	Gas Turbine Air Compressor and Control	3,606,971	1971 Sep 21
Harrison, Emmett Scott	Turbojet Afterburner Engine with Exhaust Nozzle	4,242,865	1981 Jan 6
Harrison, Jesse	Combination Tooth Brush and Paste Holder	1,844,036	1932 Feb 9
Harrison, Samuel W., et al.	Closed System Canulating Device	5,108,375	1992 Apr 28
Harrison, Samuel W., et al.	Surgical Drape	6,843,252	2005 Jan 18
Harvey, Franklin	Comb	Des229,583	1973 Dec 11
Harwell, William D.	Apparatus and Method of Capturing an Orbiting Spacecraft	4,664,344	1987 May 12
Haskins, William B.	Shoulder Pad	378,394	1888 Feb 21
Hawkins, Joseph	Gridiron	3,973	1845 Mar 26
Hawkins, Mason A.	Music Cabinet	1,135,281	1915 Apr 13
Hawkins, Mason A.	Box for Player Piano Music Rolls	1,309,030	1919 Jul 8
Hawkins, Randall	Harness Attachment	370,943	1887 Oct 4
Hawkins, Walter Lincoln	Preparation of 1,2 Di-Pimary Amines	2,587,043	1952 Feb 26
Hawkins, Walter Lincoln, et al.	Stabilized Straight Chain Hydrocarbons	2,889,306	1959 Jun 2
Hawkins, Walter Lincoln, et al.	Alpha Olefin Hydrocarbons Stabilized with Carbon Black and Carboxylic Thioether	2,967,845	1961 Jan 10

Name	Title	Number	Date
Hawkins, Walter Lincoln, et al.	Alpha Olefin Hydrocarbons Stabilized with a Fused Ring Sulfide Compounds	2,967,846	1961 Jan 10
Hawkins, Walter Lincoln, et al.	Alpha Olefin Hydrocarbons Stabilized with Carbon Black and a Compound Having R-S-S-R Structure	2,967,847	1961 Jan 10
Hawkins, Walter Lincoln, et al.	Stabilized Straight Chain Hydrocarbons	2,967,849	1961 Jan 10
Hawkins, Walter Lincoln, et al.	Compositions of Straight Chain Hydrocarbons	2,967,850	1961 Jan 10
Hawkins, Walter Lincoln, et al.	Compositions Including Saturated Hydrocarbons	3,042,649	1962 Jul 3
Hawkins, Walter Lincoln, et al.	Polyolefin Stabilized with Sulfides and Thiobisphenols	3,216,967	1965 Nov 9
Hawkins, Walter Lincoln, et al.	Stabilized Long-Chain Polymers	3,259,604	1966 Jul 5
Hawkins, Walter Lincoln, et al.	Stabilized Alpha-Mono-Olefinic Polymers	3,304,283	1967 Feb 14
Hawkins, Walter Lincoln	Multiconductor Communications Cable	3,668,298	1972 Jun 6
Hawkins, William S.	Auto Seat Cape	1,899,327	1933 Feb 28
Hayes, Claude Q. C.	Heat-absorbing Heat Sink	5,709,914	1998 Jan 20
Hayes, Claude Q. C.	Flexible Thermal Control Composite	6,759,476	2004 Jul 6
Hayes, Dorothy E.	Translucent Structural Panels	3,904,866	1975 Sep 9
Hayes, Harry C.	Condenser	1,826,540	1931 Oct 6
Hayes, Rufus	Baseball Gloves	4,891,845	1990 Jan 9
Hayes, Rufus	Baseball Gloves and Attachments	4,937,882	1990 Jul 3
Hayes, Rufus	Baseball Gloves and Attachments and Methods	5,031,238	1991 Jul 16
Headen, Minnis	Foot Power Hammer	350,363	1886 Oct 5
Hearns, Robert	Sealing Attachment for Bottles	598,929	1898 Feb 15
Hearns, Robert	Detachable Car Fender	628,003	1899 Jul 4

(Continued)

Name	Invention	Number	Issue Date
Hearns, William	Device for Removing and Inserting Taps and Plugs	1,040,538	1912 Oct 8
Helm, Tony W., et al.	Universal Joint	2,760,358	1956 Aug 28
Helm, Tony W.	Universal Joint	2,895,314	1959 Jul 21
Henderson, Henry Fairfax	Weight Loss Control System	4,111,336	1978 Sep 5
Henderson, Leonard L.	Ignition System	2,121,385	1938 Jun 21
Henderson, Robert M.	Collapsible Valet	5,022,617	1991 Jun 11
Hendrix, Willie J.	Three-Wheel Vehicle	4,373,740	1983 Feb 15
Hess, Constance R.	Combined Table & Cabinet	Des192,689	1962 May 1
Hicks, Benjamin	Machine for Stemming and Cleaning Peanuts or Green Peas	688,519	1901 Dec 10
Hill, Claudette D.	Magnetic Pick Up Attachment for Vacuum Cleaners	4,300,260	1981 Nov 17
Hill, Henry Aaron	Manufacture of Azodicarbonamide	2,988,545	1961 Jun 16
Hill, Henry Aaron	Foamable Composition Comprising a Thermoplastic Polymer and a Barium Azocarbonate and Method of Foaming	3,141,002	1964 Jul 14
Hill, Henry Aaron	Curing Furfuryl-Alcohol-Modified Urea Formaldehyde Condensates	3,297,611	1967 Jan 10
Hill, Walter A., et al.	Movable Root Contact-Pressure Plate Assembly for Hydroponic System	4,860,490	1989 Aug 29
Hill, William	Horseshoe	786,763	1905 Apr 4
Hill, William A.	High Resolution, High Speed Digital Camera	6,198,505	2001 Mar 6

Name	Title	Number	Date
Hilyer, Andrew F.	Water Evaporator Attachment for Hot Air Registers	435,095	1890 Aug 26
Hilyer, Andrew F.	Evaporator for Hot Air	438,159	1890 Oct 14
Hines, Samuel J.	Life Preserver	1,137,971	1915 May 4
Hines, Samuel J.	Lawn Mower Attachment	1,911,278	1933 May 30
Hinton, Albert R.	Mechanism for Automatically Applying Bags to Filling Machines	1,190,898	1916 Jul 11
Hightower, Adrian, et al.	LaNi.sub.5 is-based Metal Hydride Electrode in Ni-MH Rechargeable Cells	5,888,665	1999 Mar 30
Hightower, Adrian, et al.	Microfluidic Flow Control Device with Floating Element	6,739,576	2004 May 25
Hightower, Adrian, et al.	Microfluidic Flow Multi-splitter	6,845,787	2005 Jan 25
Hoagland, Jesse	Weight Lifting Bar Apparatus	4,274,628	1981 Jun 23
Hodge, John E.	Novel Reductones and Methods of Making	2,936,308	1960 May 10
Hodge, John E.	Glucose-amine Sequestrants	2,996,449	1961 Aug 15
Hodge, John E.	Substituted Benzodioxan Sweetening Compound	4,146,650	1979 Mar 27
Hodges, James L.	Slotted Rotary Shaver	6,032,365	2000 Mar 7
Holder, Neville	N-T-butyl-androst-3-5-diene-17.beta.-carboxamide-3-carboxylic Acid	5,859,266	1999 Jan 12
Hollins, James E.	Carburetor Automatic Choke Construction	4,050,427	1977 Sep 27
Holmes, Elijah H.	Gauge	549,513	1895 Nov 12
Holmes, Lydia M.	Knockdown Wheeled Toy	2,529,692	1950 Nov 14
Hooper, Francis L.	Bed Attachment	1,100,303	1914 Jun 16
Hopings, Donald B., et al.	Inspection Apparatus	4,221,053	1980 Sep 9

(Continued)

Name	Invention	Number	Issue Date
Hopings, Donald B., et al.	Apparatus for Applying a Pattern on a Substrate	4,246,866	1981 Jan 27
Hopkins, Harry C.	Preparation of Epoxy Resin-Rubber-Glass Mixture and Mixture Produced	4,256,612	1981 Mar 17
Hopkins, Harry C., et al.	Ground Effect Flying Platform	4,290,500	1981 Sep 22
Hopkins, Harry C.	Swimming Simulator	4,422,634	1983 Dec 27
Hopkins, Harry C.	Microwave Agricultural Drying and Curing Apparatus	4,430,806	1984 Feb 14
Hopkins, Harry C.	Power Controller	4,704,570	1987 Nov 3
Horad, Sewell D.	Adjustable Valve for Controlling the Amount of Water Refilling a Toilet Bowl for Flushing	5,715,860	1998 Feb 10
Horne, June B.	Emergency Escape Apparatus and Method of Using Same	4,498,557	1985 Feb 12
Howard, Darnley E.	Optical Apparatus for Indicating the Position of a Tool	2,145,116	1939 Jan 24
Howard, Darnley Moseley, et al.	Method of Making Radomes with an Internal Antenna	3,451,127	1969 Jun 24
Hubbard, James E. Jr.	Active Mirror Assembly	5,159,498	1992 Oct 27
Hubbard, James E. Jr., et al.	Center of Weight Sensor	6,223,606	2001 May 1
Hughes, Isaiah D.	Combined Excavator and Elevator	687,312	1901 Nov 26
Hull, Wilson E., et al.	Sublimation Timing Switch	3,286,064	1966 Nov 15
Hunter, John W.	Portable Weighing Scale	570,553	1896 Nov 3
Hunter, Raymond	Shower Bath Economizer	4,372,372	1983 Feb 8
Huntley, James B.	Emergency Fire Escape Mechanism	3,880,255	1975 Apr 29
Hutchings, Richard S., et al.	Process for the Manufacture of Surfactant Cleaning Blacks and Compositions	4,722,802	1988 Feb 2

Hutchings, Richard S.	Aqueous Alkali Metal Halogenite Compositions	4,790,950	1988 Dec 13
Hutchings, Richard S.	Compositions Containing Chlorine Dioxide and Their Preparation	4,861,514	1989 Aug 29
Hutchings, Richard S.	Aqueous Alkali Metal Halogenite Compositions Containing a Cobrant	4,880,556	1989 Nov 14
Hyde, Robert N.	Composition for Cleaning and Preserving Carpets	392,205	1888 Nov 6
Ingram, Clifton M.	Railroad Crossing Flag Signal	1,526,215	1925 Feb 10
Ingram, Clifton M.	Well Drilling Tool	1,542,776	1925 Jun 16
Ivey, Elwood G.	Sense-simileTransmission Machine	6,053,738	2000 Apr 25
Ivey, Elwood G.	Home Fragrance Dispenser	7,188,783	2007 Mar 13
Ivory, Brian K.	Self-Adjusting Bog Support	4,702,445	1987 Oct 27
Izevbigie, Ernest B.	Method for cAMP Production	6,541,196	2003 Apr 1
Izevbigie, Ernest B.	Phytochemotherapy for Cancer	6,713,098	2004 Mar 30
Jackson, Aaron C.	Football Board Game	5,039,107	1991 Aug 13
Jackson, André J.	Apparatus and Methods of Collecting Urine frcm Lab Animals	4,476,879	1984 Oct 16
Jackson, Benjamin F.	Heating Apparatus	599,985	1898 Mar 1
Jackson, Benjamin F.	Matrix Drying Apparatus	603,879	1898 May 10
Jackson, Benjamin F.	Gas Burner	622,482	1899 Apr 4
Jackson, Benjamin F.	Electrotyper's Furnace	645,296	1900 Mar 13
Jackson, Benjamin F.	Automobile	672,941	1901 Apr 30
Jackson, Benjamin F.	Steam Boiler	690,730	1902 Jan 7

(*Continued*)

Name	Invention	Number	Issue Date
Jackson, Benjamin F.	Trolley-Wheel Controller	771,206	1904 Sep 27
Jackson, Benjamin F.	Tank Signal	773,747	1904 Nov 1
Jackson, Benjamin F.	Gas Furnace	837,571	1906 Dec 4
Jackson, Benjamin F.	Hydrocarbon Burner System	857,808	1907 Jun 25
Jackson, Brian G.	Portable Highway Warning Device with Frangible Retainer Ring	5,775,834	1998 Jul 7
Jackson, Harry	Advertising Apparatus	1,865,374	1932 Jun 28
Jackson, Harry and Mary E.	Protective Appliance	2,038,491	1936 Apr 21
Jackson, Harry and Mary E.	Protective Appliance	2,053,035	1936 Sep 1
Jackson, Harry and Mary E.	Burglar Alarm Switch	2,071,343	1937 Feb 23
Jackson, Henry	Method and Composition for Automatically Depositing Copper	3,436,233	1969 Apr 1
Jackson, Henry A.	Kitchen Table	569,135	1896 Oct 6
Jackson, Jerome D.	Systems and Methods Employing a Plurality of Signal Amplitudes	5,864,301	1999 Jan 26
Jackson, Johnnie R.	System and Method for Portable Medical Records	11/979069	2008 Jun 12
Jackson, Joseph N.	Programmable Television Receiver Controllers	4,081,754	1978 Mar 28
Jackson, Joseph N.	Programmable Television Receiver Controllers	4,228,543	1980 Oct 14
Jackson, Joseph N., et al.	Video Viewing Censoring Supervision System	5,548,345	1996 Aug 20
Jackson, Joseph N.	Apparatus and Method of Providing a Personal Biorhythmic Cycle	6,022,323	2000 Feb 8

Jackson, Kedrich J.	Wet Wiping System for Inkjet Printheads	5,706,038	1998 Jan 6
Jackson, Kedrich J.	Constant Flexure Wiping and Scraping System for Inkjet Printheads	6,017,110	2000 Jan 25
Jackson, Kedrich J.	Wet Wiping System for Inkjet Printheads	6,290,324	2001 Sep 18
Jackson, Michael J., et al.	Method and Means for Creating Anti-Gravity Illusion	5,255,452	1993 Oct 26
Jackson, Troy	Safety System	5,593,111	1997 Jan 14
Jackson, Norman	Pneumatic Tire	1,384,134	1921 Jul 12
Jackson, William H.	Railway Switch	578,641	1897 Mar 9
Jackson, William H.	Railway Switch	593,665	1897 Nov 16
Jackson, William H.	Automatic Locking Switch	609,436	1898 Aug 23
Jamieson, Ernest J.	Gasoline Composition	3,655,351	1972 Apr 11
Jamieson, Ernest J.	Hydrocarbyl Hydrogen Phosphate Salts of Amino-Amides	3,946,053	1976 Mar 23
Jefferson, Donald E.	Forming 2-Hydroxyethyl Methacrylate Foam	3,172,868	1965 Mar 9
Jefferson, Donald E., et al.	Interpolymer Comprising Acrylic Acid and Acrylic Acid Ester	3,184,440	1965 May 18
Jefferson, Donald E., et al.	Triggered Exploding Wire Device	3,288,068	1966 Nov 29
Jefferson, Donald E.	Foamed Product and Process Thereof	3,293,198	1966 Dec 20
Jefferson, Donald E., et al.	Polyesters, Polyamides, and Polyesteramide	3,567,694	1971 Mar 2
Jefferson, Donald E., et al.	Polymers from Diesters and N-Acrylyiminodiacetic Acid	3,598,792	1971 Aug 10
Jefferson, Donald E., et al.	Increasing the Wet Strength of Cellulosic Materials	3,629,178	1971 Dec 21
Jefferson, Donald E.	Preparation of N-Allyliminodiacetimide Dioxine	3,639,364	1972 Feb 1
Jefferson, Donald E., et al.	Digital Data Storage System	3,678,468	1972 Jul 18

(Continued)

Name	Invention	Number	Issue Date
Jefferson, Donald E., et al.	Increasing the Wet Strength of Cellulosic Materials	3,681,131	1972 Aug 1
Jefferson, Donald E., et al.	Data Processing System	3,701,972	1972 Oct 31
Jefferson, Isaac	Jack	772,238	1904 Oct 11
Jenkins, Christina M.	Permanently Attaching Commercial Hair to Live Hair	2,621,663	1952 Dec 16
Jenkins, George A.	Semibouyant Aircraft	1,821,061	1931 Sep 1
Jennings, Thomas A.	Dry Scouring of Clothes	3,306X	1821 Mar 3
Jeter, Ruane, et al.	Toaster	Des289,249	1987 Apr 14
Jeter, Ruane, et al.	Hand-held, Multi-functional Devices in One Housing	Des383,783	1997 Sep 16
Jeter, Ruane, et al.	Cabinet for Housing a Medical Waste Container	Des411,008	1999 Jun 15
Jeter, Ruane, et al.	Container Installing System	5,918,762	1999 Jul 6
Jeter, Ruane, et al.	Medical Waste Disposal Container	5,947,285	1999 Sep 7
Jeter, Ruane, et al.	Combined Cabinet and Container for Housing Medical Waste	Des414,864	1999 Oct 5
Jeter, Ruane, et al.	Combined Cabinet with Glove Box and Container for Housing Medical Waste	Des415,273	1999 Oct 12
Jeter, Ruane, et al.	Medical Waste Container	Des421,122	2000 Feb 22
Jeter, Ruane, et al.	Cabinet and Container for Housing Medical Waste	Des438,964	2001 Mar 13
Jeter, Ruane, et al.	Food Pan Lid with an Elastomeric Seal	Des446,076	2001 Aug 7
Jeter, Ruane, et al.	Tray Holder with Hand Grips	Des471,400	2003 Mar 11
Jeter, Ruane, et al.	Tray Holder	Des471,401	2003 Mar 11
Jeter, Ruane, et al.	Scalpel	Des568,475	2008 May 6

Name	Title	Number	Date
Jeter, Sheila, et al.	Hand-held, Multi-functional Devices in One Housing	Des383,783	1997 Sep 16
Jetter, Milton W.	Remote-Controlled Alarm Clock	4,316,273	1982 Feb 16
Jetter, Milton W.	Alarm Deactivation System	4,352,170	1982 Sep 28
Jetter, Milton W.	Clock Alarm-Deactivating System	4,352,171	1982 Sep 28
Jetter, Milton W.	Clock Alarm Control System	4,426,157	1984 Jan 17
Jetter, Milton W.	Random Multiple Push Button Clock Alarm Deactivation System	4,430,006	1984 Feb 7
John, James A., et al.	Liniment	437,728	1890 Oct 7
Johnson, Andrew R.	Precision Digital Delay Circuit	3,376,436	1968 Apr 2
Johnson, Anthony M.	Photodetector Having Semi-insulating Material and a Contoured, Substantially Periodic Surface	4,555,622	1985 Nov 26
Johnson, Anthony M.	Integrated Optical Device Having Integral Photodetector	4,703,996	1987 Nov 3
Johnson, Anthony M.	High Speed Circuit Measurements Using Photoemission Sampling	4,721,910	1988 Jan 26
Johnson, Brenis E.	Window Insulator	5,203,129	1993 Apr 20
Johnson, Daniel	Rotary Dining Table	396,089	1889 Jan 15
Johnson, Daniel	Lawn Mower Attachment	410,836	1889 Sep 10
Johnson, Daniel	Grass Receiver for Lawn Mowers	429,629	1890 Jun 10
Johnson, George M.	Automatic Stopping and Releasing Device for Mine Cars	1,249,106	1917 Dec 4
Johnson, Isaac R.	Bicycle Frame	634,823	1899 Oct 10
Johnson, John Arthur	Wrench	1,413,121	1922 Apr 18
Johnson, John Arthur, et al.	Theft Preventing Device for Vehicles	1,438,709	1922 Dec 12

(Continued)

Name	Invention	Number	Issue Date
Johnson, Lonnie G., et al.	Digital Distance Measuring Instrument	4,143,267	1979 Mar 6
Johnson, Lonnie G.	Variable Resistance Type Sensor Controlled Switch	4,181,843	1980 Jan 1
Johnson, Lonnie G.	Smoke Detecting Timer Controlled Thermostat	4,211,362	1980 Jul 8
Johnson, Lonnie G.	Automatic Sprinkler Control	4,253,606	1981 Mar 3
Johnson, Lonnie G.	Thermal Energy Accumulation	4,476,693	1984 Oct 16
Johnson, Lonnie G.	Soil Moisture Potential Determination by Weight	4,509,361	1985 Apr 9
Johnson, Lonnie G.	Squirt Gun	4,591,071	1986 May 27
Johnson, Lonnie G.	Johnson Tube, a Thermodynamic Heat Pump	4,724,683	1988 Feb 16
Johnson, Lonnie G.	Flow Actuated Pulsator	4,757,946	1988 Jul 19
Johnson, Lonnie G., et al.	Pinch Trigger Pump Water Gun	5,074,437	1991 Dec 24
Johnson, Lonnie G., et al.	Double Tank Pinch Trigger Pump Water Gun	5,150,819	1992 Sep 29
Johnson, Lonnie G., et al.	Liquid Jet Propelled Transporter and Launcher Toy	5,197,452	1993 Mar 30
Johnson, Lonnie G., et al.	Pinch Trigger Hand Pump Water Gun with Multiple Tanks	5,238,149	1993 Aug 24
Johnson, Lonnie G., et al.	Combined Aerodynamic Glider and Launcher	Des342,551	1993 Dec 21
Johnson, Lonnie G., et al.	Pinch Trigger Water Gun with Rearwardly Mounted Hand Pump	5,292,032	1994 Mar 8
Johnson, Lonnie G., et al.	Hair Drying Curler Apparatus	5,299,367	1994 Apr 5
Johnson, Lonnie G., et al.	Pinch Trigger Hand Pump Water Gun with Non-detachable tank	5,305,919	1994 Apr 26
Johnson, Lonnie G., et al.	Low Pressure, High Volume Pressurized Water Gun	5,322,191	1994 Jun 21

Johnson, Lonnie G., et al.	Fluid Pulsator with Accumulator for Frequency Control	5,398,873	1995 Mar 21
Johnson, Lonnie G., et al.	Pressurized Air/Water Rocket and Launcher	5,415,153	1995 May 16
Johnson, Lonnie G., et al.	Fluid Powering and Launching System for a Toy Vehicle	5,499,940	1996 Mar 19
Johnson, Lonnie G.	Air Pressure Toy Rocket Launcher	5,538,453	1996 Jul 23
Johnson, Lonnie G., et al.	Toy Rocket with Velocity Dependent Chute Release	5,549,497	1996 Aug 27
Johnson, Lonnie G., et al.	Pneumatic Launcher for a Toy Projectile and the Like	5,553,598	1996 Sep 10
Johnson, Lonnie G., et al.	Electric Pump Toy Water Gun	5,586,688	1996 Dec 24
Johnson, Lonnie G., et al.	Compressed Air Gun with Magazine Indexer	5,592,951	1997 Jan 14
Johnson, Lonnie G., et al.	Compressed Air Gun with Single Action Pump	5,701,879	1997 Dec 30
Johnson, Lonnie G., et al.	Rapid Fire Compressed Air Gun	5,709,199	1998 Jan 20
Johnson, Lonnie G., et al.	Voice Activated Compressed Air Toy Gun	5,724,955	1998 Mar 10
Johnson, Lonnie G.	Vacuum Actuated Replenishing Water Gun	5,779,100	1998 Jul 14
Johnson, Lonnie G., et al	Launcher for a Toy Projectile or Similar Launchable Object	5,819,717	1998 Oct 13
Johnson, Lonnie G.	Toy Water Gun with Fluid Selection Control Valve	5,826,750	1998 Oct 27
Johnson, Lonnie G.	Wet Diaper Detector	5,838,240	1998 Nov 17
Johnson, Lonnie G., et al	Toy Water Gun with Air Siphoning Valve	5,850,941	1998 Dec 22
Johnson, Lonnie G., et al.	Multiple Barrel Compressed Air Gun	5,878,734	1999 Mar 9
Johnson, Lonnie G.	Compressed Air Toy Gun	5,878,735	1999 Mar 9
Johnson, Lonnie G.	Toy Water Gun	5,878,914	1999 Mar 9
Johnson, Lonnie G.	Compressed Air Gun with Temporary Seal	5,913,304	1999 Jun 22
Johnson, Lonnie G., et al	Rapid Fire Compressed Air Toy Gun	5,924,413	1999 Jul 29

(Continued)

Name	Number	Issue Date	Invention
Johnson, Lonnie G., et al.	5,941,751	1999 Aug 24	Fluid-launchable Sound-generating Article
Johnson, Lonnie G., et al.	5,957,745	1999 Sep 28	Gyroscopic Figurine
Johnson, Lonnie G.	5,951,345	1999 Sep 14	Toy Rocket
Johnson, Lonnie G., et al.	5,974,977	1999 Nov 2	Magnetic Propulsion Toy System
Johnson, Lonnie G., et al.	5,982,144	1999 Nov 9	Rechargeable Battery Power Supply Overcharge Protection Circuit
Johnson, Lonnie G., et al.	6,099,266	2000 Aug 8	Air Pump
Johnson, Lonnie G., et al.	6,180,281	2001 Jan 30	Composite Separator and Electrode
Johnson, Lonnie G.	6,398,824	2002 Jun 4	Method for Manufacturing a Thin-film Lithium by Direct Deposition of Battery Components on Opposite Sides of a Current
Johnson, Lonnie G.	6,439,216	2002 Aug 27	Automatic Pressurized Fluid Gun
Johnson, Lonnie G.	6,402,796	2002 Jun 11	Method of Producing a Thin Film Battery
Johnson, Lonnie G., et al.	6,408,837	2002 Jun 25	Toy Gun with Magazine
Johnson, Lonnie G.	6,540,108	2003 Apr 1	Toy Water Gun
Johnson, Lonnie G., et al.	6,511,516	2003 Jan 28	Method and Apparatus for Producing Lithium Based Cathodes
Johnson, Lonnie G., et al.	6,679,155	2004 Jan 20	Projectile Launcher
Johnson, Lonnie G., et al.	6,835,493	2004 Dec 28	Thin Film Battery
Johnson, Lonnie G.	6,899,967	2005 May 31	Electromechanical Conversion System
Johnson, Lonnie G., et al.	6,949,303	2005 Sep 27	Electromechanical Conversion System

Johnson, Lonnie G.	Portable Multimedia Projection System	6,966,651	2005 Nov 22
Johnson, Lonnie G.	Portable Multimedia Projection System	7,052,136	2006 May 30
Johnson, Lonnie G., et al.	Johnson Reversible Engine	7,160,639	2007 Jan 9
Johnson, Lonnie G., et al.	Method of Manufacturing Lithium Battery	7,540,886	2009 Jun 2
Johnson, Malcolm L., et al.	Cover Garment with Inner Garment Access Option	4,709,419	1987 Dec 1
Johnson, Malcolm L., et al.	Protective Covering for a Mechanical Linkage	4,904,514	1990 Feb 27
Johnson, Malcolm L., et al.	Melt Blown Nonwoven Wiper	4,904,521	1990 Feb 27
Johnson, Malcolm L., et al.	Melt Blown Nonwoven Wiper	5,039,431	1991 Aug 13
Johnson, Paul E.	Therapeutic Lamp	1,403,119	1922 Jan 10
Johnson, Paul E.	Base for Therapeutic Lamps	Des75,012	1928 May 1
Johnson, Paul E.	Therapeutic Lamp	Des76,542	1928 Oct 9
Johnson, Paul E.	Therapeutic Lamp	1,842,100	1932 Jan 19
Johnson, Payton	Swinging Chairs	249,530	1881 Nov 15
Johnson, Powell	Eye Protector	234,039	1880 Nov 2
Johnson, Wesley	Velocipede	627,335	1899 Jun 20
Johnson, William A.	Paint Vehicle	393,763	1888 Dec 4
Johnson, Willie Harry	Mechanism for Overcoming Dead Centers	554,223	1896 Feb 4
Johnson, Willie Harry	Overcoming Dead Centers	612,345	1898 Oct 11
Johnson, Willis	Egg Beater	292,821	1884 Feb 5
Jones, Albert A., et al.	Caps for Bottles, Jars, etc.	610,715	1898 Sep 13
Jones, Clinton	Electric Release for Toy Guns	2,474,054	1949 Jun 21

(Continued)

Name	Invention	Number	Issue Date
Jones, Felix B.	Firearm	1,685,673	1928 Sep 25
Jones, Frederick McKinley	Ticket Dispensing Machine	2,163,754	1939 Jun 27
Jones, Frederick McKinley	Air Conditioning Unit	Des132,182	1942 Apr 28
Jones, Frederick McKinley	Air Conditioner for Vehicles	2,303,857	1942 Dec 1
Jones, Frederick McKinley	Removable Cooling Unit for Compartments	2,336,735	1943 Dec 14
Jones, Frederick McKinley	Means for Automatically Stopping and Starting Gas Engines	2,337,164	1943 Dec 21
Jones, Frederick McKinley	Two Cycle Gas Engine	2,376,968	1945 May 29
Jones, Frederick McKinley	Two Cycle Gas Engine	2,417,253	1947 Mar 11
Jones, Frederick McKinley	Removable Cooling Unit for Compartments	Re.23,000	1948 May 11
Jones, Frederick McKinley	Preventing Frosting of Evaporator Heat Exchangers	2,471,692	1949 May 31
Jones, Frederick McKinley	Air Conditioning Unit	2,475,841	1949 Jul 12
Jones, Frederick McKinley	Starter Generator	2,475,842	1949 Jul 12
Jones, Frederick McKinley	Means Operated by Starter Generator for Cooling Gas Engines	2,475,843	1949 Jul 12
Jones, Frederick McKinley	Means for Thermostatically Operating Gas Engines	2,477,377	1949 Jul 26
Jones, Frederick McKinley	System for Controlling Operation for Refrigeration Units	2,509,099	1950 May 23
Jones, Frederick McKinley	Air Conditioning Unit	Des159,209	1950 Jul 4
Jones, Frederick McKinley	Engine Actuated Ventilating System	2,523,273	1950 Sep 26
Jones, Frederick McKinley	Apparatus for Heating or Cooling Atmosphere	2,526,874	1950 Oct 24
Jones, Frederick McKinley	Prefabricated Refrigerator Construction	2,535,682	1950 Dec 26

Jones, Frederick McKinley	Refrigeration Control Device	2,581,956	1952 Jan 8
Jones, Frederick McKinley	Locking Mechanism	2,647,287	1953 Aug 4
Jones, Frederick McKinley	Methods and Means for Defrosting a Cold Diffuser	2,666,298	1954 Jan 19
Jones, Frederick McKinley	Methods and Means for Air Conditioning	2,696,086	1954 Dec 7
Jones, Frederick McKinley	Methods and Means for Preserving Perishable Foodstuffs in Transit	2,780,923	1957 Feb 12
Jones, Frederick McKinley	Control Device for Internal Combustion Engine	2,850,001	1958 Sep 2
Jones, Frederick McKinley	Thermostat and Temperature Control System	2,926,005	1960 Feb 23
Jones, Howard S. Jr., et al.	Variable Waveguide Coupler	2,898,559	1959 Aug 4
Jones, Howard S. Jr., et al.	Antenna Testing Shield	3,029,430	1962 Apr 10
Jones, Howard S. Jr., et al.	Waveguide Components	3,046,507	1962 Jul 29
Jones, Howard S. Jr., et al.	Magneto-Mechanical Waveguide Line Stretcher	3,268,837	1966 Aug 23
Jones, Howard S. Jr., et al.	Electrically Scanned Microwave Antenna	3,268,901	1966 Aug 23
Jones, Howard S. Jr.	Step Twist Diode Microwave Switch	3,314,027	1967 Apr 11
Jones, Howard S. Jr.	Slot Antenna Built into a Dielectric Radome	3,346,865	1967 Oct 10
Jones, Howard S. Jr.	Multifrequency Common Aperture Manifold Antenna	3,482,248	1969 Dec 2
Jones, Howard S. Jr.	Radome Antenna	3,509,571	1970 Apr 28
Jones, Howard S. Jr.	Dielectric-Loaded Antenna with Matching Window	3,518,683	1970 Jun 30
Jones, Howard S. Jr.	Projectile with Incorporated Dielectric Loaded Cavity Antenna	3,518,685	1970 Jun 30
Jones, Howard S. Jr.	Slotted Waveguide Antenna Array	3,524,189	1970 Aug 11

(Continued)

Name	Invention	Number	Issue Date
Jones, Howard S. Jr.	Method and Apparatus for Joining Waveguide Components	3,577,105	1971 May 4
Jones, Howard S. Jr.	Dual Waveguide Horn Antenna	3,611,396	1971 Oct 5
Jones, Howard S. Jr., et al.	Re-entry Vehicle Nose Cone with Antenna	3,680,130	1972 Jul 25
Jones, Howard S. Jr.	Base-Mounted Re-entry Vehicle Antenna	3,739,386	1973 Jun 12
Jones, Howard S. Jr., et al.	Super Lightweight Microwave Circuit	3,768,048	1973 Oct 23
Jones, Howard S. Jr.	Cavity Excited Conical Dielectric Radiator	3,798,653	1974 Mar 19
Jones, Howard S. Jr.	Rearmounted Forward-Looking Radio Frequency Antenna	3,845,488	1974 Oct 29
Jones, Howard S. Jr.	Antenna System	3,858,214	1974 Dec 31
Jones, Howard S. Jr.	A Monolithic, Electrically Small, Multi-frequency Antenna	3,914,767	1975 Oct 21
Jones, Howard S. Jr., et al.	Nose Cone Capacitively Tuned Wedge Antenna	3,943,520	1976 Mar 9
Jones, Howard S. Jr., et al.	Low-Profile Quandrature-plate UHF Antenna	3,987,458	1976 Oct 19
Jones, Howard S. Jr., et al.	Conformal Radome-Antenna Structure	3,975,737	1976 Aug 17
Jones, Howard S. Jr.	Multi-function Integrated Radome Antenna System	4,010,470	1977 Mar 10
Jones, Howard S. Jr., et al.	Conformal Edge-Slot Radiator	4,051,480	1977 Sep 27
Jones, James C.	Mailbag Transferring Device	1,227,914	1917 May 29
Jones, John Leslie	Preparation of Substituted Phenols	2,497,503	1950 Feb 14
Jones, John Leslie	Personnel Restraint System for Vehicular Occupants	3,690,695	1972 Sep 12
Jones, John Leslie	Smokeless Slow Burning Cast Propellant	4,112,849	1978 Sep 12
Jones, Levonia, et al.	Soap Saving Method and Apparatus	5,030,405	1991 Jul 9
Jones, Marshall Gordon, et al.	Industrial Hand Held Laser Tool and Laser System	4,564,736	1986 Jan 14

Name	Invention	Patent Number	Date
Jones, Marshall Gordon	Underwater Laser Welding Nozzle	6,060,686	2000 May 9
Jones, Martha	Corn Husker, Sheller, etc.	77,494	1868 May 5
Jones, Sylvester S.	Manicuring Device	1,742,862	1930 Jan 7
Jones, Wilbert Leroy Jr.	Duplex Capstan	3,258,247	1966 Jun 28
Jones, William B.	Dentist Apparatus	2,096,375	1937 Oct 19
Jones, Willie G. Sr.	Basketball Rim and Net Structure	3,948,516	1976 Apr 26
Jordan, John H. Jr.	Divan	Des219,735	1971 Jan 19
Jordan, John H. Jr.	Headboard for Bed	Des219,904	1971 Feb 16
Jordan, John H. Jr.	Dresser	Des219,927	1971 Feb 16
Jordan, John H. Jr.	Cocktail Table	Des220,786	1971 May 18
Jordan, John H. Jr.	Combined Clock and Wall Plaque	Des220,965	1971 Jun 22
Joyce, James A.	Coal or Ore Bucket	603,143	1898 Apr 26
Joyner, Marjorie Stewart	Permanent Wave Machine	1,693,515	1928 Nov 27
Joyner, Marjorie Stewart	Scalp Protector	1,716,173	1929 Jun 4
Julian, Hubert	Airplane Safety Appliance	1,379,264	1921 May 24
Julian, Percy L., et al.	Recovery of Sterols	2,218,971	1940 Oct 22
Julian, Percy L., et al.	Production of a Derived Vegetable Protein	2,238,329	1941 Apr 15
Julian, Percy L., et al.	Process of Preparing Vegetable Protein	2,246,466	1941 Jun 17
Julian, Percy L., et al.	Preparation of Vegetable Phosphatides	2,249,002	1941 Jul 15
Julian, Percy L., et al.	Protein-Urea Complex	2,249,003	1941 Jul 15
Julian, Percy L., et al.	Process for the Recovering of Sterols	2,273,045	1942 Feb 17

(Continued)

Name	Invention	Number	Issue Date
Julian, Percy L., et al.	Process for Recovering Sterols	2,273,046	1942 Feb 17
Julian, Percy L., et al.	Preparation of a Soybean Plastic	2,281,584	1942 May 5
Julian, Percy L., et al.	Preparing Material Having Physiological Activity of Corpus Luteum Hormone	2,296,284	1942 Sep 22
Julian, Percy L., et al.	Process for Isolating Vegetable Proteins	2,304,099	1942 Dec 8
Julian, Percy L., et al.	Preparation of Tertiary Carbinols	2,304,100	1942 Dec 8
Julian, Percy L., et al.	Protein Composition for Paints and Paint Clears	2,304,102	1942 Dec 8
Julian, Percy L., et al.	Preparing Ketones of Cyclopentohydrophenanthrene	2,341,557	1944 Feb 15
Julian, Percy L., et al.	Preparation of Etio-Cholenic Acid Derivatives	2,342,147	1944 Feb 22
Julian, Percy L., et al.	Preparation of Oil-Soluble Phosphatide Composition	2,355,081	1944 Aug 8
Julian, Percy L., et al.	Protein Composition Resistant to Formaldehyde Coagulation	2,363,794	1944 Nov 28
Julian, Percy L., et al.	Methylation of Phospholipid, Cephalin	2,373,686	1945 Apr 17
Julian, Percy L., et al.	Alteration and Control of Viscosity of Chocolate	2,373,687	1945 Apr 17
Julian, Percy L., et al.	Increasing Oil Solubility of Phospholipids	2,374,681	1945 May 1
Julian, Percy L., et al.	Dehalogenation of Halogenated Steroids	2,374,683	1945 May 1
Julian, Percy L., et al.	Conversion of Soybean Globulin into Egg Albumin-Like Protein	2,381,407	1945 Aug 7
Julian, Percy L., et al.	Effecting Phospholipid Solubility by Acid Treatment	2,391,462	1945 Dec 25
Julian, Percy L., et al.	Refining Vegetable Oils	2,392,390	1946 Jan 8
Julian, Percy L., et al.	Unsaturated Ketones of the Cyclopentanophenanthrene	2,349,551	1946 Feb 12

Julian, Percy L., et al.	New Quaternary Compounds from Phospholipids	2,400,120	1946 May 14
Julian, Percy L., et al.	Process for Canning Soybeans and Product	2,400,123	1946 May 14
Julian, Percy L., et al.	Amines in the i-Steroid Series	2,428,368	1947 Oct 7
Julian, Percy L., et al.	Preparation of 3-Amino-Derivatives of Steroids	2,430,467	1947 Nov 11
Julian, Percy L., et al.	Procedure for Preparation of Progesterone	2,433,848	1948 Jan 6
Julian, Percy L., et al.	Preparing 3-Amino-Derivatives from i-Steriocs	2,446,538	1948 Aug 10
Julian, Percy L., et al.	Oxidation of Soya Sitosteryl Acetate Dibromide	2,464,236	1949 Mar 14
Julian, Percy L., et al.	6-Alkoxy-i-Androstene-17-ols	2,484,833	1949 Oct 18
Julian, Percy L., et al.	Rearrangement of Steroid Oximes	2,531,441	1950 Nov 28
Julian, Percy L., et al.	Steroid Dimethylamines and Their Quaternary Halides	2,561,378	1951 Jul 24
Julian, Percy L., et al.	Steroid Mannich Amines	2,562,194	1951 Jul 31
Julian, Percy L., et al.	Steroidal Ketones Containing Amino Groups	2,566,366	1951 Sep 4
Julian, Percy L., et al.	Preparation and Degradation of Steroid Amines	2,582,258	1952 Jan 15
Julian, Percy L., et al.	16-Alkyl Steroids and Process of Preparing	2,588,391	1952 Mar 11
Julian, Percy L., et al.	Improving Alkali-Soluble Acid-Perceptible Vegetable Protein	2,588,392	1952 Mar 11
Julian, Percy L., et al.	Preparation of Etio-Steroid Acids	2,606,911	1952 Aug 12
Julian, Percy L., et al.	The Hydroxylation of Phospholipids	2,629,662	1953 Feb 23
Julian, Percy L., et al.	Preparation, 3,20-Dideto-17 Alpha-Hydroxy-Steroids	2,648,662	1953 Aug 11
Julian, Percy L., et al.	Preparation of 17 Alpha-Hydroxy-Steroids	2,648,663	1953 Aug 11
Julian, Percy L., et al.	Preparation of 17 Alpha-Hydroxy-Steroids	2,662,904	1953 Dec 15

(Continued)

Name	Invention	Number	Issue Date
Julian, Percy L., et al.	Selective Dehalogenation of Certain Halogenated Ketones	2,667,498	1954 Jan 26
Julian, Percy L., et al.	Degradation of Steroid Quaternary Ammonium Salts	2,670,359	1954 Feb 23
Julian, Percy L., et al.	Procedure for Delta 16-20-Keto-Pregnanes	2,671,794	1954 Mar 9
Julian, Percy L., et al.	Preparation of 16,17-Oxido-5-Pregnenes	2,686,181	1954 Aug 10
Julian, Percy L., et al.	Preparation of Steroids of the C19 Series	2,696,490	1954 Dec 7
Julian, Percy L., et al.	16,17-Oxido-prenane-3 alpha ol-11,20-dione	2,705,233	1955 Mar 29
Julian, Percy L., et al.	Steroid-Dimenthylamines and Their Quaternary Halides	2,705,238	1955 Mar 29
Julian, Percy L., et al.	Improved Margarine	2,724,649	1955 Nov 22
Julian, Percy L., et al.	Preparation of Cortisone	2,752,339	1956 Jun 26
Julian, Percy L., et al.	Hydroxylation of Vegetable Oils	2,752,376	1956 Jun 26
Julian, Percy L., et al.	Separating Sterols from Vegetable Oils by Hydrogration	2,752,378	1956 Jun 26
Julian, Percy L., et al.	Synergistic Compositions of Matter	2,773,771	1956 Dec 11
Julian, Percy L., et al.	Process of Dehalogenating Steroids	2,773,867	1956 Dec 11
Julian, Percy L., et al.	Preparation of 21-Bromo and 21-Iodo-Steroids	2,789,989	1957 Apr 23
Julian, Percy L., et al.	Method for Introducing a 21-Hydroxy Group into 17-Oxygenated Steroids	2,816,108	1957 Dec 10
Julian, Percy L., et al.	Certain 16,17-Oxido-Steroids of the C21 Series	2,820,030	1958 Jan 14
Julian, Percy L., et al.	5,7-Pregnadiene-3-ol-one and Ester Thereof	2,876,237	1959 Mar 3
Julian, Percy L., et al.	4,5-Epoxy Derivatives of 17Alpha-Alkyltestosterones	2,885,398	1959 May 5
Julian, Percy L., et al.	Novel Method of Preparing Androstendione	2,887,478	1959 May 19

Julian, Percy L., et al.	Substituted 2,5-Androstadienes	2,891,974	1959 Jun 23
Julian, Percy L., et al.	2,5-Pregnadiene Derivatives	2,891,975	1959 Jun 23
Julian, Percy L., et al.	Androstan-3,17-diol-4-one Derivatives	2,900,399	1959 Aug 18
Julian, Percy L., et al.	Process for Preparation of 2-Acetoxy Steroids	2,910,487	1959 Oct 27
Julian, Percy L., et al.	3-Keto-4 Halo-Delta 4,5 Steroids	2,933,510	1959 Apr 19
Julian, Percy L., et al.	Method of Epimerizing 11-Bromo-Steroids	2,940,991	1960 Jun 14
Julian, Percy L., et al.	Novel Epoxy-Pregnanes	2,944,052	1960 Jul 5
Julian, Percy L., et al.	Preparation of the 12-Keto Isomer of Cortisone	2,947,765	1960 Aug 2
Julian, Percy L., et al.	Shortening Composition and Emulsifier System	3,004,853	1961 Oct 17
Julian, Percy L.	Isolation of Sapogenine	3,019,220	1962 Jan 30
Julian, Percy L., et al.	12-Alkyl-12-Hydroxyprogesterone Derivatives	3,052,694	1962 Sep 4
Julian, Percy L., et al.	Reduction of an Epoxy Group	3,055,918	1962 Sep 25
Julian, Percy L., et al.	17-Substituted 2,5-Pregnadiene Derivatives	3,153,061	1964 Oct 13
Julian, Percy L., et al.	Process for 11Beta, 12 Beta-Epoxypregnane-3,20-dione	3,153,646	1964 Oct 20
Julian, Percy L., et al.	Process for Preparing Compound "S"	3,187,025	1965 Jun 1
Julian, Percy L., et al.	Preparing 16 Alpha-Methyl Corticoids	3,231,568	1966 Jan 25
Julian, Percy L., et al.	Method for Preparing 16Alpha-Hydroxypregnenes	3,274,178	1966 Sep 20
Julian, Percy L.	Composition with Low Cholesterol Content	3,711,611	1973 Jan 16
Julian, Percy L., et al.	Process for Introducing a Delta 5,6-Double Bond into a Steroid	3,759,899	1973 Sep 18
Julian, Percy L.	Process for Manufacture of Steroid Chlorohyd=ins	3,761,469	1973 Sep 25

(Continued)

Name	Invention	Number	Issue Date
Julian, Percy L.	Process for Conversion of a 3-Hydroxy-5,6-Oxido Group of a Steroid	3,784,598	1974 Jan 8
Julian, Percy L.	Preparation, Wool Wax Alcohol of Low Cholesterol Content	3,821,121	1974 Jun 28
Julien, Leonard	Cane Planter	3,286,858	1966 Nov 22
Keelan, Harry Sanderson	Colloidal Silver Iodide Compound and Method	1,783,334	1930 Dec 2
Kelley, George W.	Steam Table	592,291	1897 Oct 26
Kelly, Kenneth C.	Linearly Polarized Monopulse Lobing Antenna	3,063,049	1962 Nov 6
Kelly, Lawrence Randolph	Automaic Telephone Alarm Apparatus	3,505,476	1970 Apr 7
Kelly, Lawrence Randolph	Programmable External Dial Operating Device	3,505,483	1970 Apr 7
Kenner, Mary Beatrice	Sanitary Belt	2,745,406	1956 May 15
Kenner, Mary Beatrice	Sanitary Belt with Moisture Proof Pocket`	2,881,761	1959 Apr 14
Kenner, Mary Beatrice	Carrier Attachment for Invalid Walkers	3,957,071	1976 May 18
Kenner, Mary Beatrice	Bathroom Tissue Holder	4,354,643	1982 Oct 19
Kenner, Mary Beatrice	Shower Wall and Bathtub Mounted Back Washer	4,696,068	1987 Sep 29
King, James	Combination Cotton Thinning and Cultivating Machine	1,661,122	1928 Feb 28
King, John G.	Power Line Sensing Appliance Theft Alarm	3,289,194	1966 Nov 29
Knox, Lawrence Howland	Production of Arecoline	2,506,458	1950 May 2
Knox, Lawrence Howland	Photochemical Preparation of Tropilidenes	2,647,081	1953 Jul 28
Knox, William Jacob Jr.	Coating Aids for Gelatin Compositions	3,038,804	1962 Jun 12
Knox, William Jacob Jr.	Gelatin Coating Compositions	3,306,749	1967 Feb 28

Name	Title	Number	Date
Knox, William Jacob Jr.	Coating Aids for Hydrophilic Colloid Layers	3,539,352	1970 Nov 10
Kornegay, Kevin T.	Low-voltage, Low-power Transimpedance Amplifier Architecture	7,042,295	2006 May 9
Lancaster, Cleo, et al.	Cytoprotective Use of Oxamate Derivatives	4,439,445	1984 Mar 27
Lancaster, Cleo, et al.	Method of Preventing Pancreatitis	4,891,382	1990 Jan 2
Latimer, Lewis Howard, et al.	Water Closets for Railway Cars	147,363	1874 Feb 10
Latimer, Lewis Howard, et al.	Electric Lamp	247,097	1881 Sep 13
Latimer, Lewis Howard	Manufacturing Carbons	252,386	1882 Jan 17
Latimer, Lewis Howard, et al.	Globe Support for Electric Lamps	255,212	1882 Mar 21
Latimer, Lewis Howard	Apparatus for Cooling and Disinfecting	334,078	1886 Jan 12
Latimer, Lewis Howard	Locking Racks for Coats, Hats, and Umbrellas	557,076	1896 Mar 24
Latimer, Lewis Howard	Book Support	781,890	1905 Feb 7
Latimer, Lewis Howard	Lamp Fixture	968,787	1910 Aug 10
Lavalette, William A.	Improvement in Printing Presses	208,184	1878 Sep 17
Lavalette, William A.	Printing Press	208,208	1878 Sep 17
Law, Kirk A., et al.	Hanging Dot Reduction System	4,616,254	1986 Oct 7
Law, Kirk A., et al.	Ditigal Correlation Indicator and Hanging Dot Reduction System	4,618,882	1986 Oct 21
Law, Kirk A., et al.	Duration-Sensitive Digital Signal Gate	4,634,984	1987 Jan 6
Law, Kirk A., et al.	Image Transistor Detector	4,656,501	1987 Apr 7
Law, Kirk A., et al.	Vertical Transition Processor for a Comb Filter	4,694,331	1987 Sep 15

(*Continued*)

Name	Invention	Number	Issue Date
Lawrence, Victor B., et al.	Object Area Network	6,812,840	2004 Nov 2
Lawrence, Victor B., et al.	Wireless Guidance System	6,830,213	2004 Dec 14
Lee, Arthur	Self-Propelled Toy Fish	2,065,337	1936 Dec 22
Lee, Henry	Improvement in Animal Traps	61,941	1867 Feb 12
Lee, Joseph	Kneading Machine	524,042	1894 Aug 7
Lee, Joseph	Bread Crumbling Machine	540,553	1895 Jun 4
Lee, Lester A.	Gas Dynamic-Transfer Chemical Laser	3,970,955	1976 Jul 20
Lee, Lester A.	Carbon Dioxide Laser Fuels	4,011,116	1977 Mar 8
Lee, Maurice William Sr.	Aromatic Pressure Cooker and Smoker	2,906,191	1959 Sep 29
Lee, Robert	Safety Attachment for Automotive Vehicles	2,132,304	1938 Oct 4
Leeo, Sterling	Railway Track Construction	1,054,852	1913 Mar 4
Leonard, Herbert Jr., et al.	Production of Hydroxylamine Hydrochloride	3,119,657	1964 Jan 28
Leonard, Herbert Jr., et al.	High Impact Polystyrene	3,586,740	1971 Jun 22
Leslie, Frank W.	Envelope Seal	590,325	1897 Sep 21
Letton, Alan, et al.	Polyether-Polycarbonate-Polyether Triblock Copolymers	4,812,530	1989 Mar 14
Letton, Alan, et al.	Crystallization Agent for Bisphenol-A-Polycarbonate	5,248,756	1993 Sep 28
Letton, Alan, et al.	Composition Containing Novel Modifier	6,214,908	2001 Apr 10
Letton, Alan, et al.	Composition Containing Novel Modifier	6,414,066	2002 Jul 2
Letton, James C.	Biodegradable Cationic Surface-Active Agents	4,228,042	1980 Oct 14
Letton, James C.	Detergent Composition	4,260,529	1981 Apr 7

Letton, James C.	Stabilized Aqueous Enzyme Composition	4,318,818	1982 Mar 9
Letton, James C.	Process for Preparing Alkyl Glycosides	4,713,447	1987 Dec 15
Letton, James C., et al.	Compositions Containing Solid, Nondigestible Compounds	4,797,300	1989 Jan 10
Letton, James C., et al.	Improved Margarine Composition	5,017,398	1991 May 21
Letton, James C., et al.	Reduced Calorie Potato Chips	5,085,884	1992 Feb 4
Letton, James C., et al.	Preparation of Mono-Condensation Derivatives	5,286,879	1994 Feb 15
Letton, James C., et al.	Solid, Nondigestible, Fat-like Compound and Food Compositions	5,306,514	1994 Apr 26
Letton, James C., et al.	Reduced Calorie Pourable Shortening, Cooking Oils	5,306,515	1994 Apr 26
Letton, James C., et al	Shortening Compositions Containing Polyol Polyesters	5,306,516	1994 Apr 26
Letton, James C.	Synthesis of Sulfated Polyhydroxy Fatty Acid Amide Sufactants	5,312,934	1994 May 17
LeVert, Francis Edward	Threshold Self-Powered Gamma Detector	4,091,288	1978 May 23
LeVert, Francis Edward	Monitor for Deposition on Heat Transfer Surfaces	4,722,610	1988 Feb 2
LeVert, Francis Edward	Continuous Fluid Level Detector	4,805,454	1989 Feb 21
Lewis, Anthony L.	Window Cleaner	483,359	1892 Sep 27
Lewis, Charles W.	Plant Supporting	4,318,247	1982 Mar 9
Lewis, Edward R.	Spring Gun	362,096	1887 May 3
Lewis, James Earl	Antenna Feed for Two Coordinate Tracking Radars	3,388,399	1968 Jun 11
Linden, Henry	Piano Truck	459,365	1891 Sep 8
Little, Ellis	Bridle Bit	254,666	1882 Mar 7

(Continued)

Name	Invention	Number	Issue Date
Loftman, Kenneth A.	Drying Agent and Process of Making	2,774,651	1956 Dec 18
Loftman, Kenneth A.	Aqueous Dispersion of Pyrogenic Silica	2,984,629	1961 May 16
Logan, Emanuel L. Jr.	Door Bar Latch	3,592,497	1971 Jul 13
Logan, Emanuel L. Jr.	Magnetic Emergency Exit Door Lock	4,257,631	1981 Mar 24
Logan, Emanuel L. Jr.	Timing Apparatus for Delaying Opening of Doors	4,314,722	1982 Feb 9
Logan, Emanuel L. Jr.	Point-of-Egress Control Device	4,324,425	1982 Apr 13
Logan, Emanuel L. Jr.	Retrofitted Point-of-Egress Control Device	4,354,699	1982 Oct 19
Logan, Emanuel L. Jr., et al.	Emergency Exit Sign Utilizing Electroluminescent Lamp	4,466,208	1984 Aug 21
Logan, Emanuel L. Jr., et al.	Emergency Exit Door Latch	4,470,625	1984 Sep 11
Logan, Emanuel L. Jr., et al.	Emergency Exit Indicators	4,489,308	1984 Dec 18
Logan, Emanuel L. Jr., et al.	Point-of-Egress Control Device	4,540,208	1985 Sep 10
Logan, Emanuel L. Jr.	Apparatus for Securing a Pivoted Member	4,651,358	1987 Mar 24
Long, Amos E., et al.	Caps for Bottle, Jars, etc.	610,715	1898 Sep 13
Loudin, Frederick J.	Sash Fastener	510,432	1893 Dec 12
Loudin, Frederick J.	Key Fastener	512,308	1894 Jan 9
Love, John Lee	Plasterer's Hawk	542,419	1895 Jul 9
Love, John Lee	Pencil Sharpener	594,114	1879 Nov 23
Love, Natalie R.	T-Top Roof Cover	5,110,178	1992 May 5
Love, Samuel D.	Fireplace Draft Adapter	4,399,806	1983 Aug 23
Love, Samuel D.	Fireplace Grate Adapter	4,429,681	1984 Feb 7

Name	Invention	Patent No.	Date
Lovelady, Herbert G.	Sound Emitting Bobber	Des314,417	1991 Feb 5
Lovell, Henry R.	Door Check	Des87,753	1932 Sep 13
Lovett, William E.	Motor Fuel Composition	3,054,666	1962 Sep 18
LuValle, James E.	Photographic Process	3,219,445	1965 Nov 23
LuValle, James E.	Sensitizing Photographic Media	3,219,451	1965 Nov 23
Lyons, Arthur W.	Oil Stove	1,730,224	1929 Oct 1
Lyons, Donald R.	Methods and Apparatus for Calibrating Gratings	5,552,882	1996 Sep 3
MacDonald, Hugh D., Jr., et al.	Rocket Catapult	3,447,767	1969 Jun 3
Mack, John Leslie	Participant Identification Recording and Playback System	4,596,041	1986 Jun 17
Madison, Shannon L.	Refrigeration Apparatus	3,208,232	1965 Sep 28
Madison, Shannon L.	Electrical Wiring Harness Termination System	4,793,820	1988 Dec 27
Madison, Walter G.	Flying Machine	1,047,098	1912 Dec 10
Madison, Walter G.	Adjustable Radiation Bracket	1,867,854	1932 Jul 19
Magee, Charles	Hand Table and Carrying Rack	5,104,168	1992 Apr 14
Majors, Walter L.	Coin Controlled Taxicab Controller	1,069,558	1913 Aug 5
Majors, Walter L.	Heater for Water Cooling Apparatus of Motor Vehicles	1,121,266	1914 Dec 15
Majors, Walter L.	Hair Drier	1,124,235	1915 Jan 5
Majors, Walter L.	Motor Controlling Device for Taxicabs and the Like	1,123,906	1915 Jan 5
Majors, Walter L.	Oil Stove	1,331,162	1920 Feb 17
Majors, Walter L.	Antiskid Device	1,422,285	1922 Jul 11
Majors, Walter L.	Machine for the Treatment of the Scalp and Hair	1,466,629	1923 Aug 28

(Continued)

Name	Invention	Number	Issue Date
Majors, Walter L.	Carburetor Auxiliary or Substitute	1,596,885	1926 Aug 24
Majors, Walter L.	Heating Apparatus	1,783,576	1930 Dec 2
Mallette, Kermit J.	Sensitive Condom	5,284,158	1994 Feb 8
Malone, Annie Minerva	Sealing Tape	Des60,962	1922 May 16
Maloney, Kenneth Morgan	Alumina Coating for Electric Lamp	3,868,266	1975 Feb 25
Maloney, Kenneth Morgan	Alumina Coating for Mercury Vapor Lamps	4,079,288	1978 Mar 14
Mangin, Anna	Pastry Fork	470,005	1892 Mar 1
Mapp, Calvin R.	Disposable Syringe	4,033,347	1977 Jul 5
Marshall, James E.	Flying Machine	1,038,168	1912 Sep 10
Marshall, Randall S.	Articles for Cooling Beverages	4,554,189	1985 Nov 19
Marshall, Randall S.	Articles for Cooling Beverages	4,761,314	1988 Aug 2
Marshall, Willis	Grain Binder	341,589	1886 May 11
Martin, Thomas J.	Fire Extinguisher	125,063	1872 Mar 26
Martin, Washington A.	Lock	407,738	1889 Jul 23
Martin, Washington A.	Lock	443,945	1890 Dec 30
Massie, Samuel P., et al.	2-Acetyl Quinoline Thiosemicarbazones	4,440,771	1984 Apr 3
Mathis, John Harrison, et al.	Automatic Stovepipe Damper	710,901	1902 Oct 7
Mathis, Nathaniel	Barber's Apron	Des327,022	1975 Oct 7
Matthews, James Elmer	Shear Guide	1,195,249	1916 Aug 22
Matthews, James Elmer	Padlock Guard	1,291,993	1919 Jan 21

Name	Invention	Patent Number	Date
Matthews, James Elmer	Sled	1,437,815	1922 Dec 5
Matthews, James Elmer	Bassinet Cradle	1,526,802	1925 Feb 17
Matthews, Virgil E.	Process for the Production of Dialkali	3,026,352	1962 Mar 20
Matthews, Virgil E.	Novel Fuel Compositions	3,365,338	1968 Jan 23
Matzeliger, Jan Earnst	Lasting Machine	274,207	1883 Mar 20
Matzeliger, Jan Earnst	Mechanism for Distributing Tacks, Nails	415,726	1889 Nov 26
Matzeliger, Jan Earnst	Nailing Machine	421,954	1890 Feb 25
Matzeliger, Jan Earnst	Tack Separating and Distributing Mechanism	432,937	1890 Mar 25
Matzeliger, Jan Earnst	Lasting Machine	459,899	1891 Sep 22
May, Edgar H.	Carpet-Cutting Machine	1,096,733	1914 May 12
Mayle, Eugene Edwin Jr.	Optical Transmitting and Receiving Apparatus	4,885,804	1989 Dec 5
Mayle, Eugene Edwin Jr., et al.	Radio Frequency Tag System	6,100,840	2000 Aug 8
Mayle, Eugene Edwin Jr., et al.	Secure Storage Disc and Disc Surveillance System	6,946,946	2005 Sep 20
Mays, Alfred T., et al.	Patterned Densified Fabric Comprising Conjugate Fiber	4,774,124	1988 Sep 27
Mays, Alfred T., et al.	Method and Apparatus for Patterned Belt Bonded Material	4,787,947	1988 Nov 29
McClennan, Walter N.	Automatic Railway Car	1,333,430	1920 Mar 9
McClennan, Walter N.	Car Door Actuating Mechanism	Re.15,388	1922 Apr 18
McClennan, Walter N.	Coin Mechanism	1,518,208	1924 Dec 9
McCoy, Admiral H., et al.	Torpedo Arrester or Insulator	2,348,094	1944 May 2
McCoy, Elijah	Lubricator for Steam Engines	129,843	1872 Jul 23
McCoy, Elijah	Lubricator for Steam Engines	130,305	1872 Aug 6

(Continued)

Name	Invention	Number	Issue Date
McCoy, Elijah	Lubricator	139,407	1873 May 27
McCoy, Elijah	Steam Lubricator	146,697	1874 Jan 20
McCoy, Elijah	Ironing Table	150,876	1874 May 12
McCoy, Elijah	Steam Cylinder Lubricator	173,032	1876 Feb 1
McCoy, Elijah	Steam Cylinder Lubricator	179,585	1876 Jul 4
McCoy, Elijah	Lubricator	255,443	1882 Mar 28
McCoy, Elijah	Lubricator	261,166	1882 Jul 18
McCoy, Elijah	Lubricator	270,238	1883 Jan 9
McCoy, Elijah	Steam Dome	320,354	1885 Jun 16
McCoy, Elijah	Lubricator	320,379	1885 Jun 16
McCoy, Elijah	Lubricator	357,491	1887 Feb 8
McCoy, Elijah	Lubricator Attachment	361,435	1887 Apr 19
McCoy, Elijah	Lubricator for Safety Valves	363,529	1887 May 24
McCoy, Elijah	Lubricator	383,746	1888 May 29
McCoy, Elijah, et al.	Lubricator	418,139	1889 Dec 24
McCoy, Elijah	Drip Cup	460,215	1891 Sep 29
McCoy, Elijah	Lubricator	465,875	1891 Dec 29
McCoy, Elijah	Lubricator	472,066	1892 Apr 5
McCoy, Elijah	Lubricator	610,634	1898 Sep 13
McCoy, Elijah	Lubricator	611,759	1898 Oct 4

McCoy, Elijah	Oil Cup	614,307	1898 Nov 15
McCoy, Elijah	Lubricator	627,623	1899 Jun 27
McCoy, Elijah	Lubricator	646,126	1900 Mar 27
McCoy, Elijah	Lubricator	663,976	1900 Dec 18
McCoy, Elijah	Journal Lubricator	783,382	1905 Feb 21
McCoy, Elijah	Scaffold Support	856,084	1907 Jun 4
McCoy, Elijah	Lubricator	890,295	1908 Jun 9
McCoy, Elijah	Lubricator	890,787	1908 Jun 16
McCoy, Elijah	Lubricator	903,306	1908 Nov 10
McCoy, Elijah	Lubricator	911,669	1909 Feb 9
McCoy, Elijah	Gauge	1,021,255	1912 Mar 25
McCoy, Elijah	Lubricator	1,031,948	1912 Jul 9
McCoy, Elijah	Locomotive Lubricator	1,097,134	1914 May 19
McCoy, Elijah	Valve and Plug Cock	1,101,868	1914 Jun 30
McCoy, Elijah	Tread for Tires	1,127,789	1915 Feb 9
McCoy, Elijah	Locomotive Lubricator	1,136,689	1915 Apr 20
McCoy, Elijah	Lubricator	1,192,983	1916 Jul 25
McCoy, Elijah	Air-Brake Pump Lubricator	1,338,385	1920 Apr 27
McCoy, Elijah	Lubricator	1,499,468	1924 Jul 1
McCoy, Elijah	Lubricator	1,558,266	1925 Oct 20
McCoy, Elijah	Lubricator	1,574,983	1926 Mar 2

(Continued)

Name	Invention	Number	Issue Date
McCoy, Elijah	Rubber Heel	Des68,725	1976 Nov 10
McCoy, Melvin	Multi-purpose Uniaxial Litter Enginery or M.U.L.E.	4,664,395	1987 May 12
McCree, Daniel	Portable Fire Escape	440,322	1890 Nov 11
McCulley, DeWayne L., et al.	Plural Mode Printer User Interface Terminal	5,038,169	1991 Aug 6
McCulley, DeWayne L., et al.	Facilitation of the Diagnosis of Malfunctions and Set-up of a Reproduction Machine	5,202,726	1993 Apr 13
McDonald, Peter	Pneumatic Tire	3,610,308	1971 Oct 5
McDonald, Peter	All-Season Pneumatic Tire Tread	4,278,121	1981 Jul 14
McDonald, Peter	Addition Members for Rubber Articles	4,317,479	1982 Mar 2
McDonald, Peter	Unified Modular Indicia Marking for Rubber Articles	4,343,342	1982 Aug 10
McDonald, Peter	Tire	Des270,723	1983 Sep 27
McDonald, Peter	Tire	Des278,228	1985 Apr 2
McElhaney, Vincent	Electrical Probe and Method	5,512,835	1996 Apr 30
McGee, Hansel L.	Method of Preparation of Carbon Transfer Inks	3,214,282	1965 Oct 26
McGuire, Lynn	Self-Contained Viscera Treatment Unit	5,093,969	1992 Mar 10
McIlwain, Ivy	Rat Trap	3,872,619	1975 Mar 25
McKindra, Clayton D., et al.	Aircraft Rocket Firing System	3,712,170	1973 Jan 23
McKnight, Alfred	Compressed Air Device	984,512	1911 Feb 14
McLurkin, James	System and Methods for Adaptive Control of Robotic Devices	7,117,067	2006 Oct 3
McLurkin, James	System and Methods for Adaptive Control of Robotic Devices	7,254,464	2007 Aug 7

Name	Title	Number	Date
McNair, Luther	Sanitary Mouth Attachment	1,034,636	1912 Aug 6
McWhorter, John E.	Flying Machine	1,114,167	1914 Oct 20
McWorter, Solomon	Improvement in Evaporators for Sorghum and Other Syrups	70,451	1867 Nov 5
Mendenhall, Albert	Holder for Driving Reins	637,811	1899 Nov 28
Mensah, Thomas O.	Method and Apparatus for Coating Optical Fibers	4,531,959	1985 Jul 30
Mensah, Thomas O.	Curing Apparatus for Coated Fiber	4,636,405	1987 Jan 13
Mensah, Thomas O.	Apparatus for Monitoring Tension in a Moving Fiber by Fourier Transform Analysis	4,692,615	1987 Sep 8
Mensah, Thomas O.	Method for Coating Optical Waveguide Fiber	4,792,347	1988 Dec 20
Mensah, Thomas O.	Optical Fiber Package and Methods	4,955,688	1990 Sep 11
Mensah, Thomas O.	Guided Vehicle System	5,035,169	1991 Jul 30
Mensah, Thomas O.	Methods of Providing an Optical Fiber	5,065,490	1991 Dec 12
Meredith, Deanna R.	Skateboard	4,458,907	1984 Jul 10
Merrill, Samuel Jr., et al.	Autopsy Apparatus	5,160,340	1992 Nov 3
Miles, Alexander	Elevator	371,207	1887 Oct 11
Miley, George H.	Plasma Pumped Laser	3,886,483	1975 May 27
Miley, George H.	Electrical Cell, Components and Methods	7,244,887	2007 Jul 17
Millington, James E.	Thermostable Dielectric Material	3,316,178	1967 Apr 25
Millington, James E.	Method of Making Expandable Styrene-type Beads	4,286,069	1981 Aug 25
Millington, James E.	Method of Making Styrene-type Polymer	4,730,027	1988 Mar 8
Mitchell, Charles Lewis	Device for Aid in Vocal Culture	291,071	1884 Jan 1

(Continued)

Name	Invention	Number	Issue Date
Mitchell, James M.	Check Row Corn Planter	641,462	1900 Jan 16
Mitchell, James Winfield, et al.	Deposition of Diamond Films	5,128,006	1992 Jul 7
Mitchell, James Winfield, et al.	Method of Growing Continuous Diamond Films	5,441,013	1995 Aug 15
Mitchell, James Winfield, et al.	Process and Apparatus for Generating Precursor Gases	5,474,659	1995 Dec 12
Mitchell, Maxwell R.	Compact Record of Human-Readable Data	5,309,655	1994 May 10
Mitchell, Roger E., et al.	Total Therapy Sauna Bed System	5,645,578	1997 Jul 8
Mitchell, Roger E., et al.	Physical Therapy Heated Personal Capsule	5,891,186	1999 Apr 6
Molaire, Michel F.	Binder Mixture/Optical Recording Layer and Elements	4,626,361	1986 Dec 2
Molaire, Michel F., et al.	Photoelectrographic Elements and Imaging Method	4,661,429	1987 Apr 29
Moliare, Michel F., et al.	Nonpolymeric Amorphous Developer Compositions	5,176,977	1993 Jan 5
Moliare, Michel F., et al.	Photoelectric Elements	5,204,198	1993 Apr 20
Moliare, Michel F., et al.	Photoconductive Element and Method	5,240,802	1993 Aug 31
Montgomery, Burgess T.	Book or Copy Holder	664,664	1900 Dec 25
Montgomery, Burgess T.	Shield for Collars and Cuffs	797,791	1905 Aug 22
Montgomery, Jay H., et al.	Food Product and Process of Producing	1,694,680	1928 Dec 11
Montgomery, Jay H.	Aeroplane Aerofoil Wing	1,910,626	1933 May 23
Montgomery, Leon M.	Headlight Lens	1,797,012	1931 Mar 17
Moody, William U.	Game Board	Des27,046	1897 May 11
Moore, Ann A.	Infant Carrier	Des277,811	1985 Mar 5
Moore, Charles C.	Toilet	1,439,748	1922 Dec 26

Moore, Mary Ann	Pain Relief Composition and Method of Preparing	4,177,266	1979 Dec 4
Moore, Milton Donald Jr.	Accident Reconstruction Device	4,524,602	1985 Jun 25
Moore, Milton Donald Jr.	Shaving Tool	4,709,481	1987 Dec 1
Moore, Milton Donald Jr.	Shaving Preparation for Treatment and Prevention of PFB (Ingrown Hairs)	4,944,939	1990 Jul 31
Moore, Milton Donald Jr.	1,2-Propylene Glycol Shaving Solution and Method of Use Thereof	5,387,412	1995 Feb 7
Moore, Milton Donald Jr.	1,2-Propylene Glycol Skin Preparation Solution and Method of Use Thereof	6,861,051	2005 Mar 1
Moore, Roy J.	Clamp Arrangement for Track Lifting and Aligning	4,565,133	1986 Jan 21
Moore, Roy J., et al.	Split Workhead	4,899,664	1990 Feb 13
Moore, Roy J., et al.	Split Tool Mechanism Vibrator	5,584,248	1996 Dec 17
Moore, Samuel	Self-Directing Headlight	1,608,903	1926 Nov 30
Moore, Samuel	Vehicle Headlight Mechanism	1,658,534	1928 Feb 7
Moore, Samuel	Locomotive Headlight	1,659,328	1928 Feb 14
Moore, Samuel	Hobby Horse	1,705,991	1929 Mar 19
Moore, Samuel	Fuel Valve Lock for Motor Vehicles	2,006,027	1935 Jun 25
Morehead, King	Reel Carrier	568,916	1896 Oct 6
Morgan, Garrett A. Sr.	Breathing Device	1,090,936	1914 Mar 24
Morgan, Garrett A. Sr.	Breathing Device	1,113,675	1914 Oct 13
Morgan, Garrett A. Sr.	Traffic Signal	1,475,024	1923 Nov 23
Morgan, Garrett A. Sr.	De-Curling Comb	2,762,382	1956 Sep 11

(Continued)

Name	Invention	Number	Issue Date
Morgan, Jerome	Mechanism Display Device	4,070,973	1978 Jan 31
Morgan, Robert W.	Body Incision Closure	3,568,276	1971 Mar 9
Morris, Joel Morton	Switching System Charging Arrangement	3,688,047	1972 Aug 29
Moses, Dennis	Automotive Grille	Des539,194	2007 Mar 27
Moses, John Ridgley Sr. et al.	Lubricating Oil Filter	4,272,371	1981 Jun 9
Moses, John Ridgley Sr.	Flat Emergency Exit Sign	4,420,898	1983 Dec 20
Moses, Robert P.	Games for Enhancing Mathematical Understanding	5,520,542	1996 May 28
Muckelroy, William L., et al.	Leadless Microminiature Inductance Element	3,691,497	1972 Sep 12
Muckelroy, William L., et al.	Ceramic Inductor	3,812,442	1974 May 21
Muckelroy, William L.	Microminiature Monolithic Ferroceramic Transformer	3,833,872	1974 Sep 3
Muckelroy, William L.	Handling Beam-Lead and Odd-Shaped Semiconductor Devices	3,731,377	1973 May 8
Muckelroy, William L.	Microminiature Leadless Inductance Element	3,585,553	1971 Jun 15
Muckelroy, William L.	Sintering Thick-Film Oxidizable Silk-screened Circuitry	3,726,006	1973 Apr 10
Muckelroy, William L., et al.	Three Dimensional Circuit Modules	3,755,891	1973 Sep 4
Mullen, Nathaniel John	Asphalt Paving Vehicles	3,880,542	1975 Apr 29
Murdock, Wilbert	Knee Alignment Monitoring Apparatus	4,608,998	1986 Sep 2
Murray, George Washington	Combined Furrow Opener and Stalk Knocker	517,960	1894 Apr 10
Murray, George Washington	Cultivator and Marker	517,961	1894 Apr 10
Murray, George Washington	Planter	520,887	1894 Jun 5
Murray, George Washington	Cotton Chopper	520,888	1894 Jun 5

Name	Title	Number	Date
Murray, George Washington	Fertilizer Distributor	520,889	1894 Jun 5
Murray, George Washington	Planter	520,890	1894 Jun 5
Murray, George Washington	Combined Cotton Seed Planter and Fertilizer Distributor	520,891	1894 Jun 5
Murray, George Washington	Planter and Fertilizer Distributor Reaper	520,892	1894 Jun 5
Murray, William	Attachment for Bicycles	445,452	1891 Jan 27
Myles, Jacquelyn	Swimwear	Des259,821	1981 Jul 14
Myles, Jacquelyn	Swimwear	Des275,476	1985 Apr 23
Myles, Jacquelyn	Swimwear	Des278,472	1985 Apr 23
Myles, Jacquelyn	Swimwear	Des278,473	1985 Apr 23
Myles, Jacquelyn	Swimwear	Des278,474	1985 Apr 23
Myles, Jacquelyn	Swimwear	Des278,475	1985 Apr 23
Myles, Jacquelyn	Swimwear	Des278,476	1985 Apr 23
Myles, Jacquelyn	Swimwear	Des278,568	1985 Apr 30
Myles, Jacquelyn	Swimwear	Des278,569	1985 Apr 30
Myles, Jacquelyn	Swimwear	Des279,936	1985 Aug 6
Myles, Jacquelyn	Swimwear	Des280,252	1985 Aug 27
Myles, Jacquelyn	Swimwear	Des282,116	1986 Jan 14
Nance, Lee	Game Apparatus	464,035	1891 Dec 1
Napier, Dennis K.	Earth Splitter	5,109,930	1992 May 5
Nash, Henry H.	Improvement in Life Preserving Stools	168,519	1875 Oct 5
Nauflette, George W.	Synthesis of 2-Fluoro-2,2-Dinitroethanol	3,652,686	1972 Mar 28

(Continued)

Name	Invention	Number	Issue Date
Nauflette, George W., et al.	Plasticizer for Nitropolymers	4,457,791	1984 Jul 3
Nauflette, George W., et al.	Preparation of 2,24-Dinitro-2,4-Diazapentane	4,469,888	1984 Sep 4
Neal, Lonnie George	Electromagnetic Gyroscope Float Assembly	3,475,795	1969 Nov 4
Neal, Theophilus Ealey	Automatic Blow-off	1,885,466	1932 Nov 1
Neal, Theophilus Ealey	Shower Bath Spray	1,893,435	1933 Jan 3
Neblett, Richard Flemon	Gasoline Composition	2,955,928	1960 Oct 11
Neblett, Richard Flemon	Motor Fuel Composition	3,054,666	1962 Sep 18
Neblett, Richard Flemon	Oil-Soluble Ashless Dispersant-Detergent-Inhibitors	3,511,780	1970 May 12
Newell, Florine, et al.	Hair Relaxer Cream	4,950,485	1990 Aug 21
Newell, Florine, et al.	Hair Relaxer Cream	5,068,101	1991 Nov 29
Newell, Florine, et al.	Conditioning Hair Relaxer System with Conditioning Activator	5,077,042	1991 Dec 31
Newell, Florine, et al.	Hair Relaxer Cream	5,171,565	1992 Dec 15
Newman, Lyda D.	Brush	614,335	1898 Nov 15
Newson, Simeon	Oil Heater or Cooker	520,188	1894 May 22
Nicholson, Jerome	Bags	5,913,606	1999 Jun 22
Nicholson, Jerome	Toothpick Holder	6,076,658	2000 Jun 20
Nicholson, Jerome	Mini-Blind/Curtain Rod Bracket	6,382,295	2002 May 7
Nickerson, William J.	Mandolin and Guitar Attachment for Pianos	627,739	1899 Jun 27
Nichols, Barbara A., et al.	Information Repository for Storing Information for Enterprise Computing System	5,727,158	1998 Mar 10

Name	Title	Number	Date
Nicol, Evelyn C.	Urokinase Production	3,930,944	1976 Jan 6
Nix, Ceoma	Mobility Aid	4,451,080	1984 May 29
Nokes, Clarence David	Venetian Blind Restringer	2,836,882	1958 Jun 3
Nokes, Clarence David	Lawn Mower	3,077,066	1963 Feb 12
Nokes, Clarence David	Programmed Steering Means for Moving Apparatus	3,650,097	1972 Mar 21
Nokes, Clarence David	Lawn Mower Apparatus	4,354,339	1982 Oct 19
Nokes, Clarence David	Snap-off Key	4,402,201	1983 Sep 6
Norfleet, George	Model Building	6,073,404	2000 Jun 13
Norwood, James P.	Bread Wrapping, Labeling, and Sealing Machine	1,191,029	1916 Jul 11
Nwoko, Luck	Enhanced Speed Lacing Device	4,916,833	1990 Apr 17
Nwoko, Luck	Hook-Type Speed Fastening Device	4,970,763	1990 Nov 20
Nwoko, Luck	Spring Actuated Fastening Device	5,050,915	1991 Sep 24
Oliphant, Adam L.	Portable Cooking Grill	4,646,711	1987 Mar 3
Oliphant, Adam L.	Portable Barbeque Grill Assembly	4,878,476	1989 Nov 7
Oliphant, Adam L.	Portable Grill	Des301,106	1989 May 16
Oliver, Lee Grant	Auto Accessories	4,915,274	1990 Apr 10
Okonkwo, Chidi	Modern Sports Car Body	Des484,440	2003 Dec 30
Okonkwo, Chidi	Luxury Vehicle Body	Des491,107	2004 Jun 8
Omohundro, Robert Johnson, et al.	Scintillation Counter	3,087,060	1963 Apr 23
Omohundro, Robert Johnson, et al.	Selective Detector for Fission Neutrons	3,612,872	1971 Oct 12
Onley, John H.	Method and Apparatus for Removal of Carbon Monoxide	4,464,349	1984 Aug 7

(Continued)

Name	Invention	Number	Issue Date
Outlaw, John W.	Horse Shoes	614,273	1898 Nov 15
Ozanne, Leroy	Wall Panel	4,037,379	1977 Jul 26
Ozanne, Leroy, et al.	Composite Building Panel	5,265,389	1993 Nov 30
Ozanne, Leroy	Wall Panel Construction	5,566,523	1996 Oct 22
Overstreet, Tannis L.	Security Mail Receptacle	5,071,063	1991 Dec 10
Page, Lionel F.	Auxilliary Circulating Device for Automobile Heaters	2,170,032	1939 Aug 22
Parker, Alice H.	Heating Furnace	1,325,905	1919 Dec 23
Parker, Alonzo E. Jr.	Passive Exercising Apparatus	4,723,537	1988 Feb 9
Parker, Alonzo E. Jr.	Passive Exercising Apparatus	4,827,913	1989 May 9
Parker, Alonzo E. Jr.	Oscillating Reclining Chair	4,860,733	1989 Aug 29
Parker, Denson	Fluid Velocity Actuated Structure for a Wind Mill/Water Wheel	4,276,481	1981 Jun 30
Parker, Denson	Centrifugal Force Magnetic Field Variator	5,053,659	1991 Oct 1
Parker, George A.	Multipurpose Light Duty Garden Tool	4,334,583	1982 Jun 15
Parker, John Percial	Follower-Screw for Tobacco Presses	304,552	1884 Sep 2
Parker, John Percial	Portable Screw Press	318,285	1885 May 19
Parker, Joseph F.	Apparatus for Printing and Delivering Transfer Slips	1,113,783	1914 Oct 13
Parker, Joseph F.	Means for Securing License Tags to Vehicles	1,358,872	1920 Nov 16
Parsons, James A. Jr.	Iron Alloy	1,728,360	1929 Sep 17
Parsons, James A. Jr.	Method of Making Silicon Iron Compounds	1,819,479	1931 Aug 18

Parsons, James A. Jr.	Process for Treating Silicon Alloy Castings	1,972,103	1934 Sep 4
Parsons, James A. Jr.	Corrosion Resisting Ferrous Alloys	2,134,670	1938 Oct 25
Parsons, James A. Jr.	Corrosion Resisting Ferrous Alloys	2,185,987	1940 Jan 2
Parsons, James A. Jr.	Corrosion Resisting Ferrous Alloys	2,200,208	1940 May 7
Parsons, James A. Jr.	Cementation Process of Treating Metal	2,318,011	1943 May 4
Parsons, James A. Jr.	Nickel Base Alloy	2,467,288	1949 Apr 12
Payne, Moses	Horseshoe	394,388	1888 Dec 11
Pelham, Robert	Pasting Apparatus	807,685	1905 Dec 19
Perry, George W.	Sleeve Sports	4,985,934	1991 Jan 22
Perry, John Jr., et al.	Biochemical Fuel Cell	3,284,239	1966 Nov 8
Perry, John Jr.	Method of Making Fuel Cell Electrode and Fuel Cell	3,464,862	1969 Sep 2
Perry, John Jr.	Fuel Cell Anode Electrode, Method of Making and Fuel Cell	4,141,801	1979 Feb 27
Perryman, Frank R.	Caterers' Tray Table	468,038	1892 Feb 2
Peterson, Charles A. Jr.	Power Generating Apparatus	3,391,903	1968 Jul 9
Peterson, Charles A. Jr.	Method and Apparatus for Generating Power by Sea Wave Action	4,086,775	1978 May 2
Peterson, Henry	Attachment for Lawn Mowers	402,189	1889 Apr 30
Pettigrew, Roderic I., et al.	Flow-induced Artifact Elimination in Magnetic Resonance Images	5,438,992	1995 Aug 8
Petty, Claudius M.	Aeroplane	1,561,108	1925 Nov 10
Petty, Claudius M.	Convenient Union-alls	1,737,803	1929 Dec 3

(Continued)

Name	Invention	Number	Issue Date
Phelps, William Henry	Apparatus for Washing Vehicles	579,242	1897 Mar 23
Philips, Raymond P.	Radiotelephone System Featuring Switching Circuit	2,894,121	1959 Jul 7
Pickering, John F.	Air Ship	643,975	1900 Feb 20
Pickett, Henry	Improvement in Scaffolds	152,511	1874 Jun 30
Pickett, James Henry	Trophy Lamp	4,059,752	1977 Nov 22
Pickett, James Jr.	Combined Lamp, Ornament & Container	Des289,694	1987 May 5
Pierre, Leo	Combination tool	Des142,263	1945 Aug 21
Pinn, Traverse B.	File Holder	231,355	1880 Aug 17
Polite, William D.	Gun	1,218,458	1917 Mar 6
Polk, Austin J.	Bicycle Support	558,103	1896 Apr 14
Poole, Leonard	Donkey Calf Exercising Machine	4,346,887	1982 Aug 31
Pope, Jessie T.	Croquingnole Iron	2,409,791	1946 Oct 22
Porter, James H.	Gas Well Sulfur Removal by Diffusion through Polymer Membranes	3,534,538	1970 Oct 20
Posey, Leroy R.	Educational Device	2,188,723	1940 Jan 30
Powell, Aaron	Illuminating Dance Shoes	4,130,951	1978 Dec 26
Powell, Manual, et al.	Self-Generated Lighted Hubcap	4,893,877	1990 Jan 16
Prather, Alfred G. B.	Movable Prefabricated Fireplace and Handling Hanger Attachment	3,289,666	1966 Dec 6
Prather, Alfred G. B.	Method and Means for Instantly Filling and Sealing an Envelope	3,623,820	1971 Nov 20

Prather, Alfred G. B.	Gravity Escape Means	3,715,011	1973 Feb 6
Prather, Alfred G. B.	Man-Powered Glider Aircraft	3,750,981	1973 Aug 7
Prather, Alfred G. B.	Collapsible Propeller for Man-Powered Glider Aircraft	3,811,642	1974 May 21
Prather, Alfred G. B.	Fan-like Tail Section for Man-Powered Glider Aircraft	3,813,062	1974 May 28
Price, Frank Osalo	Quarterback Draw Football Device	4,706,959	1987 Nov 17
Prillerman, Kathleen O. Johnson	Card Game Having Cards with Graphic and Pictorial Illustrations of Geographic, Historical and Health Related Facts	6,457,716	2002 Oct 1
Prince, Frank R.	Production of 2-Pyrrolidones	3,637,743	1972 Jan 25
Pryde, Arthur Edward	Portable Sound Manifold	Des227,485	1973 Jun 26
Pugsley, Abraham	Blind Stop	433,306	1890 Jul 29
Pugsley, Samuel	Gate Latch	357,787	1887 Feb 15
Purdy, John E. & Sadgwar, Daniel A.	Folding Chair	405,117	1889 Jun 11
Purdy, Walter	Device for Sharpening Edged Tools	570,337	1896 Oct 27
Purdy, Walter	Device for Sharpening Edged Tools	609,367	1898 Aug 16
Purdy, Walter	Device for Sharpening Edged Tools	630,106	1899 Aug 1
Purdy, William H.	Spoon	Des24,228	1895 Apr 23
Purvis, William B.	Bag Fastener	256,856	1882 Apr 25
Purvis, William B.	Hand Stamp	273,149	1883 Feb 27
Purvis, William B.	Paper Bag Machine	293,353	1884 Feb 12
Purvis, William B.	Fountain Pen	419,065	1890 Jan 7

(Continued)

Name	Invention	Number	Issue Date
Purvis, William B.	Paper Bag Machine	420,099	1890 Jan 28
Purvis, William B.	Paper Bag Machine	430,684	1890 Jun 24
Purvis, William B.	Paper Bag Machine	434,461	1890 Aug 19
Purvis, William B.	Paper Bag Machine	435,524	1890 Sep 2
Purvis, William B.	Paper Bag Machine	460,093	1891 Sep 22
Purvis, William B.	Electric Railway	519,291	1894 May 1
Purvis, William B.	Paper Bag Machine	519,438	1894 May 8
Purvis, William B.	Paper Bag Machine	519,349	1894 May 8
Purvis, William B.	Paper Bag Machine	530,650	1894 Dec 1
Purvis, William B.	Magnetic Car Balancing Device	539,542	1895 May 21
Purvis, William B.	Paper Bag Machine`	578,361	1897 Mar 9
Purvis, William B.	Electric Railway System	588,176	1897 Aug 17
Purvis, William B.	Cutter for Roll Holders	630,267	1899 Aug 1
Purvis, William B., et al.	Electric Railway	1,044,819	1912 Nov 19
Queen, William	Guard for Companion Ways or Hatches	458,131	1891 Aug 18
Quick, Brothella	Pocketed Underwear	Des342,470	1993 Nov 23
Quick, Nathaniel R., et al.	Carbon Transducer with Electrical Contact	4,387,276	1983 Jun 7
Quick, Nathaniel R.	Apparatus and Method for Processing Wire Strand Cable	4,401,479	1983 Aug 30
Quick, Nathaniel R., et al.	Electrical Contact Means with Gold Nickel Overlay	4,480,014	1984 Oct 30
Quick, Nathaniel R.	Apparatus and Method for Processing Wire Strand Cable	4,529,566	1985 Jul 16

Quick, Nathaniel R.	Apparatus and Method for Processing Wire Str and Cable	4,534,310	1985 Aug 13
Quick, Nathaniel R., et al.	Direct Wiring of Conductive Patterns	4,691,091	1987 Sep 1
Quigless, Kirk	Dispensable-Head Manual Toothbrush	5,737,792	1998 Apr 14
Raines, Morris A.	Receptacle for Growing Plants	2,026,322	1935 Dec 31
Raines, Morris A.	Method and Receptacle for Propagating Plants	2,431,890	1947 Dec 2
Randall, Carol C.	Ear Bruce	4,971,072	1990 Nov 20
Randolph, John B.	Combined Furnace and Stove or Range	540,365	1895 Jun 4
Ransom, Victor Llewellyn	Traffic Data Processing	3,231,866	1966 Jan 25
Ransom, Victor Llewellyn	Method and Apparatus for Gathering Peak Load Traffic Data	3,866,185	1975 Feb 11
Ratchford, Debrilla M.	Suitcase with Wheels and Transporting Hook	4,094,391	1978 Jun 13
Ray, Ernest P.	Chair Supporting Device	620,078	1899 Feb 21
Ray, Lloyd P.	Dust Pan	587,607	1897 Aug 3
Redding, James Thomas	Tourist Seat	2,094,410	1937 Sep 28
Redmond, Sidney D.	Mine Sweeper	2,320,986	1943 Jun 1
Redmond, Sidney D., et al.	Torpedo Arrester or Insulator	2,348,094	1944 May 2
Redmond, Joseph M., et al.	Resistor Sensing Bit Switch	3,736,573	1973 May 29
Reeberg, Christian	Hold Steady Strap	4,155,636	1979 May 22
Reed, Judy W.	Dough Kneader and Roller	305,474	1884 Sep 23
Reid, Patricia B., et al.	Electrically Heatable Vision Unit	4,725,710	1988 Feb 16

(*Continued*)

Name	Invention	Number	Issue Date
Reid, Patricia B., et al.	Method of Increasing the Visible Transmittance of an Electrically Heated Window and Product Produced Thereby	4,771,167	1988 Sep 13
Reid, Tahira, et al.	Jump Rope Device	5,961,425	1999 Oct 5
Reynolds, Humphrey H.	Window Ventilator for Railroad Cars	275,271	1883 Apr 3
Reynolds, Humphrey H.	Safety Gate for Bridges	437,937	1890 Oct 7
Reynolds, Mary Janes	Hoisting and Loading Mechanism	1,337,667	1920 Apr 20
Reynolds, Robert R.	Non-Refillable Bottle	624,092	1899 May 2
Rhodes, Jerome Bonaparte	Water Closet	639,920	1899 Dec 19
Richards, Donna E.	Loose Leaf Retainer for File Folders	4,932,804	1990 Jun 12
Richards, Levie	Ointment for Treatment of Arthritis	4,271,154	1981 Jun 2
Richardson, Albert C.	Hame Fastener	255,022	1882 Mar 14
Richardson, Albert C.	Churn	445,470	1891 Feb 17
Richardson, Albert C.	Casket-Lowering Device	529,311	1894 Nov 13
Richardson, Albert C.	Insect Destroyer	620,362	1899 Feb 28
Richardson, Albert C.	Bottle	638,811	1899 Dec 12
Richardson, Alfred G., et al.	Method for Fabricating an Optical Fiber Cable	4,484,963	1984 Nov 27
Richardson, George J., et al.	Method of Reproducing Pictures and Designs	1,518,863	1924 Dec 9
Richardson, William H.	Cotton Chopper	343,140	1886 Jun 1
Richardson, William H.	Child's Carriage	405,599	1889 Jun 18
Richardson, William H.	Child's Carriage	405,600	1889 Jun 18

Name	Invention	Patent Number	Date
Richey, Charles V.	Car Coupling	584,650	1897 Jun 15
Richey, Charles V.	Railroad Switch	587,657	1897 Aug 3
Richey, Charles V.	Railroad Switch	592,488	1897 Oct 26
Richey, Charles V.	Fire Escape Bracket	596,427	1897 Dec 28
Richey, Charles V.	Combined Cot, Hammock, and Stretcher	615,907	1898 Dec 13
Richey, Charles V.	Telephone Call Register	1,037,053	1912 Aug 27
Richey, Charles V.	Telephone Register and Lock-out Device	1,063,599	1931 Jun 3
Richey, Charles V.	Lockout for Outgoing Calls for Telephone Systems	1,812,984	1931 Jul 7
Richey, Charles V.	Time Control System for Telephones	1,897,533	1933 Feb 14
Richman, Alvin Longo	Overshoe	598,816	1898 Feb 8
Ricks, James	Horseshoe	338,781	1886 Mar 30
Ricks, James	Overshoes for Horses	626,245	1899 Jun 6
Rillieux, Norbert	Improvement of Sugar-Works	3,237	1843 Aug 26
Rillieux, Norbert	Improvement of Sugar-Making	4,879	1846 Dec 10
Rillieux, Norbert	Improvement in Sugar-Making	Re. 439	1857 Mar 17
Rivers, Cecil, Jr., et al.	Circuit Breaker with Single Test Button Mechanism	6,731,483	2003 Feb 14
Roberson, William A.	Portable Laundry	748,896	1904 Jan 5
Roberson, William A.	Convertible Cot	780,815	1905 Jan 24
Robert, Andre	Method of Reducing the Undesirable Gastrointestinal Effects of Prostaglandin Synthetase Inhibitor	4,061,742	1977 Dec 6
Robert, Andre	Cytoprotective Prostaglandins	4,081,553	1978 Mar 28

(Continued)

Name	Invention	Number	Issue Date
Robert, Andre	Treatment of Inflammatory Diseases of the Mammalian Large Intestine	4,083,998	1978 Apr 11
Robert, Andre	Cytoprotective Prostaglandins	4,088,784	1978 May 9
Robert, Andre	Gastric Cytoprotection with Non-Antisecretory Doses of Prostaglandins	4,097,603	1978 Jun 27
Robert, Andre	Method for Preventing Renal Papillary Necrosis	4,397,865	1973 Aug 9
Robert, Andre	Cytoprotective Use of Oxamate Derivatives	4,439,445	1984 Mar 27
Robert, Andre	Method of Preventing Pancreatitis Utilizing 2-Amino Cycloaliphatic Amides	4,891,382	1990 Jan 2
Roberts, Edgar E., et al.	Electro-Hydraulic Control Module for Activating Intake and Exhaust Valves	6,481,409	2002 Nov 19
Roberts, Harold A., et al.	Channel Selection for a Hybrid Fiber Coax Network	6,334,219	2001 Dec 5
Roberts, Harold A., et al.	Fast Fourier Transform Apparatus and Method	6,434,583	2002 Aug 13
Roberts, Louis W.	High-Frequency-Transmission Control Tube	2,678,408	1954 May 11
Roberts, Louis W., et al.	Electrode Support for Electron Discharge Devices	2,945,983	1960 Jul 19
Roberts, Louis W.	High Power Microwave Switching Device	3,017,534	1962 Jan 16
Roberts, Louis W.	Gaseous Discharge Device	3,072,865	1963 Jan 8
Roberts, Louis W.	Device for Gas Amplification by Stimulated Emission and Radiation	3,257,620	1966 Jun 21
Roberts, Louis W., et al.	Gallium-Wetted Movable Electrode Switch	3,377,576	1968 Apr 9
Robinson, Daniel E., et al.	Cord Sets with Power Factor Control	4,417,196	1983 Nov 22

Name	Title	Number	Date
Robinson, Daniel E., et al.	Remotely Actuable Line Disconnect Device	4,485,271	1984 Nov 27
Robinson, Daniel E., et al.	Remotely Controlled Crossconnection System	4,533,914	1985 Aug 6
Robinson, Elbert R.	Electric Railway Trolley	505,370	1893 Sep 19
Robinson, Elbert R.	Casting Composition or Other Car Wheels	594,286	1897 Nov 23
Robinson, Elbert R.	Switch	866,306	1907 Sep 17
Robinson, Elbert R.	Rail	886,541	1908 May 5
Robinson, Elbert R.	Cast-Iron Axle	887,848	1908 May 19
Robinson, Hassel	Traffic Signal Casing	Des66,703	1925 Feb 24
Robinson, Hassel	Traffic Signals for Automobiles	1,580,218	1926 Apr 13
Robinson, Ira C.	Sustained Release Pharmaceutical Tablets	3,577,514	1971 May 4
Robinson, James H.	Life-Saving Guard for Locomotives	621,143	1899 Mar 14
Robinson, James H.	Life-Saving Guard for Street Cars	623,929	1899 Apr 25
Robinson, John	Dinner Pail	356,852	1887 Feb 1
Robinson, John Carter	Comb	1,894,832	1933 Jan 17
Robinson, Natalie F. G.	Time to Win	5,513,852	1996 May 7
Robinson, Neale Moore	Vehicle Wheel	1,422,479	1922 Jul 11
Rocke, Leonora	Corner Cleaning Brush	Des235,942	1975 Jul 22
Rolls, James P.	Delta1 Dehydrogenation of Corticoids without Side Chain	4,088,537	1978 May 9
Romain, Arnold	Passenger Register	402,035	1889 Apr 23
Rose, Raymond E.	Control Apparatus	3,618,388	1971 Nov 9
Ross, Archia L.	Runner for Stoops	565,301	1896 Aug 4

(Continued)

Name	Invention	Number	Issue Date
Ross, Archia L.	Bag Closure	605,343	1898 Jun 7
Ross, Archia L.	Trousers Support or Stretcher	638,068	1899 Nov 28
Ross, Joseph	Hay Press	632,539	1899 Sep 5
Ross, Leonard W. Jr.	Tarp Enclosure for Flat Bed Trailer and Truck Bodies	4,342,480	1982 Aug 3
Roston, David N.	Feather Curler	556,166	1896 Mar 10
Rowe, V. Lopez	Bicycle Drinking Apparatus	4,095,812	1978 Jun 20
Royster, Ronald B. Sr.	Rotable Surveillance Capsule	Des223,086	1972 Mar 7
Royster, Ronald B. Sr.	Computer Controlled Stolen Vehicle Detection System	3,656,111	1972 Apr 11
Royster, Ronald B. Sr.	Plate for Chain Door Locks	Des230,009	1974 Jan 22
Ruffin, Paul B.	Efficient Design Technique for Wavelength Division Multiplexing	4,606,020	1986 Aug 12
Ruffin, Paul B., et al.	Device for Controlling Optical Fiber Lag Angle for Fiber Wound on a Bobbin	4,655,410	1987 Apr 7
Russell, Edwin Roberts, et al.	Adsorption-Bismuth Phosphate Method for Separating Plutonium	2,942,937	1960 Jun 28
Russell, Edwin Roberts, et al.	Removal of Cesium from Aqueous Solution by Ion Exchange	3,296,123	1967 Jan 3
Russell, Edwin Roberts, et al.	Thorium Oxide or Thorium-Uranium Oxide with Mg Oxide	3,309,323	1967 Mar 14
Russell, Edwin Roberts, et al.	Base Station for Mobil Radio Telecommunication System	5,084,869	1992 Jan 28
Russell, Jesse E., et al.	Multi-band Wireless Radiotelephone Operative in a Plurality of Air Interface of Differing Wireless Communication System	5,406,615	1995 Apr 11

Russell, Jesse E., et al.	Universal Wireless Radiotelephone System	5,574,775	1996 Nov 12
Russell, Jesse E., et al.	Intelligent Wireless Signaling Overlay for a Telecommunication Network	5,583,914	1996 Dec 10
Russell, Jesse E., et al.	Broadband Wireless System & Network Architecture Providing Broadband/Narrowband Service	5,592,470	1997 Jan 7
Russell, Jesse E., et al.	Wireless Telecommunication Base Station for Integrated Wireless Services with ATM Processing	5,600,633	1987 Feb 4
Russell, Jesse E, et al.	Multiple Call Waiting in a Packetized Communication System	6,633,635	2003 Oct 14
Russell, Joseph L., et al.	Preparation of Tungsten Hexafluoride	3,995,011	1976 Nov 30
Russell, Lewis A.	Guard Attachment for Beds	544,381	1895 Aug 13
Ryder, Earl	High Silicon Cast Iron	3,129,095	1964 Apr 14
Saab, Acie J.	Picture Postcard	4,079,881	1978 Mar 21
Sammons, Walter H.	Comb	1,362,823	1920 Dec 21
Sammons, Walter H.	Hair-Dressing Device	1,483,988	1923 Feb 19
Sammons, Walter H.	Comb	Re.15,808	1924 Apr 1
Samms, Adolphus	Rocket Engine Pump Feed System	3,000,179	1961 Sep 19
Samms, Adolphus	Multiple Stage Rocket	3,199,455	1965 Aug 10
Samms, Adolphus	Air-Breathing Rocket Booster	3,218,974	1965 Nov 23
Samms, Adolphus	Rocket Motor Fuel Feed	3,310,938	1967 Mar 28
Samms, Adolphus	Emergency Release for Extraction Chute	3,257,089	1966 Jun 21
Sampson, Charles T. Sr.	Fishhook	2,591,013	1952 Apr 1

(Continued)

Name	Invention	Number	Issue Date
Sampson, Charles T. Sr.	Fishing Device	2,736,980	1956 Mar 6
Sampson, George T.	Sled Propeller	312,388	1885 Feb 17
Sampson, George T.	Clothes Dryer	476,416	1892 Jun 7
Sampson, Henry T.	Binder System for Propellants and Explosives	3,140,210	1964 Jul 7
Sampson, Henry T.	Case Bonding System for Cast Composite Propellants	3,212,256	1965 Oct 19
Sampson, Henry T.	Gamma-Electric Cell	3,591,860	1971 Jul 6
Sampson, Henry T.	Process for Case Bonding Cast Composite Propellant Grains	3,734,982	1973 May 22
Samuels, Donald H.	Toy Race Track for Miniature Cars	Des257,272	1980 Oct 7
Samuels, Donald H.	Toy Fire Truck	Des258,973	1981 Apr 21
Samuels, Donald H.	Toy Tow Truck	Des258,974	1981 Apr 21
Samuels, Donald H.	Toy Wheeled Vehicle	4,270,305	1981 Jun 2
Samuels, Donald H.	Jack-in-the-Box	Des261,293	1981 Oct 13
Samuels, Donald H.	Ball Game Board	Des270,458	1983 Sep 6
Samuels, John Clifton	A Cathode-Follower Oscillator	2,874,290	1959 Feb 17
Sanders, Estelle, et al.	Scalp Massaging Implement	4,308,860	1982 Jan 5
Sanderson, Dewey S. C.	Urinalysis Machine	3,522,011	1970 Jul 28
Sanderson, Ralph	Hydraulic Shock Absorber	3,362,742	1968 Jan 9
Saxton, Olivia	Anchor for Furniture Including TV Sets	4,118,902	1978 Oct 10
Saxton, Richard L.	Pay Telephone with Sanitized Tissue Dispenser	4,392,028	1983 Jul 5
Scharschmidt, Virginia	Safety Window Cleaning Device	1,708,594	1929 Apr 9

Name	Invention	Patent No.	Date
Scott, Blanton, Jr.	Photographic Film Magazine	3,719,130	1973 Mar 6
Scott, Henry	Spinal Traction and Support Unit Used While Seated	4,881,528	1989 Nov 21
Scott, Howard L.	Treating Human, Animal, and Synthetic Hair with Water-Proofing Composition	3,568,685	1971 Mar 9
Scott, J. C.	Shadow Box	Des212,334	1968 Oct 1
Scott, Linzy	Knee Brace	4,275,716	1981 Jun 30
Scott, Robert P.	Corn Silker	534,224	1894 Aug 7
Scottron, Samuel R.	Adjustable Window-Cornice	224,732	1880 Feb 17
Scottron, Samuel R.	Cornice	270,851	1883 Jan 16
Scottron, Samuel R.	Pole Tip	349,525	1886 Sep 21
Scottron, Samuel R.	Curtain Rod	481,720	1892 Aug 30
Scottron, Samuel R.	Supporting Bracket	505,008	1893 Sep 12
Seale, Glenn C., et al.	Genealogy Apparatus	4,201,386	1980 May 6
Shanks, Stephen C.	Sleeping Car Berth Register	587,165	1897 Jul 21
Shaw, Earl D.	Free-Electron Amplifier Device with Electromagnetic Radiation Delay Element	4,529,942	1985 Jul 16
Shaw, Fred C.	Pediatric Lumbar Puncture Immobilizer	5,357,982	1994 Oct 25
Sheffield, Abner Barto	Caster for Besteads	766,068	1904 Jul 26
Shelby, Jerry A. Jr.	Engine Protection System for Recoverable Rocket Booster	5,328,132	1994 Jul 12
Shields, Willie A.	Appliance for Applying and Removing Garment Bags	1,304,913	1919 May 27
Shields, Willie A.	Bag Mounting	1,533,666	1925 Apr 14

(Continued)

Name	Invention	Number	Issue Date
Shields, Willie A.	Garment Bagging Machine	1,808,824	1931 Jun 9
Shields, Willie A.	Garment Bag Applying and Removing Device	2,439,148	1948 Apr 6
Shivers, Clarence L.	Passive Ambience Recovery System for Reproduction of Sound	4,837,825	1989 Jun 6
Shivers, Clarence L.	Passive Ambience Recovery System for the Reproduction of Sound	4,882,753	1989 Nov 21
Shorter, Dennis W.	Feed Rack	363,089	1887 May 17
Sigur, Wanda A.	Method of Fabricating Composite Structures	5,084,219	1992 Jan 28
Sill, Donald E.	Telephone Set	Des294,496	1988 Mar 1
Simpson, Joycelyn O., et al.	Thermally Stable Piezoelectric and Pyroelectric Polymeric Substrates	5,891,581	1999 Apr 6
Simpson, Joycelyn O., et al.	Method of Making Thermally Stable Piezoelectric and Pyroelectric Polymeric Substrates	5,909,905	1999 Jun 8
Simpson, Joycelyn O., et al.	Thermally Stable Piezoelectric and Pyroelectric Polymeric Substrates and Method Relating Thereto	6,379,809	2002 Apr 30
Simpson, Joycelyn O., et al.	Thin Layer Composite Unimorph Ferroelectric Driver and Sensor	6,734,603	2004 May 11
Silvera, Esteban	Ram-Valve Level Indicator	3,718,157	1973 Feb 27
Skanks, Stephen Chambers	Sleeping Car Berth Register	587,165	1897 Jul 27
Sluby, Thomas Buchanan	Milk Bottle Stopper	1,052,289	1913 Feb 4
Small, Isadore	Universal On-Delay Timer	3,814,948	1974 Jun 4
Smartt, Brinay	Reversing-Valve	799,489	1905 Sep 12

Name	Title	Number	Date
Smartt, Brinay	Reversing-Valve	837,427	1906 Dec 4
Smartt, Brinay	Valve Gear	935,169	1909 Sep 28
Smartt, Brinay	Rotary Valve	981,019	1911 Jan 10
Smartt, Brinay	Wheel	1,052,290	1913 Feb 4
Smith, Bernard	Glass Laser Window Sealant Technique	3,616,523	1971 Nov 2
Smith, Bernard, et al.	Method of Making a High Current Density Long Life Cathode	4,078,900	1978 Mar 14
Smith, Bernard	Method of Forming an Efficient Electron Emitter Cold Cathode	4,149,308	1979 Apr 17
Smith, Bernard	Method of Making Ruggedized High Current Density Cathode	4,236,287	1980 Dec 2
Smith, Bernard, et al.	EBS Device with Cold-Cathode	4,410,832	1983 Oct 18
Smith, Bernard, et al.	Method of Preparing Nonlaminating Anisotrcpic Boron Nitride	4,544,535	1985 Oct 1
Smith, Bernard, et al.	Method of Making Long Lived High Current Density Cathode	4,708,681	1987 Nov 24
Smith, Bernard, et al.	Method of Making a Cathode from Tungsten and Iridium Powders	4,808,137	1989 Feb 28
Smith, Bernard, et al.	Method of Making a Cathode from Tungsten and Iridium Powders	4,818,480	1989 Apr 4
Smith, Betty L., et al.	Multicharacter Doll	4,921,459	1990 May 1
Smith, Bruce K., et al.	Soap Saving Method and Apparatus	5,030,405	1991 Jul 9

(Continued)

Name	Invention	Number	Issue Date
Smith, Charles R. Sr.	Hoist	2,305,202	1942 Dec 15
Smith, Herman W.	Omega-Aryl-13,14-Didehydro-PGF Compounds	4,276,429	1981 Jun 30
Smith, Herman W.	Structural Analogues of 5,6-Dihydro PG.sub.1	4,294,759	1981 Oct 13
Smith, Herman W.	Trans-4,5,13,14-Tetrahydro-PGI.sub.1	4,301,078	1981 Nov 17
Smith, Herman W.	6-Aryluracils	4,495,349	1985 Jan 22
Smith, Herman W.	Analogs of 5,6-Dihydro PGI.sub.2	4,496,742	1985 Jan 29
Smith, Herman W., et al.	Process for the Preparation of 1,3-Oxazine-4-ones	4,521,599	1985 Jun 4
Smith, Herman W.	Use of 5,6,7,8-Tetrahydroquinoline and 5,6-Dihydropyridines	4,576,949	1986 Mar 18
Smith, Herman W.	Process for the Preparation of 6-Aryluracils	4,578,466	1986 Mar 25
Smith, Herman W.	Use of 6-Aryluracils as Anti-inflammatory and Antiarthritic Agents	4,593,030	1986 Jun 3
Smith, Herman W.	6-Aryluracils and Selected Novel Intermediates	4,625,028	1986 Nov 25
Smith, Herman W.	Cyclopentapyrazole and Tetrahydroindazole Compounds and Their Use	4,851,425	1989 Jul 25
Smith, Herman W.	Phosphonic Acid Derivatives	5,298,498	1994 Mar 29
Smith, Herman W.	Biphosphonic Acid Derivatives	5,360,797	1994 Nov 1
Smith, Herman W.	Diaromatic Substituted Compounds as Anti-HIV-1 Agents	5,563,142	1996 Oct 8
Smith, James	Aeroplane	1,047,581	1912 Dec 17
Smith, James Henry	Peach Cutter and Stoner	474,927	1892 May 17
Smith, James Henry	Machine for Stoning Fruit	913,571	1909 Feb 23

Name	Title	Number	Date
Smith, John Winsor	Improvement in Games	647,887	1900 Apr 17
Smith, Jonathan S. II, et al.	Yttrium, Dysprosium, and Ytterbium Alkoxides and Process	3,278,571	1966 Oct 11
Smith, Jonathan S. II, et al.	Yttrium, Dysprosium, and Ytterbium Alkoxides	3,356,703	1967 Dec 5
Smith, Jonathan S. II, et al.	Transparent Zirconia Composition	3,432,314	1969 Mar 11
Smith, Jonathan S. II, et al.	Method for Making High Purity and High Yield Tertiary-Amyl Acetate	3,489,796	1970 Jan 13
Smith, Jonathan S. II, et al.	Transparent Zirconia and Process for Making	3,525,597	1970 Agu 25
Smith, Jonathan S. II, et al.	Producing High Purity Submicron Barium and Strontium Titanate	3,647,364	1972 Mar 7
Smith, Joseph H.	Lawn Sprinkler	581,785	1897 May 4
Smith, Joseph H.	Lawn Sprinkler	601,065	1898 Mar 22
Smith, Leonard	Grain Door Table	1,652,802	1927 Dec 13
Smith, Mildred Austin	Family Relationship Card Game	4,230,321	1980 Oct 28
Smith, Morris L.	Chemically Treated Paper Products	4,882,221	1989 Nov 21
Smith, Morris L.	Chemically Treated Paper Products	4,883,475	1989 Nov 28
Smith, Peter D.	Potato Digger	445,206	1891 Jan 27
Smith, Peter D.	Grain Binder	469,279	1892 Feb 23
Smith, Robert T.	Spraying Machine	1,970,984	1934 Aug 21
Smith, Robert W.	Method of Making Fiber Glass Parts with Stud Supports	4,088,525	1978 May 9
Smith, Robert W.	Reinforced Stud Supports in Fiberglass Parts	4,234,633	1980 Nov 18
Smith, Samuel C.	Hardness Tester	3,956,925	1976 May 18

(Continued)

Name	Invention	Number	Issue Date
Smith, Wilson W.	Portion of Shoe Upper	Des397,856	1998 Sep 8
Smith, Wilson W.	Spat for a Shoe	Des456,121	2002 Apr 30
Smith-Green, E. D.	Mechanism for Cleaning Shell-Fillers	1,232,401	1917 Jul 3
Smithea, Clarence O.	Auxiliary Retention Belt and Support for Seat of Open Vehicles	3,940,166	1976 Feb 24
Smoot, Laney S.	Optical Receiver Circuit and Active Equalizer	4,565,974	1986 Jan 21
Smoot, Laney S.	Teleconferencing Facility with High Resolution	4,890,314	1989 Dec 26
Smoot, Laney S.	Teleconferencing Terminal and Camera behind Display Screen	4,928,301	1990 May 22
Snow, William, et al.	Liniment	437,728	1890 Oct 7
Snowden, Maxine W.	Rain Hat	4,378,606	1983 Apr 5
Souther, Benjamin F.	Hose Storage Reel	2,438,306	1948 Mar 23
Spain, Andrew J.	Cotton Cultivator and Chopper	554,153	1896 Feb 4
Speers, Horde	Improvement in Portable Shields for Infantry and Artillery	110,599	1870 Dec 27
Spencer, Jerrald D., et al.	Light Show Mechanism	5,269,719	1993 Dec 14
Spencer, Jerrald D.	Hand Held Light Display	6,589,094	2003 Jul 8
Spencer, Jerrald D.	Electronic Pinball	6,861,962	2005 Mar 1
Spight, Carl	Machine Vision System Utilizing Programmable Optical Parallel Processing	4,462,046	1984 Jul 24
Spikes, Richard B.	Billiard Rack	972,277	1910 Oct 11
Spikes, Richard B.	Combination Milk Bottle Opener and Bottle Cover	1,590,557	1926 Jul 29

Name	Invention	Patent No.	Date
Spikes, Richard B.	Method and Apparatus for Obtaining Average Samples and Temperature of Tank Liquids	1,828,753	1931 Oct 27
Spikes, Richard B.	Automatic Gear Shift	1,889,814	1932 Dec 6
Spikes, Richard B.	Transmission and Shifting Means	1,936,996	1933 Nov 28
Spikes, Richard B.	Horizontally Swinging Barber's Chair	2,517,936	1950 Aug 8
Spikes, Richard B.	Automatic Safety Brake System	3,015,522	1962 Jan 2
Stafford, Osbourne C.	Microwave Phase Shift Device	3,522,558	1970 Aug 4
Stallworth, Elbert	Electric Heater	1,687,521	1928 Oct 16
Stallworth, Elbert	Electric Chamber	1,727,842	1929 Sep 10
Stallworth, Elbert	Alarm Clock Electric Switch	1,972,634	1934 Sep 4
Stanard, John	Oil Stove	413,689	1889 Oct 29
Stanard, John	Refrigerator	455,891	1891 Jul 14
Stancell, Arnold F.	Separating Fluids with Selective Membranes	3,657,113	1972 Apr 18
Stanton, Horace D., et al.	In Situ Cured Booster Explosive	4,385,948	1983 May 31
Stanton, Horace D., et al.	Polymer Modified TNT Containing Explosives	4,445,948	1984 May 1
Stanton, Horace D., et al.	Extrudable PBX Molding Powder	4,952,255	1990 Aug 28
Starks, Zeston	Protector for Plants	1,904,700	1933 Apr 18
Starks, Zeston	Container	1,910,646	1933 May 23
Starks, Zeston	Protector and Supporter for Plants	1,916,868	1933 Jul 4
States, John B. Sr.	Material and Methods for Oil Spill Control and Cleanup	4,248,733	1981 Feb 3
States, John B. Sr., et al.	Odor-Reducing, Nutrient-Enhancing Composition	5,574,093	1996 Nov 12

(Continued)

Name	Invention	Number	Issue Date
Stephens, George B. Davis	Cigarette Holder and Ash Tray	2,762,377	1956 Sep 11
Stevens, Emeline	Pillow-like Body Supports and Protectors and System of Same	5,103,516	1992 Apr 14
Stewart, Albert Clifton	Redox Couple Radiation Cell	3,255,044	1966 Jun 7
Stewart, Albert Clifton	Electric Cell	3,255,045	1966 Jun 7
Stewart, Earl M., et al.	Arch and Heel Support	2,031,510	1936 Feb 18
Stewart, Enos	Punching Machine	362,190	1887 May 3
Stewart, Enos	Machine for Forming Vehicle Seat Bars	373,698	1887 Nov 22
Stewart, Eugene	Fare Computer	4,800,502	1989 Jan 24
Stewart, Isaac Jr.	Sno-Rak	4,547,011	1985 Oct 15
Stewart, Jeffrey D.	Rack Apparatus for Barbecuing	5,158,009	1992 Oct 27
Stewart, Marvin Charles	Arithmetic Unit for Digital Computers	3,395,271	1968 Jun 30
Stewart, Marvin Charles	System for Interconnecting Electrical Components	3,605,063	1971 Sep 14
Stewart, Thomas	Metal Bending Machine	375,512	1887 Dec 27
Stewart, Thomas W.	Mop	499,402	1893 Jun 13
Stewart, Thomas W., et al.	Station Indicator	499,895	1883 Jun 20
Stilwell, Henry F.	Means for Delivery of Mail and Other from Aeroplanes while in Motion	1,841,766	1932 Jan 19
Stilwell, Henry F.	Means for Delivery of Mail and Other Matter from Aeroplanes while in Motion	1,911,248	1933 May 30
St. John, Stella	Umbrella Boot Holder	Des284,618	1986 Jul 15

Stokes, Rufus	Exhaust Purifier	3,378,241	1968 Apr 16
Stokes, Rufus	Air Pollution Control Device	3,520,113	1970 Jul 14
Sutton, Edward H.	Improvement in Cotton Cultivators	149,543	1874 Apr 7
Sweeting, James A.	Device for Rolling Cigarettes	594,501	1897 Nov 30
Sweeting, James A.	Combined Knife and Scoop	605,209	1898 Jun 7
Tankins, Sacramenta G.	Comb	1,339,632	1920 May 11
Tankins, Sacramenta G.	Method and Means for Treating Human Hair	1,845,208	1932 Feb 16
Tate, Charles	Flexible and Transparent Lubricant Housing	3,423,959	1969 Jan 28
Taylor, Aiken C.	Combined Cotton Planter and Fertilizer Distributor	827,328	1906 Jul 31
Taylor, Aiken C.	Invalid Bed	847,619	1907 Mar 19
Taylor, Aiken C.	Combined Curtain, Pole and Shade Roller Support	882,180	1908 Mar 17
Taylor, Aiken C.	Extension Step Ladder	886,737	1908 May 5
Taylor, Asa J.	Machine for Assembling and/or Disassembling the Parts of Spring Tensioned Devices	2,286,695	1942 Jun 16
Taylor, Asa J.	Device for Dislodging Valve-Assemblies of Internal-Combustion Engines	2,365,023	1944 Dec 12
Taylor, Asa J.	Fluid Joint	2,434,629	1948 Jan 13
Taylor, Benjamin H.	Improvement in Rotary Engines	202,888	1878 Apr 23
Taylor, Benjamin H.	Side Valve	585,798	1897 Jul 6
Taylor, Christopher L.	Combination Toothbrush and Dentifrice Dispenser	2,807,818	1957 Oct 1
Taylor, Don A.	Individually Packaged Frozen Confection	2,735,778	1956 Feb 21

(Continued)

Name	Invention	Number	Issue Date
Taylor, Don A.	Floor Mats for Automobiles	2,810,671	1957 Oct 22
Taylor, Don A.	Floor Mats for Automobiles	2,810,672	1957 Oct 22
Taylor, Don A.	Baton	3,003,385	1961 Oct 10
Taylor, Don A.	Air Intake Scoop for Ventilating Seat Cushion	3,039,817	1962 Jan 19
Taylor, Don A.	Measuring Tape Tension Holder	3,100,941	1963 Aug 20
Taylor, Don A.	Detachable Ventilating Seat Cover for Automobile Seats	3,101,037	1963 Aug 20
Taylor, Don A.	Ventilating Hood for Seat Cushions	3,101,660	1963 Aug 27
Taylor, Don A.	Finger Grip Pad for Bowling Balls	3,113,775	1963 Dec 10
Taylor, Don A.	Toy Play Table	Des176,740	1970 Jan 24
Taylor, Don A.	Molding Apparatus	3,748,075	1973 Jul 24
Taylor, Don A.	Apparatus for Molding Strip Material	3,829,271	1974 Aug 13
Taylor, Don A.	Method for Forming Hollow Article	3,832,437	1974 Aug 27
Taylor, Don A.	Molding Apparatus	3,836,307	1974 Sep 17
Taylor, Don A.	Apparatus for Transfer Molding Thermosetting Materials	3,843,289	1974 Oct 22
Taylor, Don A.	Particle Filled Self-Conformable Cushion and Method	3,971,839	1976 Jul 27
Taylor, Don A.	Injection Cylinder Unit Mold and Mold Handling Apparatus	3,981,661	1976 Sep 21
Taylor, Don A.	Heating System	3,993,244	1976 Nov 23
Taylor, Don A.	Heater Adaptor	Des244,450	1991 May 4
Taylor, Don A.	Combined Display	Des244,570	1991 Jun 7

Name	Title	Date
Taylor, Moddie D.	Preparation of Anhydrous Alkaline Earth Halides	2,891,899	1957 Aug 6
Taylor, Moddie D.	Ion Exchange Adsorption Process for Plutonium Separation	2,992,249	1961 Jul 11
Taylor, Moddie D.	Preparation of Anhydrous Lithium Salts	3,049,406	1962 Aug 14
Taylor, Richard	Leaf Holder	Des105,037	1937 Jun 22
Thomas, Arend J.	Electric Heating Apparatus for Heat Treating Pharmaceuticals	4,273,992	1981 Jun 16
Thomas, Darrell	Training Apparatus for Cattle Roping	5,192,210	1993 Mar 9
Thomas, Edward H. C.	Automobile Key and License Holder	1,693,006	1928 Nov 27
Thomas, Henry	Method of Refining Iron and Steel	1,453,734	1923 May 1
Thomas, Henry	Method of and Flux for Refining Brass	1,454,351	1923 May 8
Thomas, Samuel E.	Waste Trap	286,746	1883 Oct 16
Thomas, Samuel E.	Waste Trap for Basins, Closets, etc.	371,107	1887 Oct 4
Thomas, Samuel E.	Process of Casting	386,941	1888 Jul 31
Thomas, Samuel E.	Pipe Connection	390,821	1888 Oct 9
Thomas, Valerie	Illusion Transmitter	4,229,761	1980 Oct 21
Thompson, Asa	Cotton Chopper and Cultivator	830,113	1906 Sep 4
Thompson, John P.	Motor Vehicle Elevating and Parking Device	2,086,142	1937 Jul 6
Thompson, Joseph Ausbon Jr.	Foot Warmer	2,442,026	1948 May 25
Thompson, Joseph Ausbon Jr.	Moist/Dry Lavatory and Toilet Tissue	3,921,802	1975 Nov 25
Thompson, Levi Jr., et al.	High Surface Area Nitride, Carbide and Boride Electrodes and Methods of Fabrication Thereof	5,680,292	1997 Oct 21

(Continued)

Name	Invention	Number	Issue Date
Thompson, Levi Jr., et al.	High Surface Area Mesoporous Desigel Materials and Methods for Their Fabrication	5,837,630	1998 Nov 17
Thompson, Levi Jr., et al.	Transition Metal-Based Ceramic Material and Articles Fabrication Therefrom	5,888,669	1999 Mar 30
Thompson, Levi Jr., et al.	Transition Metal-Based Ceramic Material and Electrodes Fabricated Therefrom	6,190,802	2001 Feb 20
Thompson, Levi Jr., et al.	Catalyst	6,297,185	2001 Oct 2
Thompson, Levi Jr., et al.	Transition Metal Carbides, Nitrides and Borides, and Their Oxygen Containing Analogs Useful as Water Gas Shift Catalysts	6,623,720	2003 Sep 23
Thompson, Levi Jr., et al.	Carbide/Nitride Based Fuel Processing Catalysts	6,897,178	2005 May 24
Thompson, McKinley W.	Toboggan	Des235,982	1975 Jul 22
Thompson, Neil E. S., et al.	Methods for Treating Hydrocarbon Recovery Operations and Industrial Waters	5,089,619	1992 Feb 18
Thompson, Oliver L.	Vehicle Parking Attachment	1,541,670	1925 Jun 9
Thornton, Benjamin F.	Apparatus for Automatically Recording Telephonic Messages	1,831,331	1931 Nov 10
Thornton, Benjamin F.	Apparatus for Automatically Transmitting Messages Over a Telephone Line	1,843,849	1932 Feb 2
Thornton, Benjamin F.	Underarm Perspiration Pad	2,911,647	1959 Nov 10
Thornton, Robert L. et al.	Temperature Controlled Light Source for Interlaced Printer	5,138,340	1992 Aug 11
Thornton, Robert L. et al.	Near-field Laser and Detector Apparatus and Method	6,574,257	2003 Jun 3

Author	Title	Patent Number	Date
Thurman, John S.	Vehicle Motion Signalling System	4,594,574	1986 Jun 10
Todd, Melvin I., et al.	Hoodliner	5,164,254	1992 Nov 17
Toland, Mary H.	Float-Operated Circuit Closer	1,339,239	1920 May 4
Toliver, George	Propeller for Vessels	451,086	1891 Apr 28
Tolliver, Peter M.	Termistor and Diode Bridge Circuit for Thermal Compensation of Resistive Load	3,207,984	1965 Sep 21
Tolliver, Peter M.	Electronically Tunable High Frequency Network Using Pin Diodes	3,414,833	1968 Dec 3
Tolliver, Peter M.	Staple Remover	3,484,080	1969 Dec 16
Tolliver, Peter M.	Gun Holster	3,664,558	1972 May 23
Tolliver, Peter M.	Paraboloidal Reflectors	3,784,836	1974 Jan 8
Tolliver, Peter M.	IR Generator Having Ellipsoidal and Paraboloidal Reflectors	3,959,660	1976 May 25
Tolliver, Peter M.	Corona Generating Device with Improved Built-in Cleaning Mechanism	3,965,400	1976 Jun 22
Tolliver, Peter M.	Lateral View Extender Device	4,493,538	1985 Jan 15
Tolliver, Peter M.	Lawn Rake with Debris Pile Capability	5,303,536	1994 Apr 19
Tolliver, Peter M.	Low Profile Staggered Treble Fish Hook	5,901,493	1999 May 11
Toomey, Richard E. S., et al.	Airplane Appliance to Prevent Ice Formation	1,749,858	1930 Mar 11
Truedell, Brenda A., et al.	2-N-Acylated and 2-N-Alkylated Derivatives and Process	4,424,344	1984 Jan 3
Truedell, Brenda A., et al.	1-N-Acylated and 1-N-Alkylated Derivatives and Process	4,424,345	1984 Jan 3
Truedell, Brenda A., et al.	1-N-Acylated and 1-N-Alkylated Derivatives	4,468,512	1984 Aug 28

(Continued)

Name	Invention	Number	Issue Date
Truedell, Brenda A., et al.	2'-N-Acylated and 2'-N-Alkylated Derivates	4,468,513	1984 Aug 28
Truesdale, Carlton M., et al.	Increasing the Retention of GeO.sub.2 during Production of Glass Articles	5,641,333	1997 Jun 24
Tucker, Cleveland T.	Door Car Starter	4,291,653	1981 Sep 29
Turner, Albert Walter	Lever Assemblies for Augmenting Prime Mover Power	4,113,047	1978 Sep 12
Turner, Allen H., et al.	Electrostatic Paint System	3,017,115	1962 Jan 16
Turner, Allen H., et al.	Electrostatic Painting	3,054,697	1962 Sep 18
Turner, Allen H., et al.	Electrodeposition Process and Apparatus	3,399,126	1968 Aug 27
Turner, Allen H., et al.	Electron Discharge Control	3,418,155	1968 Dec 24
Turner, Allen H.	Electron Induced Deposition of Organic Coatings	3,462,292	1969 Aug 19
Turner, Collatinus, et al.	Alarm for Boilers	566,612	1896 Aug 25
Turner, Collatinus, et al.	Steam Cage	566,613	1896 Aug 25
Turner, Collatinus, et al.	Alarm for Water Containing Vessels	598,572	1898 Feb 8
Turner, Cyril	Sloped Gutter Assembly	5,678,359	1997 Oct 21
Turner, George W.	Spring Motor for Fans	1,214,848	1917 Feb 6
Turner, Jason E.	Penile Volumetric Measuring Device	7,147,609	2006 Dec 12
Turner, John R.	Method and Apparatus for Polishing Glass and Like Substances	2,380,275	1945 Jul 10
Turner, Madeline M.	Fruit Press	1,180,959	1916 Apr 25
Turner, Posie C.	Compact Foldable Bootjack with Positive Locking Device	4,226,346	1980 Oct 7

Name	Title	Number	Date
Turner, Ronald Leon	Eating Container	Des428,767	2000 Aug 1
Turner, Ronald Leon	Food Container	6,269,964	2001 Aug 7
Turner, Rufus J.	Nut or Bolt Lock	1,195,877	1916 Aug 22
Turner, Willie L.	De-ending Shears	4,428,119	1984 Jan 31
Turpin, Robert A. Jr., et al.	Odor-Reducing Nutrient-Enhancing Composition	5,574,093	1996 Nov 12
Udofot, Bassey J.	Electrodeposition of Manganese and Other Hard to Deposit Metals	5,965,002	1999 Oct 12
Valdes, Mario A.	Pipeable Gelled Food and Ethyl Alcohol Beverages	5,019,414	1991 May 28
Van Allen, David E., et al.	Light Deflector for a Photographic Camera	Des218,363	1970 Aug 11
Van Allen, David E.	Photographic Fluid-Spreading Apparatus	3,625,129	1971 Dec 7
Van Allen, David E., et al.	Stepped Photographic Processing Fluid-Spreading Apparatus	3,625,130	1971 Dec 7
Van Allen, David E., et al.	Unique Waste-Free Camera System	3,722,383	1973 Mar 27
Van Allen, David E.	Photographic Flash Assembly	3,786,737	1974 Jan 22
Van Allen, David E., et al.	Modular Constructed Sequencing System for Photographic Apparatus	3,967,304	1976 Jun 29
Van Allen, David E., et al.	Exposure Counter for an Automatic Camera	3,984,852	1976 Oct 5
Van Allen, David E., et al.	Photographic Apparatus with Sequencing System	4,047,192	1977 Sep 6
Van Allen, David E., et al.	Photographic Strobe-Light or Similar Article	Des255,457	1980 Jun 17
Van Allen, David E.	Photographic Lighting Apparatus	4,304,479	1981 Dec 8
Van Allen, David E., et al.	Handheld Viewer for Transparency Film	4,491,434	1985 Jan 1

(Continued)

Name	Invention	Number	Issue Date
Van Allen, David E., et al.	Method and Apparatus for Delaminating a Laminate	5,520,776	1996 May 28
Vincent, Simon	Woodworking Machine	1,361,295	1920 Dec 7
Wade, Forrest L., et al.	System and Method for Data Recovery in Multiple Head Assembly Storage	5,163,162	1992 Nov 10
Wade, Forrest L., et al.	Method and System for Perfecting Data in a Bridge System	6,502,157	2002 Dec 31
Wade, William L. Jr.	Method of Making Magnetic Ferrite Films	3,096,206	1963 Jul 2
Wade, William L. Jr., et al.	Method of Coating a Substrate with Magnetic Ferrite Film	3,197,334	1965 Jul 27
Wade, William L. Jr., et al.	Method of Making a Porous Carbon Cathode, a Porous Carbon Cathode So Made, and Electrochemical Cell	4,514,478	1985 Apr 30
Wade, William L. Jr., et al.	Method of Pretreating Carbon Black Powder	4,526,881	1985 Jul 2
Wade, William L. Jr., et al.	Method of Pretreating Carbon Black Powder	4,543,305	1985 Sep 24
Walker, Donald P.	Afro American Educational Quiz Game	5,454,569	1995 Oct 3
Walker, M. Lucius Jr., et al.	Laminar Fluid NOR Element	3,478,764	1969 Nov 18
Walker, Moses Fleetwood	Cartridge	458,026	1891 Aug 18
Walker, Moses Fleetwood	Film End Fastener for Motion Picture Film Reels	1,328,408	1920 Jan 20
Walker, Moses Fleetwood	Motion Picture Film Reel	1,348,813	1920 Jul 6
Walker, Moses Fleetwood	Alarm for Motion Picture Film Reel	1,348,609	1920 Aug 3
Walker, Peter	Machine for Cleaning Seed Cotton	577,153	1897 Feb 16
Walker, Peter	Bait Holder	600,241	1898 Mar 8
Wallace, Richard W.	Analog Computer System for Solving Heat Flow Problems	3,436,534	1969 Apr 1

Name	Title	Number	Date
Wallace, Richard W.	Light Scattering Photometer and Sample Handling System Therefor	4,178,103	1979 Dec 11
Wallace, Richard W., et al.	Multi Quasi Phase Matched Interactions in a Non-linear Crystal	5,640,405	1997 Jun 17
Waller, Joseph W.	Shoemaker's Cabinet or Bench	224,253	1880 Feb 3
Walton, Ulysses S.	Denture	2,314,674	1943 Mar 23
Warde, Cardinal, et al.	Microchannel Spatial Light Modulator	4,481,531	1984 Nov 6
Warde, Cardinal, et al.	Charge Transfer Signal Processor	4,794,296	1988 Dec 27
Warde, Cardinal, et al.	Completely Cross-Talk Free High Speed Resolution 2-D Bistable Light Modulation	4,800,263	1989 Jan 24
Warde, Cardinal, et al.	Low-Cost Substantially Cross-Talk Free High Spatial Resolution 2-D Bistable Light Modulator	4,822,993	1989 Apr 18
Warde, Cardinal, et al.	High Spatial Resolution 2-D Bistable Light Modulator	4,851,659	1989 Jul 25
Warde, Cardinal, et al.	Charge Transfer Signal Processor and Charge Transfer, Feedthrough Plate Fabrication Assembly & Method	4,863,759	1989 Sep 5
Warner, Isiah M., et al.	Degassing Process and Apparatus for Removal of Oxygen	4,516,984	1985 May 14
Warren, Richard	Display Rack	1,619,900	1927 Mar 8
Washington, Andrew D.	Shoe Horn	728,788	1903 May 19
Washington, Wade	Corn Husking Machine	283,173	1883 Aug 14
Watkins, Boyd G.	Integrated Latch Circuit	3,401,319	1968 Sep 10
Watkins, Boyd G.	Synchronized Watch Movement	3,892,066	1975 Jul 1
Watkins, Isaac	Scrubbing Frame	437,849	1890 Oct 7

(Continued)

221

Name	Invention	Number	Issue Date
Watts, Julius R.	Bracket for Miner's Lamp	493,137	1893 Mar 7
Watts, Orlando	Stencil Cutting Machine	1,305,847	1919 Jun 3
Weatherby, Dennis W.	Automatic Dishwasher Detergent Composition	4,714,562	1987 Dec 22
Weaver, Rufus J.	Stairclimbing Wheelchair	3,411,598	1968 Nov 19
Webb, Henry C.	Clearing Plow	1,226,425	1917 May 15
Webster, John W.	Method and Apparatus for Visually Comparing Files in a Data Processing System	5,142,619	1992 Aug 25
Weir, Charles	High-Pressure Optical Cell	3,079,505	1963 Feb 26
Weir, Charles	High-Pressure Optical Cell for Raman Spectrography	3,610,757	1971 Oct 5
Welburn, Edward T. Jr.	Vehicle Wheel	Des259,484	1981 Jun 9
Welburn, Edward T. Jr.	Vehicle Body	Des293,310	1987 Dec 22
West, Edward H.	Weather Shield	632,385	1899 Sep 5
West, James E., et al.	Electroacoustic Transducer	3,118,022	1964 Jan 14
West, James E., et al.	Electroacoustic Transducer	3,118,979	1964 Jan 21
West, James E., et al.	Method of Measuring the Volume Resistivity of Thin, Solid Dielectric Material	3,496,461	1970 Feb 17
West, James E., et al.	Directional Microphone	3,573,399	1971 Apr 6
West, James E., et al.	Directional Microphone	3,573,400	1971 Apr 6
West, James E., et al.	Method of Producing Permanent Electret Charges in Dielectric Materials	3,644,605	1972 Feb 22
West, James E., et al.	Method and Apparatus for Measurement of Surface Charge of an Electret	3,652,932	1972 Mar 28

Inventor	Title	Patent No.	Date
West, James E., et al.	Touch-Sensitive Switch Employing Electret Foil	3,668,417	1972 Jun 6
West, James E., et al.	Preparation of Electret Transducer Elements	3,705,312	1972 Dec 5
West, James E., et al.	Fabrication of Electret Transducer Elements	3,711,941	1973 Jan 23
West, James E., et al.	Unidirectional Microphones	3,715,500	1973 Feb 6
West, James E., et al.	Multi-unit Electret Touch Selector	3,750,149	1973 Jul 31
West, James E., et al.	Technique for Fabrication of Foil Electret	3,930,066	1975 Dec 30
West, James E., et al.	Technique for Fabrication of Foil Electret	3,945,112	1976 Mar 23
West, James E., et al.	Loudspeaking Teleconferencing Circuit	4,008,376	1977 Feb 15
West, James E.	Technique for Removing Surface and Volume Charges	4,248,808	1981 Feb 3
West, James E., et al.	Electret Transducer with a Selectively Metalized Backplate	4,429,189	1984 Jan 31
West, James E., et al.	Electret Transducer with Variably Charged Electret Foil	4,429,191	1984 Jan 31
West, James E., et al.	Electret Transducer with Variably Electret Foil Thickness	4,429,192	1984 Jan 31
West, James E., et al.	Electret Transducer with Variably Effective Air Gap	4,429,193	1984 Jan 31
West, James E., et al.	Electret Transducer with Variably Actual Air Gap	4,434,327	1984 Feb 28
West, James E., et al.	Integrated Electroacoustic Transducer with Built-in Bias	4,524,247	1985 Jun 18
West, James E., et al.	Electret Transducer for Blood Pressure Measurement	4,598,590	1986 Jul 8
West, James E., et al.	Method for Producing Electret-Containing Devices	4,612,145	1986 Sep 16
West, James E., et al.	Second Order Toroidal Microphone	4,675,906	1987 Jun 23
West, James E., et al.	Unidirectional Second Order Gradient Microphone	4,742,548	1988 May 3
West, James E., et al.	Noise Reduction Processing Arrangement for Microphone Arrays	4,802,227	1989 Jan 31

(Continued)

Name	Invention	Number	Issue Date
West, James E., et al.	Image Derived Directional Microphones	4,965,775	1990 Oct 23
West, James E., et al.	Discriminating Electret Radioactivity Detector System and Method for Measuring Radon Concentration	5,093,570	1992 Mar 3
West, James E., et al.	Adjustable Filter for Differential Microphones	5,303,307	1994 Apr 12
West, James E., et al.	Electret Transducer Array and Fabrication Technique	5,388,163	1995 Feb 3
West, James E., et al.	Adjustable Filter for Differential Microphones	5,586,191	1996 Dec 17
West, John W.	Improvement in Wagons	108,419	1870 Oct 18
West, Thomas P.	Clasp for Shoes or Other Articles	320,104	1885 Jun 16
West, Willis H.	Window Ventilator	1,209,366	1916 Dec 19
Wharton, Ferdinand D.	Treatment of Diarrhea Employing Certain Basic Polyelectrolyte Polymers	3,655,869	1972 Apr 11
White, Charles Fred	Timing Device	1,018,799	1912 Feb 27
White, Daniel L.	Extension Step for Cars	574,969	1897 Jan 12
White, John T.	Lemon Squeezer	572,849	1896 Dec 8
White, Joseph C., et al.	Apparatus for Determining Specific Gravity of an Acid Solution	2,844,532	1958 Jul 22
White, Samuel G. Jr.	Article of Footwear with Improved Tension Distribution Closure System	4,780,969	1988 Nov 1
Wicks, Jerome L.	Patio Door and Window Guard System	4,325,203	1982 Apr 20
Wicks, Jerome L., et al.	Door Security	4,601,503	1986 Jul 22
Wiggins, Reatha L.	Plurality of Aspirators	3,430,628	1969 Mar 4

Name	Title	Number	Date
Wiles, Joseph S.	Injection Pistol	3,538,916	1970 Nov 10
Willard, John Wesley Sr.	Method of Washing Soiled Culinary Articles	3,874,927	1975 Apr 1
Willard, John Wesley Sr.	Method of Cleaning Glass Windows and Mirrors	3,915,738	1975 Oct 28
Willard, John Wesley Sr.	Method of Washing Textile Materials	2,923,456	1975 Dec 2
Willard, John Wesley Sr.	Method of Growing Plants in Soil	4,067,712	1978 Jan 10
Willard, John Wesley Sr.	Method of Improving the Fertility of Soil and the Soil thus Prepared	4,067,713	1978 Jan 10
Willard, John Wesley Sr.	Method of Watering Plants and/or Feeding Nutrients to Plants	4,067,714	1978 Jan 10
Willard, John Wesley Sr.	Method of Transplanting Plants	4,067,715	1978 Jan 10
Wilkerson, Wendell W.	Antihypercholesterolemic	4,900,744	1990 Feb 13
Williams, Carter	Canopy Frame	468,280	1892 Feb 2
Williams, Eugene Sr.	Audiovisual Interview Portfolio	4,255,872	1981 Mar 17
Williams, Isaac C.	Fire Place	315,368	1885 Apr 7
Williams, James P.	Pillow Sham Holder	634,784	1899 Oct 10
Williams, Kevin M.	Fluid-Collecting Receptacle Having Hinged Mat	Des414,642	1999 Oct 5
Williams, Kevin M.	Fluid-Collecting Receptacle	Des414,972	1999 Oct 12
Williams, Kevin M.	Fluid-Collecting Receptacle	6,102,073	2000 Aug 15
Williams, Kevin M.	Fluid-Collecting Receptacle Having Hinged Upper Sheet	6,202,689	2001 Mar 20
Williams, Kevin M.	Sofa Lovers Sofa	6,811,214	2004 Nov 2
Williams, Kevin M.	Privacy Screens	6,942,002	2005 Sep 13

(Continued)

225

Name	Invention	Number	Issue Date
Williams, Kevin M.	Sofa Lovers Sofa	7,134,727	2006 Nov 14
Williams, Louise H.	Collapsible Receptacle	2,405,627	1946 Aug 13
Williams, Paul E.	Helicopter	3,065,933	1962 Nov 27
Williams, Philip B.	Electromagnetic Electric Railway Track Switch	648,092	1900 Apr 24
Williams, Philip B.	Electrically Controlled and Operated Railway Switch	666,080	1901 Jan 15
Williams, Robert	Method and Apparatus for Disinfecting Objects	5,171,523	1992 Dec 15
Williamson, Michael A., et al.	Accelerator Combinations for Anaerobic Polymerization	4,631,325	1986 Dec 23
Williamson, Samuel R., et al.	Acoustic Light Deflection Cells	3,614,204	1971 Oct 19
Willis, Lovell, J.	Portable Miniature Waterfall	3,901,439	1975 Aug 26
Willis, Robert E.	Orthopedic Apparatus for Protecting and Supporting a Bone Joint	4,256,097	1981 Mar 17
Wilson, Donald Claude	Flying Saucer Toy	4,228,616	1980 Oct 21
Wilson, Donald Claude	Simulative Toy Vehicle	Des262,291	1981 Oct 13
Winge, Ralph C.	Combined Brush for Teeth and Gums and Stand Therefor	Des363,820	1995 Nov 7
Winn, Frank	Direct Acting Steam Engine	394,047	1888 Dec 4
Winters, Joseph R.	Fire Escape Ladder	203,517	1878 May 7
Winters, Joseph R.	Improvement in Fire Escape Ladders	214,224	1879 Apr 8
Wise, John D.	Driverless Lawn Mower	3,415,335	1968 Dec 10
Wise, John D.	Driverless Lawn Mower	3,566,988	1971 Mar 2
Wise, John D.	Automatic House Painter	3,611,983	1971 Oct 12
Wise, John D.	Automatic House Painter	3,847,112	1974 Nov 12

Wise, John D.	Envelope Contents Removal	4,866,915	1989 Sep 19
Withers, Charles A.	Ventilator for Ships	744,950	1903 Nov 24
Withers, Charles A.	Ventilator	757,534	1904 Apr 19
Wood, Francis J.	Potato Digger	537,953	1895 Apr 23
Wood, Robert	Wheeled Trundle Toy	Des270,847	1983 Oct 4
Woodward, Dudley G.	Vinylidene Chloride Copolymer Latices and Products	3,235,525	1966 Feb 15
Woodward, Dudley G.	Preparation of Water Soluble Acrylic Copolymers	3,574,175	1971 Apr 6
Woodward, Dudley G., et al.	Polyvinyldene Chloride Latex and Process	3,317,449	1967 May 2
Woodward, Dudley G.	Stringed Instruments with Improved Strings Due to Irradiation and Process	3,842,705	1974 Oct 22
Woodward, Dudley G.	Rapidly Crystallizing Vinylidene Chloride-Acrylonitrile Copolymer	3,642,735	1972 Feb 15
Woods, Granville T.	Steam Boiler Furnace	299,894	1884 Jun 3
Woods, Granville T.	Apparatus for Transmitter of Messages by Electricity	315,368	1885 Apr 7
Woods, Granville T.	Relay Instrument	364,619	1887 Jun 7
Woods, Granville T.	Polarized Relay	366,192	1887 Jul 5
Woods, Granville T.	Electromechanical Brake	368,265	1887 Aug 16
Woods, Granville T.	Telephone System and Apparatus	371,241	1887 Oct 11
Woods, Granville T.	Electromagnetic Brake Apparatus	371,655	1887 Oct 18
Woods, Granville T.	Railway Telegraphy	373,383	1887 Nov 15
Woods, Granville T.	Induction Telegraph System	373,915	1887 Nov 29

(Continued)

Name	Invention	Number	Issue Date
Woods, Granville T.	Overhead Conducting System for Electric Railway	383,844	1888 May 29
Woods, Granville T.	Electromotive Railway System	385,034	1888 Jun 26
Woods, Granville T.	Tunnel Construction for Electric Railway	386,282	1888 Jul 17
Woods, Granville T.	Galvanic Battery	387,839	1888 Aug 14
Woods, Granville T.	Railway Telegraphy	388,803	1888 Aug 28
Woods, Granville T.	Automatic Safety Cut-out for Electric Circuit	395,533	1889 Jan 1
Woods, Granville T.	Electric Railway System	463,020	1891 Nov 10
Woods, Granville T.	System of Electrical Distribution	569,443	1896 Oct 13
Woods, Granville T.	Amusement Apparatus	639,692	1899 Dec 19
Woods, Granville T.	Incubator	656,760	1900 Aug 28
Woods, Granville T.	Electric Railway	667,110	1901 Jan 29
Woods, Granville T.	Electric Railway System	678,086	1901 Jul 9
Woods, Granville T.	Regulating and Controlling Electrical Translating Device	681,768	1901 Sep 3
Woods, Granville T.	Electric Railway	687,098	1901 Nov 19
Woods, Granville T.	Automatic Air Brake	701,981	1902 Jun 10
Woods, Granville T.	Electric Railway System	718,183	1903 Jan 13
Woods, Granville T. and Lyates	Electric Railway	729,481	1903 May 26
Woods, Granville T. and Lyates	Railway Brake Apparatus	755,825	1904 Mar 29
Woods, Granville T. and Lyates	Railway Brake Apparatus	795,243	1905 Jul 18
Woods, Granville T. and Lyates	Safety Apparatus for Railways	833,193	1906 Oct 16

Name	Invention	Patent No.	Date
Woods, Granville T. and Lyates	Safety Apparatus for Railways	837,022	1906 Nov 27
Woods, Granville T. and Lyates	Vehicle Controlling Apparatus	867,180	1907 Sep 24
Woolery, Andre A.	Product Display	Des551,551	2007 Sep 25
Woolfork, James B.	Shoe Shining Machine	1,762,005	1930 Jun 3
Wormley, James	Life-Saving Apparatus	242,091	1881 May 24
Wright, Louis T.	Device for Treatment of Bone	2,561,550	1951 Jul 24
Yaeger, Ivan	Artificial Arm and Hand Assembly	4,685,928	1987 Aug 11
Yaeger, Ivan	Therapeutic Device for Hands and Wrists	7,110,810	2006 Sep 19
Young, James E.	Battery Performance Control	4,564,798	1986 Jan 14
Young, Joseph	Stimulant Massager	Des404,139	1999 Jan 12
Young, Patricia	Combined Backpack and Stereo	Des 351,943	1994 Nov 1

Notes

The noncited characterization of an innovation is taken from the patent grant itself. The appendix provides the listing of inventor, invention, patent number, and date.

PREFACE

1. John Sibley Butler, *Entrepreneurship and Self-Help among Black Americans* (Albany: State University of New York Press, 2005), p. 46; Abram L. Harris, *The Negro as Capitalist* (College Park, Md.: McGrath, 1936), p. 6.

2. R. R. Wright, "The Negro as an Inventor," *A.M.E. Church Review* 2, no. 14 (April 1886): 397.

3. Ali A. Mazrui, *The Africans* (Boston: Little, Brown, 1986), p. 4.

4. See James M. Trotter, *Music and Some Highly Musical People* (Boston: 1878; reprint, Chicago: Afro-American Press, 1969), pp. 114–30; Giles B. Jackson and D. Webster Davis, *The Industrial History of the Negro Race of the United States* (Richmond, Va.: Giles B. Jackson, 1908), p. 129; and Benjamin Verdery, "Contemporary Classical, Justin Holland, Classical Pioneer," *Guitar Player*, May 1989, p. 112.

CHAPTER 1: SETTING THE STAGE: EARLY INVENTIVE SPIRIT

1. Worthington G. Snethen, *The Black Code of the District of Columbia* (New York: Published for the A. & F. Anti-Slavery Society, 1848), pp. 34–35, 38, 41, 43.

2. Kimberly Melton, "Text Fills in History of Oregon's Racist Acts," *The Oregonian*, p. A1, May 12, 2008.

3. Patricia Carter Sluby, *The Inventive Spirit of African Americans: Patented Ingenuity* (Westport, Conn.: Praeger, 2004), pp. 43–44.

4. John Sibley Butler, *Entrepreneurship and Self-Help among Black Americans* (Albany: State University of New York Press, 2005), p. 83.

5. Ibid., p. 43.

6. John H. Hewitt, *Protest and Progress: New York's First Black Episcopal Church Fights Racism* (New York: Garland, 2000), p. 98. See also Katharine Greider, "The Schoolteacher's Stand," *American Legacy*, Summer 2006, p. 12.

7. *Anglo-African*, April 1859, vol. 1, pp. 126–28; C. G. Gibbs, *Black Inventors from Africa to America* (Silver Spring, Md.: Three Dimensional, 1995), p. 72; *A Documentary History of the Negro People in the United States*, ed. Herbert Aptheker (New York: Citadel, 1951), pp. 420–22; and Sluby, *Inventive Spirit*, p. 16.

8. On May 17, 1861, the Statutes at Large of the Confederate States of America provided talented slaves with patent rights. After Jefferson Davis became president of the Confederate States of America, he endorsed the following legislation to provide for slave inventors: *And be it further enacted, That in case the original inventor or discoverer of the art, machine or improvement for which a patent is solicited is a slave, the master of such slave may take oath that the said slave was the original; and on complying with the requisites of the law shall receive a patent for said discovery or invention, and have all the rights to which a patentee is entitled by law.* See *Statutes at Large of the Confederate States of America*, ed. James M. Matthews, July 1861, p. 54.

9. Sluby, *Inventive Spirit*, pp. 11–12. Literature asserts that Forten patented an improved invention relative to a sail-handling concept that reaped economic reward as it came into general use on the market. Many searches by the author were made in the United States Patent and Trademark Office patented files and published lists of issued patents to locate a patent in the name of James Forten, to no avail. With none found or assigned to him to substantiate the claim, it can be safely assumed that Forten did not receive a grant in the American patent system. We can theorize, however, that Forten may have filed a patent application but never received the grant because the invention was not novel or new in the eyes of patent law, or he could have abandoned the invention for any number of possible reasons, one being that he had placed the improved device or technique in the marketplace and was receiving already a substantial income from its manufacture. Exploring another theory, Forten may have applied for and received a foreign patent, perhaps from Great Britain in the early 1800s, because of his familiarity with England resulting from the year he spent overseas just after Britain's defeat in America's Revolutionary War. A search of this foreign patented file might be feasible. Then, too, he may have kept all knowledge as a trade secret.

10. Julie Winch, *A Gentleman of Color: The Life and Times of James Forten* (New York: Oxford University Press, 2002), p. 151.

11. Portia James, *The Real McCoy* (Washington, D.C.: Smithsonian Institution Press, 1989), pp. 33–39; Rayford W. Logan and Michael R. Winston, eds., *Dictionary of American Negro Biography* (New York: Norton, 1982), pp. 234–35; and Winch, *A Gentleman of Color*, pp. 93, 239, 246, 249, 326, 328.

12. Winch, *A Gentleman of Color*, pp. 365–66; Sluby, *Inventive Spirit*, p. 56.

13. Abram L. Harris, *The Negro as Capitalist* (College Park, Md.: McGrath, 1936), pp. 17–18; James, *The Real McCoy*, pp. 39–40.

14. Louis Haber, *Black Pioneers of Science and Invention* (New York: Harcourt, Brace & World, 1970), pp. 13–15; Logan and Winston, *Dictionary*, p. 25.

15. Sluby, *Inventive Spirit*, pp. 25–27.

16. Logan and Winston, *Dictionary*, p. 526.

17. Rayvon Fouché, *Black Inventors in the Age of Segregation* (Baltimore: Johns Hopkins University Press, 2003), p. 27.

18. Vital Records, State of Ohio; Sluby, *Inventive Spirit*, p. 72.

19. Fouché, *Black Inventors*, p. 28; U.S. Census, 1860, Martinsburg, Clay Township, County of Knox, State of Ohio, page 141, lines 24–29. Woods's sister Henrietta Woods Wilborn is listed in the 1880 U.S. Census as living with her husband, John Wilborn, in Springfield, Clark County, State of Ohio, on page 22, Supervisor's District no. 2, Enumeration District no. 45, line 46, with place of birth given as Ohio, as was given for her mother and father as well. This Ohio place of birth for her father is inconsistent with the information given in the 1860 census at line 24 for her father, who is listed as head of household and named Cyrus Woods (not Tailer Woods as expected). Curiously, in the 1860 U.S. Census Woods's brother Lyates is not listed; most likely he was not born at the time the 1860 census was enumerated. However, subsequent federal censuses do not list him either. Granville's age in 1860 is given as 10.

20. William J. Simmons, *Men of Mark: Eminent, Progressive, and Rising* (1887; Chicago: Johnson, 1990 [1887]), pp. 107–8; Fouché, *Black Inventors*, pp. 29–30.

21. Fouché, *Black Inventors*, p. 43.

22. Ibid., p. 46.

23. Ibid., p. 47.

24. Simmons, *Men of Mark*, p. 111.

25. Fouché, *Black Inventors*, 74.

26. Middleton Harris, Morris Levitt, Roger Furman, and Ernest Smith, *The Black Book* (New York: Random House, 1974), p. 122.

27. Haber, *Black Pioneers*, p. 48.

28. Booker T. Washington, *The Negro in Business* (Coshocton, Ohio: Vail, 1907), p. 113; Sluby, *Inventive Spirit*, p. 47.

29. Scottron, Samuel, "Manufacturing Household Articles," *Colored American Magazine*, October 1904, p. 622.

30. Washington, *The Negro in Business*, p. 115.

31. Ibid., p. 116.

32. Ibid., pp. 116–17.

33. Ibid., pp. 621–24; *The Proceedings of the National Negro Business League, Boston, 1900* (Boston: J. R. Hamm, 1901), p. 276; James, *The Real McCoy*, p. 90.

34. *Proceedings*, p. 190.

CHAPTER 2: SELF-HELP—A BEGINNING: BUSINESS IN THE MAKING

1. Juliet E. K. Walker, *The History of Black Business in America: Capitalism, Race, Entrepreneurship* (New York: Macmillan Library Reference USA, 1998), p. 126.

2. Ibid., p. 150.

3. Booker T. Washington, *The Negro in Business* (Coshocton, Ohio: Vail, 1907), p. 11.

4. John Sibley Butler, *Entrepreneurship and Self-Help among Black Americans*, revised edition (Albany: State University of New York Press, 2005), p. 52; Robert H. Kinzer and Edward Sagarin, *The Negro in American Business* (New York: Greenberg, 1950), p. 36.

5. G. F. Richings, *Evidences of Progress among Colored People* (Philadelphia: George S. Ferguson, 1905), p. 342.

6. Ibid., p. 342.

7. Ibid., p. 342; Patricia Carter Sluby, *The Inventive Spirit of African Americans: Patented Ingenuity* (Westport, Conn.: Praeger, 2004), p. 217.

8. *The Proceedings of the National Negro Business League, Boston, 1900* (Boston: J. R. Hamm, 1901), pp. 13–17.

9. Frederick D. Wilkinson, ed., *Directory of Graduates, Howard University, 1870–1963* (Washington, D.C.: Howard University, 1965), p. 175; Sluby, *Inventive Spirit*, p. 49; and "Genius of the Colored Man," *New Ideas, Philadelphia*, September 1895, p. 31.

10. *The Evening Star*, January 14, 1925; Paul E. Sluby Sr., *Records of the Columbian Harmony Cemetery, Washington, D.C.* (Washington, D.C.: Columbian Harmony Society, 1996), p. 351; Giles B. Jackson and D. Webster Davis, *The Industrial History of the Negro Race of the United States* (Richmond, Va.: Giles B. Jackson, 1908), pp. 188, 260.

11. W. P. Burrell and D. E. Johnson Sr., *Twenty-Five Year History of the Grand Fountain of the United Order of True Reformers, 1881–1905* (Richmond, Va.: Grand Fountain of United Order of True Reformers, 1909), passim; Richings, *Evidences of Progress*, pp. 336–37.

12. *Proceedings*, pp. 32–33; Sluby, *Inventive Spirit*, p. xv.

13. Abram L. Harris, *The Negro as Capitalist* (College Park, Md.: McGrath, 1936), pp. 45, 62–73.

14. In the 1880s employees of the Patent Office, one of whom was Henry Edwin Baker, undertook to collect a list of "Negro" inventors for the Cotton States Centennial in 1884 but were not fully successful. Another fairly successful effort was attempted in 1892 for the Chicago World's Fair, and another effort was made a year later for the Negro Exhibit at Atlanta. However, the very best results came in 1900 for the Paris Exposition, compiled by the United States Commissioner, T. J. Galloway. Notwithstanding a number of negative responses from patent attorneys and other sources, hundreds of black patentees were positively identified.

15. Sluby, *Inventive Spirit*, p. 42.

16. Ibid., pp. 64–67.

17. Paul E. Sluby Sr. and Stanton L. Wormley Jr., *The Columbian Harmony Society, A Brief History* (Washington, D.C.: The Columbian Harmony Society, 1976), p. 56; Harris, *The Negro as Capitalist*, p. 104; *Washington* [D.C.] *Star*, September 2, 1918.

18. G. F. Richings, *Evidences of Progress*, p. v.

19. *Proceedings*, p. 87

20. Ibid., p. 88.

21. Richings, *Evidences of Progress*, p. x.

22. Virginius Dabney, *Richmond, the Story of a City* (New York: Doubleday, 1976), p. 257.

23. Luther Porter Jackson, *Negro Office-Holders in Virginia* (Norfolk, Va.: Guide Quality Press, 1945), passim; see H. J. McGuinn and T. L. Spraggins, "Negro in Politics in Virginia," *Journal of Negro Education*, Summer 1957; Patricia Carter Ives, "Jackson Ward . . . Citadel of Black Business," *Richmond Afro-American*, February 13, 1982, pp. 29, 31.

24. J. L. Nichols and William H. C. Crogman, *Progress of a Race* (1920; reprint, New York: Arno Press, 1969), p. 247; Jackson and Davis, *Industrial History*, pp. 210, 247; and Washington, *The Negro in Business*, pp. 143–46.

25. Washington, *The Negro in Business*, p. 146.

26. Jackson and Davis, *Industrial History*, pp. 210, 250, 251; U.S. Census, 1900, City of Charleston, State of South Carolina, sheet no. 5, line 60.

27. Washington, *The Negro in Business*, p. 108.

28. Ibid., p. 106.

29. Ibid.

30. Ibid., pp. 107–8.

31. "Hunter Haynes Dead," *Chicago Defender*, January 19, 1918.

32. "Great Exposition at Richmond, Virginia July 5 to 27, 1915," *Richmond Evening Journal*, June 15, 1915; "Negro Industrial Exposition," *Richmond Planet*, 1932.

33. Sluby, *Inventive Spirit*, p. 58.

34. Ibid.

CHAPTER 3: FOLLOWING THEIR PASSION—IN THE MARKETPLACE

1. Patricia Carter Sluby, *The Inventive Spirit of African Americans: Patented Ingenuity* (Westport, Conn.: Praeger, 2004), p. 117.

2. Louis Haber, *Black Pioneers of Science and Invention* (New York: Harcourt, Brace & World, 1970), p. 89.

3. Sluby, *Inventive Spirit*, p. 116.

4. Haber, *Black Pioneers*, p. 99.

5. Sluby, *Inventive Spirit*, p. 118.

6. Alex Severinsky and Andrew Hirsch, "Inventing as a Business," unpublished paper, circa 2006, p. 1.

7. Haber, *Black Pioneers*, p. 104.

8. Juliet E. K. Walker, *The History of Black Business in America: Capitalism, Race, Entrepreneurship* (New York: Macmillan Library Reference USA, 1998), p. 243.

9. Virginia Ott and Gloria Swanson, *Man with a Million Ideas: Fred Jones, Genius/Inventor* (Minneapolis: Lerner, 1977), p. 14.

10. Ibid., p. 17.

11. Ibid., pp. 60–62.

12. Ibid., p. 75; US Patent 2,163,754 (see Roster of African America Patentees).

13. Ott and Swanson, *Man with a Million Ideas*, pp. 77–78.

14. US Patent 2,303,857 (see Roster of African American Patentees).

15. Ott and Swanson, *Man with a Million Ideas*, p. 80.

16. Ibid., pp. 81, 86; Sluby, *Inventive Spirit*, pp. 118–19.

17. Ott and Swanson, *Man with a Million Ideas*, pp. 87–89.

18. Ibid., p. 99.

19. Ibid., p. 106.

20. A'Lelia Bundles, *On Her Own Ground* (New York: Scribner, 2001), p. 65.

21. Walker, *History of Black Business*, p. 208; John N. Ingham and Lynne B. Feldman, *African American Business Leaders* (Westport, Conn.: Greenwood Press, 1994), p. 634.

22. Bundles, *On Her Own Ground*, p. 64; Ingham and Feldman, *African American Business Leaders*, p. 635.

23. *Official Gazette*, United States Patent Office, vol. 308, March 27, 1923, p. 687.

24. Walter L. Majors, US Patent 1,069,558, Coin Controlled Taxicab Controller, August 5, 1913; US Patent 1,121,266, Heater for Water Cooling Apparatus of Motor

Vehicles, December 15, 1914; US Patent 1,123,906, Motor Controlling Device for Taxicabs and the Like, January 15, 1915; and US Patent 1,124,235, Hair Drier, January 5, 1915 (see Roster of African American Patentees).

25. U.S. Census Population, 1910, St. Louis, Missouri. Majors acquired nine patents from 1913 to 1930, mostly on automotive devices. He assigned his invention for a machine for the treatment of the scalp and hair to the Majors Oxford College, incorporated in St. Louis, more than likely a training school for hair care practitioners.

26. Annie M. Malone, United States Design Patent 60,962, May 16, 1922.

27. Ingham and Feldman, *African American Business Leaders*, p. 635; and *The Federal Reporter,* vol. 273, August–September 1921, p. 363. Federal trademark registration has several advantages, including the right to sue for infringement in federal courts. Other federal intellectual property protections confer the same advantages.

28. U.S. Trademark Registration Number 502,991, October 19, 1948.

29. Annie Turnbo Malone, http://www.novelguide.com/a/discover/ewb23/ewb2308247.html.

30. Sluby, *Inventive Spirit,* p. 113.

31. A'Lelia Bundles, *Madam C. J. Walker* (New York: Chelsea House, 1991), pp. 29–39; and Sluby, *Inventive Spirit,* p. 131.

32. "Madame" is spelled variously. Bundles uses the title without the final e; Madame C. J. Walker's trademarks are registered with the title "Mme.," but on one occasion both spellings are in the same document. U.S. Patent and Trademark Office; Sluby, *Inventive Spirit,* p. 133.

33. Bachelor–Benedict Club Debutante Program, Washington, D.C., 1948; U.S. Patent and Trademark Office.

34. Bundles, *On Her Own Ground,* pp. 229, 270–75.

35. Walker, *History of Black Business,* pp. 210, 303–4; Bundles, *On Her Own Ground,* p. 133; and Victoria Sherrow, *Encyclopedia of Hair: A Cultural History* (Westport, Conn.: Greenwood Press, 2006), pp. 395–96.

36. Bachelor–Benedict Club Debutante Program, Washington, D.C., 1948.

37. U.S. Census, Population, 1920, Chicago, Illinois; Walker, *History of Black Business,* pp. 210; and Anthony Overton, U.S. Trademark Registration Number 173,245, September 18, 1923.

38. Bundles, *On Her Own Ground,* p. 134.

39. Walker, *History of Black Business,* p. 210.

40. Ibid.

41. Ibid.; Harris, *The Negro as Capitalist,* pp. 150, 161.

42. Joe L. Dudley Sr., *Walking By Faith—I Am, I Can & I Will* (Kernersville, N.C.: Executive Press, 1998), p. 72.

43. Walker, *The History of Black Business in America,* p. 297.

44. Ibid., p. 298; Dudley, *Walking By Faith,* p. 103.

45. Dudley, *Walking By Faith,* pp. 103–8.

46. Ibid., pp. 96–97.

47. Ibid., pp. 100–101; U.S. Trademark Registration Number 1,286,716.

48. Ibid., pp. 131–41.

49. Ibid., pp. 123–24; U.S. Trademark Registration Number 2,335,779; personal communication, telephone interview with Lucky Kizure, 2010.

50. Ingham and Feldman, p. 592.

51. Ibid., p. 594; U.S. Trademark Registration Number 978,681.

52. U.S. Trademark Registration Number 978,681.

53. Ingham and Felman, p. 595.

54. Walker, *History of Black Business,* p. 306.

55. Ibid., p. 310; see U.S. Trademark Registration Numbers 784,137, and 3,200,502.

56. Walker, *History of Black Business,* p. 311.

CHAPTER 4: COMMERCIALIZED CONCEPTS: CAPITAL AND ENTERPRISES OF TODAY

1. Alex Severinsky and Andrew Hirsch, "Inventing as a Business," unpublished paper, circa 2006, pp. 5–6.

2. Radio program on the National Patent Law Association (now National Intellectual Property Law Association), WHUR, Howard University, Washington, D.C., February 15, 1976. Participants: patent examiners Hosea Taylor and Patricia C. Ives, patent attorney Richard Gaither, and inventor attorney Charles R. Beckley. At that time a patent's monopoly (the exclusive right to bar others from practicing one's invention without permission) lasted 17 years from the date of issuance by the federal government.

3. Bridget McCrea, "Bringing Luxury to the Masses," *Black Enterprise,* September 2005, p. 54; personal communication, telephone conversation with Terry Phillips of Astute Advance, March 1, 2010; see also "Black Car Designers," *Ebony,* February 2000, pp. 142–44.

4. "Historic Inventor Honored in Washington," *JET,* October 30, 2006, p. 27; www. alifesdesign.com. See also Charles E. Harrison, *A Life's Design* (Chicago: Ibis Design, 2005).

5. "Business Based on Invention," speech by Robert G. Bayless before the Detroit, Michigan, National Inventors Meeting, 1981.

6. Ibid.

7. Tony Lang, "Global Answers Go to Waste," *Cincinnati Enquirer,* February 14, 1989.

8. Ibid.

9. Bayless, "Business Based on Invention."

10. Amy Harper-Gault, "One Scientist's Work: Making Possibilities Real," *Yellow Springs News,* November 25, 1987.

11. Telephone interview with inventor Dr. Robert G. Bayless, March 13, 2009.

12. Bayless, "Business Based on Invention."

13. Ibid.

14. Telephone interview with inventor Dr. Lonnie G. Johnson, March 21, 2005.

15. Dr. Lonnie G. Johnson, resume, personal communication.

16. Ibid.

17. Ibid.

18. US Patent 4,143,267; US Patent 4,181,843; US Patent 4,211,362 (see Roster of African American Patentees).

19. US Patent 4,591,071 (see Roster of African American Patentees); Jay Mathes, "Escaping the Office to Unlock Ideas," *Washington Post,* December 27, 1991; and "The Man Behind the Curtain (of Water)," *Washington Post,* July 9, 2002, p. C14.

20. Johnson, resume; William J. Broad, "Rocket Science, Served Up Soggy," *New York Times,* July 31, 2001.

21. Ibid.

22. Johnson, resume.

23. Johnson, telephone interview.

24. Telephone interview with inventor Sharon B. Duncan, May 18, 2009.

25. Telephone interview with inventor Clyde Bethea, December 8, 2007.

26. Clyde Bethea, resume.

27. Barbara Bell, "John Dove, 20th Century Inventor," February 9, 2007, www.as
sociatecontent.com; US Patent 3,226,696 (see Roster of African American Patentees).

28. R. Patrick Corbett, "Rome Scientist Dove Dies at 79," News, January 23, 2004,
www.uticaod.com.

29. Telephone interview with inventor Johnny G. Allen Sr., March 7, 2010.

30. Ibid.

31. Ibid.

32. Ibid.

33. Ibid.

34. Ibid.

35. Black History Month, Albany-Dougherty Georgia Web site, 2004.

36. Telephone interview with inventor Dr. Frances Christian Gaskin, August 23,
2009.

37. Johnnie R. Jackson, Ph.D., Career Highlights, personal communication, January 5, 2010.

38. Ibid.; personal interview with inventor Dr. Johnnie R. Jackson, January 15,
2010.

39. Johnnie J. Jackson, Ph.D., *Genocide of Americans—the Healthcare Tsunamis*
(Camp Springs, Md.: Diabetes Informatics Corporation, 2008), acknowledgment; personal interview, January 15, 2010.

40. Personal interview with inventor Dr. Johnnie R. Jackson, March 22, 2010.

41. Personal interview with Samuel Merrill, March 9, 2010.

42. Ibid.

43. Ibid.

44. "Moore Unique Skin Care" advertisement; www.mooreunique.com.

45. Telephone interview with inventor Dr. Milton D. Moore, March 10, 2010.

46. US Patent 5,255,452 (see Roster of African American Patentees); http://
en.wikipedia.org/wiki/Michael_Jackson.

47. United States Patent and Trademark Office.

48. Joy T. Bennett, "Michael," *Ebony*, December 2007, pp. 82, 100.

49. Gladys Knight, on national television, July 7, 2009.

50. Berry Gordy, on national television, July 7, 2009.

51. http://en.wikipedia.org/wiki/Michael_Jackson

52. *Washington Post*, June 29; July 2; and July 8, 2009.

53. Michele Hoskins with Jean A. Williams, *Sweet Success* (Avon, Mass.: Adams
Media, 2004), pp. 9–23.

54. Ibid., pp. xxiii–xvi.

55. Ibid., p. 168.

56. US Patent Design 342,470; Brothella Quick seen on *Invent This!*, TechTV cable
television show, January 6, 2004.

57. Sibylla Nash, "Got a Great Idea for an Invention?" *Turning Point*, November/
December 2004, p. 21.

58. Pamela Gold Waldo, "The Inventor Beware," *Black Enterprise*, February 2007.

59. Telephone interview with inventor Calvin Flowers, June 15, 2010.

60. Telephone interview with Gail E. Wright, president/chief executive officer,
Wright Alternatives, LLC, March 5, 2010, and communications, March 30, 2010.

61. Ibid.

62. Ibid.; *Advantage, The NASA Glenn Garrett Morgan Commercialization Initiative*,
Winter 2000, p. 5.

Bibliography

Adams, Russell L. *Great Negroes Past and Present.* Chicago: Afro-American, 1969.

"A Look Ahead to the Dawn of the Next Millennium." *Newsweek,* January 27, 1997.

Anglo-African, April 1859, volume 1, pp. 126–28.

Aptheker, Herbert, ed. *A Documentary History of the Negro People in the United States.* New York: Citadel, 1951.

"Architects of the Future." *Black Enterprise,* February 1990, pp. 79–116.

Bachelor-Benedict Club Debutante Program, Washington, D.C., 1948.

Baker, Henry Edwin. *The Colored Inventor: A Record of Fifty Years.* New York: Crises, 1913.

Ball, Edward. *Slaves in the Family.* New York: Farrar, Straus and Giroux, 1998.

Bundles, A'lelia. *On Her Own Ground—the Life and Times of Madam C.J. Walker.* New York: Scribner, 2001.

Burrell, W.P., and D.E. Johnson Sr. *Twenty-Five Years History of the Grand Fountain of the United Order of True Reformers.* Richmond, Va.: Grand Fountain, United Order of True Reformers, 1909.

Butler, John Sibley. *Entrepreneurship and Self-Help among Black Americans.* Albany: State University of New York Press, 2005.

Chappell, Kevin. "How Black Inventors Changed America." *Ebony,* February 1997, pp. 40, 46, 48, 50.

Dudley, Joe L. Sr. *Walking By Faith—I Am, I Can & I Will.* North Carolina: Executive Press, 1998.

Fouché, Rayvon. *Black Inventors in the Age of Segregation: Granville T. Woods, Lewis H. Latimer & Shelby J. Davidson.* Baltimore: Johns Hopkins University Press, 2003.

Gibbs, Carroll R. *Black Inventors from Africa to America: Two Million Years of Invention and Innovation.* Silver Spring, Md.: Three Dimensional, 1995.

Gray, Garry. "H.C. Haynes, Barber and Inventor." *Negro History Bulletin* 40, no. 5 (September–October 1977): 750–52.

"Great Exposition at Richmond, Virginia July 5 to 27, 1915." *Richmond Evening Journal,* June 15, 1915.

Haber, Louis. *Black Pioneers of Science and Invention.* New York: Harcourt, Brace & World, 1970.

Harris, Abram L. *The Negro as Capitalist.* College Park, Md.: McGrath, 1936.

Harris, Middleton, Morris Levitt, Roger Furman, and Ernest Smith. *The Black Book.* New York: Random House, 1974.

Harris, Wendy. *Against All Odds.* New York: Wiley, 2001.

Harrison, Charles. *A Life's Design.* Chicago: Ibis Design, 2005.

Hewitt, John H. *Protest and Progress: New York's First Black Episcopal Church Fights Racism.* New York: Garland, 2000.

"Historic Inventor Honored in Washington." *JET,* October 30, 2006.

Holmes, Keith C. *Black Inventors, Crafting Over 200 Years of Success.* Brooklyn, NY: Global Black Inventor Research Projects, 2008.

Hoskins, Michelle, with Jean A. Williams. *Sweet Success.* Avon, Mass.: Adams Media, 2004.

"Hunter Haynes Dead." *Chicago Defender,* January 19, 1918.

Ingham, John N., and Lynne B. Feldman. *African American Business Leaders.* Westport, Conn.: Greenwood Press, 1994.

Ives, Patricia Carter. *Creativity and Inventions: The Genius of Afro-Americans and Women in the United States and Their Patents.* Arlington, Va.: Research Unlimited, 1987.

Ives, Patricia Carter. "Minority Inventive Genius: A Look at Spirited American People." In *Bicentennial Celebration, United States Patent and Copyright Laws: Proceedings, Events, Addresses, May 7 through 11, 1990, Washington, D.C.* Washington, D.C.: Foundation for a Creative America, Port City Press, Crabtree & Jamison-Clark Boardman, 1991.

Jackson, Giles B., and Daniel Webster Davis. *The Industrial History of the Negro Race of the United States.* Richmond, Va.: Presses of the Virginia Press, 1908.

Jackson, Johnnie J., Ph.D. *Genocide of Americans—the Healthcare Tsunamis.* Camp Springs, Md.: Diabetes Informatics Corporation, 2008.

James, Portia. *The Real McCoy: African American Invention and Innovation, 1619–1930.* Washington, D.C.: Smithsonian Institution, 1989.

Kinzer, Robert H., and Edward Sagarin. *The Negro in American Business.* New York: Greenberg, 1950.

Logan, Rayford W., and Michael R. Winston, eds. *Dictionary of American Negro Biography.* New York: Norton, 1982.

Marshall, Randall S. *Roulettechess.* Washington, D.C.: Privately printed, 2008.

Mazrui, Ali A. *The Africans.* Boston: Little, Brown, 1986.

McCrea, Bridget. "Bringing Luxury to the Masses." *Black Enterprise,* September 2005, p. 54.

Melton, Kimberly. "Text Fills in History of Oregon's Racist Acts." *The Oregonian,* May 12, 2008.

Miller, Kelly, and Joseph R. Gay. *Progress and Achievements of the Colored People.* Washington, D.C.: Austin Jenkins, 1917.

"Negro Industrial Exposition." *Richmond Planet,* 1932.

Peiss, Kathy L. "American Women and the Making of Modern Consumer Culture." *Journal for Multi Media History* 1, no. 1 (Fall 1998).

Peterson, John L. *The Road to 2015: Profiles of the Future.* Corte Madera, Calif.: Waite Group Press, 1994.

Proceedings of the National Negro Business League. Boston, Mass.: J. R. Hamm, 1901.

Quarles, Benjamin. *The Negro in the Making of America.* New York: Collier, 1964.

Richings, G. F. *Evidences of Progress among Colored People.* Philadelphia: Ferguson, 1905.

Scottron, Samuel R. "Manufacturing Household Articles." *Colored American Magazine,* December 1906, pp. 621–24.

Simmons, William J. *Men of Mark: Eminent, Progressive, and Rising.* Chicago: Johnson, 1990 [1887].

Sluby, Patricia Carter. *The Inventive Spirit of African Americans: Patented Ingenuity.* Westport, Conn.: Praeger, 2004.

Sluby, Paul E. Sr. *Bury Me Deep.* Washington, D.C.: Privately printed, 2009.

Sluby, Paul E. Sr., and Stanton L. Wormley Jr. *History of the Columbian Harmony Society and of Harmony Cemetery.* Washington, D.C.: Privately printed, revised 2001.

Smith, Cheryl A. *Market Women—Black Women Entrepreneurs: Past, Present, and Future.* Westport, Conn.: Praeger, 2005.

Snethen, Worthington G. *The Black Code of the District of Columbia.* New York: Published for the A. & F. Anti-Slavery Society, 1848.

Sterrett, Mrs. N. B. "Negro Exhibit at Charleston [South Carolina] Exposition." *African Methodist Episcopal Church Review* 19, no. 1 (July 1902): 465.

Trotter, James M. *Music and Some Highly Musical People.* Boston: 1878; reprint, Chicago: Afro-American Press, 1969.

Van Sertima, Ivan. *Blacks in Science: Ancient and Modern.* London: Transaction Books, 1983.

Verdery, Benjamin, "Contemporary Classical, Justin Holland, Classical Pioneer." *Guitar Player.* May 1989, p. 112.

Walker, Juliet E. K. *The History of Black Business in America: Capitalism, Race, Entrepreneurship.* New York: Macmillan Library Reference USA, 1998.

Washington, Booker T. *The Negro in Business.* Witchita, Kans.: Hertel, Jenkins, 1907.

Williams, Michael Paul. "Was Black Inventor Ripped Off?" *Richmond* [Virginia] *Times-Dispatch,* June 15, 1998.

Winch, Julie. *A Gentleman of Color.* New York: Oxford University Press, 2002.

Woodson, Carter G., and Charles H. Wesley. *The Negro in Our History.* Washington, D.C.: Associated, 1972.

Wright, R. R. "The Negro as an Inventor." *A.M.E. Church Review* 2, no. 14 (April 1886): 397.

Index

About the Author

PATRICIA CARTER SLUBY is a Registered Patent Agent and former U.S. primary patent examiner with a background in organic chemistry. Ms. Sluby, a lecturer and freelance writer, has written numerous journal articles and is the author of *The Genius of Afro-Americans and Women in the United States and Their Patents* and *The Inventive Spirit of African Americans: Patented Ingenuity.*